THE SINGING DETAINEE AND
THE LIBRARIAN WITH ONE BOOK

Before you start to read this book, take this moment to think about making a donation to punctum books, an independent non-profit press,

@ https://punctumbooks.com/support/

If you're reading the e-book, you can click on the image below to go directly to our donations site. Any amount, no matter the size, is appreciated and will help us to keep our ship of fools afloat. Contributions from dedicated readers will also help us to keep our commons open and to cultivate new work that can't find a welcoming port elsewhere. Our adventure is not possible without your support.

Vive la Open Access.

Fig. 1. Detail from Hieronymus Bosch, *Ship of Fools* (1490–1500)

THE SINGING DETAINEE AND THE LIBRARIAN WITH ONE BOOK: ESSAYS ON EXILE. Copyright © 2025 by Michael Beltran. This work carries a Creative Commons BY-NC-SA 4.0 International license, which means that you are free to copy and redistribute the material in any medium or format, and you may also remix, transform, and build upon the material, as long as you clearly attribute the work to the author (but not in a way that suggests the author or punctum books endorses you and your work), you do not use this work for commercial gain in any form whatsoever, and that for any remixing and transformation, you distribute your rebuild under the same license. http://creativecommons.org/licenses/by-nc-sa/4.0/

First published in 2023 by Ateneo de Manila University Press.
Published in a new edition in 2025 by punctum books, Earth, Milky Way.
https://punctumbooks.com

ISBN-13: 978-1-68571-270-9 (print)
ISBN-13: 978-1-68571-271-6 (ePDF)

DOI: 10.53288/0529.1.00

LCCN: 2025936447
Library of Congress Cataloging Data is available from the Library of Congress

Editing: Vincent W.J. van Gerven Oei and SAJ
Book design: Hatim Eujayl
Cover image: Miguel Robleza
Cover design: Vincent W.J. van Gerven Oei

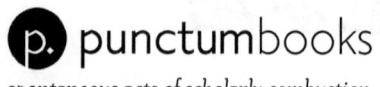

spontaneous acts of scholarly combustion

HIC SVNT MONSTRA

Michael Beltran

THE SINGING DETAINEE
and
THE LIBRARIAN WITH ONE BOOK

Essays on Exile

Contents

* * *

Foreword	15
Author's Preface	19
Introduction	25

* * *

A Particular Purgatory	29
Mangoes and Escape Plans	41
Family of Exiles	49
Superstar	59
The Sentinel	71
Knockin' on Heaven's Door	79
Memories of Socialism	91
Yet Again	101
A Bottle of Wine	113
Fighting Makes You Stronger	129
Puri and Art	143
The Singing Detainee and the Librarian with One Book	151
Therein Lies the Difference	161
The Workhorse	171
Baptism by War	181
Off-Center	187
No Binaries	199
Out of the Attic	207
Murmurs on a Train	213
Turning Back the Tide	223

The Polite Man	239
Parting Suggestions	251

***

References	257

Acknowledgments

This book would not have been possible had Jose Maria Sison and Julieta de Lima ignored my pitch. They welcomed me, practically a stranger, like a friend into their life and home. Our unique time together was a gift and I am filled with gratitude.

I must mention the National Democratic Front – Philippines (NDFP) personnel and the Filipino migrants who also opened up about their lives and longing. May they find a way back to a better homeland.

The Kurdish and Belgian revolutionaries, and all who agreed to be interviewed are likewise an essential part of the book.

The patient Larissa Mae Suarez took my sloppy drafts and helped the most to churn these into something meaningful. She scrapped my worst ideas, and helped me make something of the half-decent ones.

Special thanks to the trusted eyes of Antares Bartolome, Meg Yarcia, and Teo S. Marasigan. They made crucial comments on the text and also did much of the copyediting.

The bright presence of Kim Garcia was indispensable to this project as she took pictures, documented conversations, and helped me get around town besides being an overall good person who livens up any situation.

Miguel Robleza, who designed the cover, I've known since we worked on our high school paper. Louie De Guzman and Jessica Mari De Guzman took me into their home, no questions asked, many times while I worked on this project.

Sarah Raymundo and Joi Barrios-Leblanc provided valuable advice in, and support for, the publishing of this book. Likewise, Karina Bolasco and the Ateneo University Press granted a first-time author a chance and were extremely welcoming throughout the whole process.

I met Vincent W.J. van Gerven Oei somewhat randomly for the first time just days after the passing of Joma. I had sought out punctum books and was lucky to learn to that he was in town. Thankfully, that brief meeting led to the publication of the English edition of this text at punctum books.

Rappler's Chay Hofilena helped to give space for one of the book's chapters, publishing part of the text when it was needed in the public discourse.

Additional thanks to the endorsements of Faye Cura, Jonathan De Santos, Emily Drabinski, and J. Paul Moufawad.

The always supportive Kalipunan ng Damayang Mahihirap or Kadamay and The General Strike crowd pushed me to finish the manuscript. The *Pinoy Weekly* colleagues helped me promote the book.

I must also thank all the people who contributed to the initial crowd-funding for the book, especially Alison Hsiao, Paulette Keating, Yin Yu, Andre Ortega, Chelsea B. Carl, Nazia Hussain, Patrick Macatangga, and Jonna Baldres.

I'm grateful for great friends and loved ones, Genevieve Inumerable, Luis Clarin and Dolly Recto, (Free) Amanda Echanis, Kai Duque, Soleil Santoalla, and Issa Baguisi.

*For Carlets, Randall, Fidel, Kim, and Joma.
For my mother, whose absence is always felt.*

Foreword

Larissa Mae Suarez

Just a few weeks before the first major lockdown in the Philippines, Michael asked if he could meet me at University of the Philippines Diliman to consult regarding a writing project. Over fishballs and bottled juice, he made his pitch: he had just traveled to the Netherlands to meet with Jose Maria Sison and Julieta de Lima, and he wanted me to edit the essays he would write about the couple.

In the next few months, as COVID-19 swept through the world, the project proceeded. That it was completed within a year, despite the lockdowns and quarantines and stress and anxiety and disruption caused by the pandemic, is remarkable, and a testament to Michael's skills and tenacity as a journalist.

Much has already been written about Joma and Julie, though the former has no doubt proven the more popular subject (or target) for reporters, biographers, academics, propagandists, mouthpieces, and all kinds of commentators. *The Singing Detainee and the Librarian with One Book* joins this vast body of existing work, with several unique contributions: first, it is about both Joma and Julie, highlighting the crucial but often overlooked role of Julie in the revolutionary movement in the Philippines; second, it focuses on their life post-exile, not just the rise and development of the communist revolution in the Philippines; and three, extant throughout the essays is the discerning perspective of Michael, himself a young Filipino activist and journalist. Though he has sought to be fair and factual, he makes no pretensions of objectivity or neutrality, and openly discusses the influence of Joma and Julie's ideas and actions on the direction of both his own life and Philippine history.

It's easy to mistake the accessibility of Michael's essays with simplicity. In fact, every essay was rigorously planned and meticulously executed, and the outcome of months of interaction with Joma and Julie and the Filipino community in Utrecht. The twenty-two essays in this collection mingle narrative, memory, and analysis; they are readable and incisive, giving readers another — and distinctively valuable — vantage point into the lives of two Filipinos whose massive impact on political thought and practice in the Philippines has made them a lifelong focus of scrutiny.

*　*　*

In December 2022, Jose Maria Sison passed away. Michael was among the first to contact me to talk about the news; he was agitated that his book had not been completed in time for Joma to see the finished product, and determined to see it published as soon as possible. By then the manuscript was complete and had been submitted to several publishers for consideration. It was an auspicious — or inauspicious, depending on your point of view — time to seek publication. Between 2019 and 2022, as Michael worked on his essays, Ferdinand Marcos Jr. became president of the Philippines, and the political climate became more dangerous for any who professed sympathy for Joma and his ideas. However, the need for rigorous research and writings about the country's past has also become stronger than ever, and Michael's book slots neatly into that category: a counter-history and alternative perspective to the reductive red-tagging of the government; a challenge to the disparaging and belittling narratives about Joma, Julie, and revolution that have dominated the public sphere over the past decade.

Perhaps Joma's most famous creative literary work, and the basis for the title of one of the essays in this collection, is the poem "Sometimes the Heart Yearns for Mangoes" (1994). Since his death, however, lines from a different poem have resonated more deeply with me:

I shall smile with satisfaction
If some people sometimes remember
That I did what I could in my time
To add to what is now commonplace.

That poem, written in 2013, is titled "I Wish to Be Taken for Granted."

This enduring belief in the eventual triumph of the revolution, and Joma's willing effacement of his own magnified status in the movement, is consistent with the depiction that emerges in this collection. I consider myself fortunate to have had the opportunity to help with this timely project. Like Michael, Joma and Julie's work has loomed large in the formation of my own political consciousness, and the death of Joma was more than tragic — it was disconcerting, agitating, and particularly foreboding in the context of ongoing distortions of history in the Philippines. For all their lives, the activists of my generation have had Joma's authoritative voice as a ballast amid the increasing complexity of public discourse, tirelessly articulating sharp, in-depth, and uncompromisingly pro-people analyses of current events and new developments. Now that it is gone, many other capable and respected voices will fill the void, while others take up the task of piecing together for posterity the various aspects of Joma's long life and works. This book is an invaluable addition to that record, all the more significant for being one of the last texts written based on firsthand interactions between the author and Joma himself.

February 2023

Author's Preface

In June 2019, I pitched the idea of publishing an in-depth article to Joma about his life in exile. I had interviewed him quite a few times before, and I felt we had developed a level of rapport common between journalists and their usual sources.

At the time, he was ever-present in the news, releasing statements and trading barbs with then President Rodrigo Duterte. Jose Maria Sison, or Joma, is well-recognized as the founder of the Communist Party of the Philippines (CPP) and New People's Army (NPA), arguably the government's greatest adversaries. He has also been living in the Netherlands as a political refugee since 1987.

Not much is publicly known about the nature of his life in exile — not just the politics of it, but also the personal toll that asylum exacts from its seekers. I was curious about that aspect — and mindful that one of my editors always pushed for writers to file more human-interest stories — so I sent Joma a message, and he responded via email later that day, a lot sooner than I expected. His answer got me off my seat. I went outside to smoke a cigarette with my thoughts racing.

Joma proposed I write a book instead of an article. I had never produced any book-length or book-worthy output before, nor had I even remotely considered it. But now that the suggestion was on the table, how could I say no? The offer was too enticing; it gave me the leeway to explore his history and character with a scope I hadn't imagined. Thinking it over, I was suddenly overwhelmed by the sheer number of ways I could approach the subject of a man who had been making headlines for over half a century. Even with all the preexisting literature on him and the revolutionary movement, there was still a lot of story to be told.

I also had other reasons for pursuing this project. I was raised by a single mother who spent seven years as an NPA guerrilla and many more years as a women's rights activist. I grew up emotionally connected to the revolutionary movement and with a deep affection for it. Its martyrs became my bedtime stories; its hymns were my lullabies; its history, my after-school lessons. My mother's friends always told me the most fascinating tales of champions in upheavals, of loss and isolation. Because of the tyrannical times we live in, I thought maybe a few more stories like these could serve us well.

Joma's ideas and actions have been a constant feature of Philippine politics for most of the postwar period, but he didn't attain that prominence by himself. There's bound to be a web of other stories and people tied to him, all beneath the surface of the public narrative. There was so much ground to cover. No portrait of Jose Maria Sison can be complete without including his wife and brilliant partner Julieta de Lima, as comfortable behind the scenes as her husband is in the spotlight.

Joma and Julie are two of the most important figures in Filipino contemporary history. On the one hand, they are heroes to Filipino revolutionaries back home and beacons of international solidarity in the global communist movement. On the other hand, they're also considered villains to a host of governments, reactionaries, ex-communists, and all manner of paper tigers. This dichotomy — celebrated and vilified for the majority of their lives — was worth investigating.

I was nervous about my pitch. To fill an entire book, I wanted to study their lives in exile, what led to it and likewise who was there to witness and share the ordeal with the couple. I wasn't sure if this was enough to satisfy any group of readers.

Throughout the project, the couple agreed to surrender creative control to me. I thought they might reconsider given the amount of polarization surrounding them, but they were pretty casual about the whole affair. We also decided that documentation in preparation for writing the book would have to take place in the Netherlands, where Joma, Julie, and the rest of the National Democratic Front of the Philippines (NDFP) agreed to meet with me for a series of interviews. I had the intimidating task of traveling a continent away to try and sift through a lifetime of experience and find new stories to tell.

Thankfully, when I arrived in the Netherlands with just this vague idea for the project, I encountered more and more people and events that would make their way into the book.

To secure funding for the project, I posted in the crowd-funding website Indiegogo. Before I left, a number of friends, relatives, obscure acquaintances, and nosey onlookers took the opportunity to weigh in on what I should write. Some of the top recommendations urged me to speak truth to power and to dig up any controversy hidden by the couple. Others wanted me to add to the parade of commemorative literature about their achievements.

The barrage of suggestions confounded me, though I took it all in with respect and understood it as a way to wish me well. At the very least, I thought it best to avoid the role of the insidious journalist out to serialize for the sake of the sensational.

To be clear, this project is not and was never intended to be a comprehensive report on the Philippine Left, or on Joma and Julie. I doubt such a task could be done in a single book. My contribution is only another addition to the large body of work about the revolutionary movement in the Philippines and its leaders. There are numerous reports and recorded accounts on the split in the movement that happened in the late 1980s, the mistakes made along the way, and its rectification and triumphs which led to a resurgence later on.

The couple have shared so much of their ideas with the world. What else is there to add? What I did know, as I prepared to rummage through their lives and ideology, is that it is impossible to treat the latter as incidental.

Despite allusions to historical events, this book is meant to be a portrait of the present. Written from my own perspective from late 2019, it hopes to explore areas of the movement and their humanity that, for the most part, is left out of the written conversation. It is divided into four sections. The first introduces the asylum conditions of Joma and Julie and a few other refugee companions. It juxtaposes this with the diaspora of the Filipino migrant community, and how exile — whether political or economic, as in the case of many migrant workers — is imprisonment by displacement.

The second looks at a few snapshots from the past of the revolutionary movement which inextricably shaped the lives of Joma and Julie. Who would have thought that purchasing a bottle of wine might have helped usher the undoing of the first Communist Party of the Philippines, leading to the establishment of a new one in 1968? Which lesser-known martyrs had saved and made a profound impact on the pair?

The third section focuses on Julieta de Lima. Julie is decidedly reserved; she is one of the longest-serving women revolutionaries in the country, on par with Tandang Sora and Gabriela Silang, and yet there is a dearth of information about her.

The last section chronicles my encounters with revolutionaries and thinkers in Europe: the Dutch activist group Revolutionaire Eenheid, the Kurdistan Workers Party, and the Worker's Party of Belgium. Case studies of these groups attempt to analyze their impact, and those of Joma's and Julie's, on the global class struggle and the relationships between movements. The section also includes a lengthy interview with CPP critic and Dutch Trotskyist Alex de Jong. His divergent and cynical views on Third-World revolutions are pitted against those of Joma's, which guide the CPP today.

After two months in Europe, I returned to the Philipines right into the pandemic lockdown. An upside was that it offered more than sufficient writing time, albeit not under the best conditions. However, the events that followed made finishing the manuscript all the more urgent. Ferdinand "Bongbong" Marcos Jr. was elected president in 2022, completing a Marcos restoration and fascist reboot. I thought of all the exiles on election night, of Joma, Julie, and the rest of their companions who were led to the Netherlands, in large part, by their actions against the dictatorship. With all the disinformation going around, sharing the narratives of exiled Martial Law veterans became added motivation for the project.

While going over the interviews, I gained a renewed sense of admiration for those who had sacrificed so much to fight the dictatorship. Given the current dangerous political climate in the Philippines, several sources reached out with reservations while I was finalizing this book. Some were worried about the dangers of red-tagging.

In the first draft of the manuscript, I included detailed descriptions of the people I interviewed, complete with names, places, and current circumstances. To accommodate the concerns of my sources, I obscured those aspects. Particulars about some interview subjects have been altered or omitted in consideration of their safety and security.

Now more than it has ever been since the people toppled a madman, those who are deep in the trenches of the struggle for freedom are hunted and vilified. The exiles and sources for this book are among them.

In December 2022, I welcomed a trip back to the Netherlands to work on a different project. I planned to stop by Joma's house and talk again like we did three years ago. I sent him an email in advance declaring there would be mangoes when I arrive. The only reply I received was about funeral preparations.

Strangely, I thought I'd never see the passing of Joma in my lifetime. It was hard to imagine a time that wasn't punctuated by his thoughts or shaped by actions he and many others had taken. Hard to imagine how a man who shaped our national history could succumb to mortal limitations.

The loss hurt many—myself included. It was like learning that a character from your favorite story had suddenly stopped his adventures, and no more new tales would be told.

As he lay in great pain for weeks on his hospital bed, he issued his last statement, proclaiming the revolution to be "invincible." I felt it was Joma saying that death would not be his or the revolution's undoing. That for many, if not all, the pursuit was enough for others to carry on. The body suffers terribly. The struggle prevails.

I sought the good and the true about the revolution throughout the nearly three years I spent working on this book. Indeed, Joma lives on and our talks ring clear in my memory. Three people, Joma, Kim and Fidel, who helped me to finish this text have already passed. This book is anchored by memories of them.

I also think back to one of the last things my mother said to me before she passed. *"Walang masama sa Kaliwa. Mabuti ang Kaliwa* (There's nothing bad about the Left. There is goodness in the Left)." I had that in mind every time I switched on my recorder.

January 2023

Introduction

I might have stayed out there forever. It was an early autumn afternoon in Utrecht. The wind scraped me with a skin-piercing chill. In a few days, November would usher in the height of the year's gloom, the dreary period between the previous months' warmer, milder weather and the December festivities. I stood at the doorstep of the office of the National Democratic Front of the Philippines (NDFP), and a terrifying anticipation washed over me. I couldn't bring myself to ring the doorbell. I had arrived at my destination with a severely incomplete idea of what I intended to write. The subjects at hand were about to surrender the details of their lives for my book, yet here I was, outside on the Utrecht sidewalk, still wondering what to do. An old friend, Kim had just picked me up at Schiphol Airport in Amsterdam. We caught up with each other's lives on the train ride to Utrecht Central Station. I stared at some of her new tattoos, including one underneath her bleach blonde and violet bangs that read *"sa digma sisilang ang payapa* (from war, peace will be born)." But my lively friend implored me to focus as she suggested people to meet for the project. From the station, we disembarked for a five-minute walk to the office. I wasn't used to the biting cold. It wasn't just the weather, I was also frozen by thoughts of the task at hand.

Through the window blinds of the NDFP, I saw a glimpse of an old man in a threadbare red cardigan seated at a table, deep in discussion with several others. Beside me, Kim had her hands on her hips, her eyebrows cocked and waiting for me to do something. I asked her if we could delay entering. I needed a few minutes to take it all in — what I was about to do and whether I would be able to pull it off. She said I worry too much; she's right.

The people inside the office were expecting us. We rang the doorbell, stepped inside, and disrupted an ongoing meeting with our exchange of introductions and pleasantries.

"*Uy, si Michael* (Hey, it's Michael)." Jose Maria Sison stood to greet me.

I attempted a wave, but my hand was left hanging in the air like I was about to answer a question in class. I managed to pull off a crooked smile. Kim noticed my whole body stiffen so she dragged me closer to them.

I sat between Joma and Julie. We agreed to conduct most of the interviews at the couple's home, but here in the office Joma already appeared excited, gushing at the prospect of storytelling. I mentioned my family's hometown in Pangasinan. He responded by digging into some internal archive. He named several mayors of my ancestral town and noted the variety of languages therein. Then he traced my lineage back to Spanish colonial times, correctly naming my great-grandparents. I had never met anyone who could do that. It's like a party trick. I was impressed and began to feel somewhat at ease.

Julie let Joma did most of the talking. At 4:00 p.m. she rose to fetch her lunch. She barely looked up from her small cup of food, but muttered corrections to Joma whenever he misremembered a detail or lagged behind in the conversation because he could not hear well even when he wore his hearing aid.

* * *

A few days after my arrival, I biked to Joma and Julie's private residence, or as the Philippine government likes to call it, their luxurious European mansion. I carried my notebook filled with out-of-sequence questions. Luckily, this trip provided plenty of insight to shape the entire text. So much of Joma and Julie's life is tied to their Dutch dwelling.

Inside the apartment, Joma settled down into the faded upholstery of his favorite chair. The afternoon sunlight slanted into the room and bounced off his glasses whenever he looked at the window. His attention was caught by the sight of a passing barge on the Amsterdam–Rhine Canal, the only visible outdoor attraction.

Good conversation is one of Joma's greatest pleasures in life. If you had an assortment of random topics in a hat, he'd be happy to discuss any of them at length. *"Naikwento ko na ba ito?* (Have I told you this?)" he often began, leaning in and committing his entire attention to the exchange. As soon as we sat, he started answering questions I hadn't even asked.

He described the neighborhood and how it turned noisy without warning. On some nights, gunshots and local scuffles roused them from their sleep.

Julie sat in front of her computer. At one point during the 1990s she enjoyed photography with her vintage camera. The hobby ended when a man snatched her camera while she was taking pictures around the block. When I asked to see pictures, they suggested taking a short neighborhood tour instead.

We made our way down the stretch of road on the banks of the Amsterdam–Rhine Canal to climb the Prins Claus bridge at the edge of the neighborhood. On the way back, a conversational high gripped Joma. Although panting from exertion, he insisted on speaking between every labored breath.

Joma's lust for life and conversation struck me as something instinctive; an attempt to bypass, even rebel against, his own physical containment.

The sky had darkened by the time we returned to their house. Julie rushed to her workstation, her face illuminated by three lit monitor screens and a desk lamp. She gave Kim instructions about another task. Joma returned to his chair, rapped on its armrest with his fingers, and started to hum.

Later that evening — notebook in hand, spare change in one pocket, cigarettes in the other, and a dysfunctional laptop open in front of me — I sat on my bed inside my quarters at the NDFP office and tried to invoke some conviction for this book. I didn't know where to go in this huge sandbox. There's so much room for error. But the first few days of meeting the NDFP folks and the Filipino community had led to some key impressions. I went out for a cigarette. It felt like the deep breath I had needed since my plane landed.

The experience of one exile was wildly different from the next. Dealing with separation from the Philippines was a Herculean task or burden, depending on whom you ask. But they all had to rely on each other. They are all, after all, Filipino revolutionaries fighting to liberate a homeland they cannot set foot on.

I had also come upon an unexpected variable: the way Filipino migrant workers and refugees permeated every dialogue. Filipino communities have sprung up throughout the world, pulling their compatriots into orbit. Joma, Julie, and the NDFP were no different.

For approximately the next two months, I spent almost every day gathering data and conducting interviews. I hopped on trains, buses, trams, and bikes or walked to interviews I had booked on the fly. I spoke to migrants, communists, and opponents of the movement, among others, who were added to the developing cast of characters in this book.

Along the way I picked up quite a few surprising details, sources, and angles which would shape the entire book. I didn't know it at the beginning, but my own fears of banishment and homesickness were much greater than my initial anxieties. Predictably, these same fears helped guide and connect everything in these pages. What started out initially as a human-interest piece on the famous couple's current life grew into a collection of portraits examining exile.

A Particular Purgatory

Every month, Joma makes a mandatory appearance before the Dutch police. Sometimes when the situation between him and the Philippine government is more volatile than usual, he is obliged to appear once a week. No other asylum seeker in the Netherlands is asked to report to the authorities so he can personally demonstrate that he hasn't skipped town.

Today, Joma is expected at 10:00 a.m. He's running late, still standing at the door of the apartment complex at 9:45 a.m. with Dennis, the NDFP's security personnel who is always by his side. I'm a bit late too, but arrive in time to catch them as Gary, another staff member, and his car pulls up to the apartment complex to fetch us. Joma has been under increased surveillance from the authorities ever since Dutch law enforcement got wind of an assassination plot by Filipino state forces in 2001, and again because of his arrest in 2007.

"*Mas mabait na din pulis dito ngayon* (The police here are nicer now)," says Joma from the front seat. "They tolerate refugees." The whole trip has the air of a mundane chore, as if we're simply on our way to pick up groceries.

For the past three days, Joma had been sick with a slight fever. No illness, however, was a good enough excuse to forego the compulsory visit. In ten minutes, we reach the station. The old communist stumbles out of the car then asks for a moment as he stomps his right foot on the ground, trying to get the blood flowing in his limbs.

Joma hobbles into the receiving area. He's quite conspicuous, an old Asian man in a bright red cardigan, and the only one grinning ear to ear as he joins others on the lobby bench. The cops are courteous, using *please* and *thank you*, calling him over to a small desk. They ask Joma to sign a few things, nod at him assuredly, and the errand is over. Once we'd left, they told me this was one of the more routine checks Joma has undergone. These encounters were much more heated when he was still on the European Union's terrorist list. In those days, he faced invasive questioning about his daily life more frequently. When politics are turbulent, so too are his trips to station, they say.

* * *

Early on a typical sunless morning, I find myself under an icicled waiting shed, queuing for a bus to Brussels. I care to probe the more unique aspects to Joma and Julie's prolonged stay in the Netherlands besides the visits to the police station.

I'm meeting Jan Fermon, the primary legal counsel for Joma and Julie. I hope he can elaborate on the prickly situation of his clients, as Joma is both legally classified as a refugee and denied residence.

Jan is an affable, widely built man, an independent *advocaat* or attorney, splitting his duties with the progressive counsels of the International Association of Democratic Lawyers. He shows me into his modest office filled with stacked papers and binders, leaving not much room to set down my notepad. He offers me a seat as if I am a prospective client. It isn't quite the expanse of space I expected for a lawyer, and in Europe at that. He doesn't seem to mind the tight quarters and slanted ceiling which might bump one's head when standing in the wrong spot. In a slow baritone voice reverberating around his office walls, Jan begins to explain the peculiar particulars of Joma's decades-long case.

Jan met Joma and Julie when they first arrived in Europe in 1987. He was an activist studying law who helped organize a series of talks for the couple across Belgian universities. To the aspiring lawyer, learning of a dynamic revolution in a distant country meant a broadening of what he had imagined to be possible. Since then, Jan has been a consistent partner in their legal affairs.

Before navigating the wilderness of laws governing asylum status and terrorism, it is important to note that the Dutch government has loathed Joma's presence since he arrived in the country. He is a strain on the Netherlands' relations with the Philippine and US governments. For a time, Jan shares, the website of the Holland's Ministry of Foreign Affairs singled out the presence of Jose Maria Sison in Utrecht as the biggest impediment to Philippine–Dutch relations. Meanwhile, US authorities have made no secret of their desire for him to be classified as a war criminal.

The Dutch and US governments have had a prosperous relationship in the postwar period. The former tends to revere the latter for liberating them from the Nazis, a national gratitude anchoring many of their political decisions to this day. For both governments, the fact that Joma is not in jail — and not planning to leave the Netherlands — is a continuing affront.

* * *

When Joma and Julie first applied for asylum in 1988, their primary counsel was a Mr. Boekman. Jan was their secondary counsel. Sadly, Mr. Boekman was preoccupied with his professional and personal troubles. He found himself in one unfortunate predicament after another while working with Joma. So distressed was Mr. Boekman that he was forced to sell his home and resign from his post after suffering a nervous breakdown.

Luckily for Joma and Julie, Jan would not be short of a helping hand. Quite a few attorneys wanted to make a name for themselves by handling the high-profile asylum suits of two revolutionary leaders. The case threatened to reshape the politico-legal notions of refugee-related law, thereby making it attractive to any ambitious attorney to lend a hand.

"Active ako sa kung anu-anong circles eh, kaya marami akong nakikilala at marami nagpapakilala o nagpipresenta na maging abogado. Pero kadalasan kumukuha kami mula sa referral of foreign comrades (I'm active in many circles, that's why I've met many lawyers, and many also introduced themselves to me and offered to provide me with counsel. But we often hire lawyers based on the referral of foreign comrades)," Joma told me before I interviewed Jan. "And if the refugee has no means to pay, it's the state who pays the lawyers."

In 1990, Joma's appeal for asylum was rejected (PILC 2004).[1] "The Dutch government for political reasons didn't want him to be there," said Jan.[2]

In a turn of fortune, the Raad van State (Dutch State Council) in 1992 ruled that under existing law Joma should not be excluded from international protections, even if the Dutch government had rejected his application. The court also affirmed he had legitimate fears of persecution and danger should he return to the Philippines. Several appeals on both sides were contested. When Joma's asylum was challenged in the courts once more in 1993, the ruling of the Raad van State stood firm by 1995. The judgement states Joma had "well-founded fear of persecution (in the Philippines) on account of his political beliefs" and there was "no sufficient evidence" to suggest Joma carried out serious crimes in his country (PILC 2004).[3]

---

1 Using information provided by the Philippine government against Sison, the Dutch Minister of Justice decided to reject his application for asylum, invoking Article 1F of the Geneva Convention. The article excludes individuals from refugee protection if they have committed serious crimes and are looking to avoid any kind of judicial punishment. In subsequent decisions by the Dutch Minister of Justice, Article 1F has been a constant feature.

2 "By judgment of 17 December 1992, the Raad van State annulled the implied decision to reject. It held essentially that the State Secretary had not demonstrated to the requisite legal standard which of the acts allegedly committed by the applicant had led him to conclude that the applicant fell within the scope of Article 1F of the Geneva Convention." *Sison v Council of the European Union* (2009), §48.

3 An excerpt from the February 21, 1995 Raad van State Decision referring to the evidence presented against Joma reads: "Those pieces, however, do

The Dutch government reacted by changing the law, seeking to nullify the Raad van State's decision and, along with it, Joma's hopes for residency. His appeal was withdrawn from the Raad van State and transferred to a lower administrative court (PILC 2004).[4] Then this other court with newly anointed powers echoed the Raad van State ruling. They said Joma Sison should be recognized as a refugee, but with a catch. They also sided with the Dutch Minister of Justice who said the Dutch state can refuse to give legal admission and residence permit to a refugee who is also a threat to the "public interest." The Dutch minister's position invoked "freedom of policy" in asylum cases, meaning he ascribed to Joma the Dutch government's political agenda coded into policy. Joma's lawyers share that he was denied residence because the Dutch took into account how he would "damage the integrity and credibility of the Netherlands as a sovereign state, in particular in relation to its responsibilities to other states" (PILC 2004).

This was a notable mutation of the law and understanding of what constitutes a refugee. It was commonly accepted, consistent with the 1951 Convention Relating to the Status of Refugees (also known as the Geneva Convention), that residence followed recognition of asylum. The Dutch government insisted otherwise.

---

not offer sufficient evidence for the fundamental judgment that the appellant to that extent has given direction and carries responsibilities for such activities that it can be held that there are serious reasons to suppose that appellant in the sense of the abovementioned article parts have carried out those mentioned crimes." Cited in PILC (2004).

4   The new court was dubbed the Law Unity Chamber of the Aliens Court or the REK and was created in 1996. "The REK held that the Dutch government would not be in violation of Prof. Sison's right if he is not admitted to the Netherlands or permitted to stay therein so long as he is not actually expelled. This judicial hairsplitting has actual practical effects, chief among them being that Prof. Sison, not being a legal resident, has been denied the right to seek employment in the Netherlands. His claim to social benefits such as social security, accommodation and study financing has also been made 'extraordinarily difficult' as a result of his non-admission." Cited in PILC (2004).

Joma faced a bizarre dilemma. He wasn't allowed to stay in the Netherlands, but neither was the Dutch government allowed to send him back to the Philippines or even to a third country, because that put him at risk of being extradited. Such a move violated Article 3 of the European Convention on Human Rights and Fundamental Freedoms, which prohibits putting anyone in certain danger or allowing them to be tortured. The Philippine state had already tortured Joma when he was imprisoned during Martial Law from 1977 to 1986. Any visit back was sure to put him in harm's way again.

These contradictions made Joma an immovable individual with no permission to stay put in Holland. He belonged neither here nor there; in limbo, a purgatory of sorts. His case remains an anomaly of Dutch jurisprudence. Residency should have granted Joma all the benefits of being a citizen. Instead, the Dutch government submitted to tolerating his presence while placing restrictions to make his stay as intolerable as possible. He cannot leave without risk, is constantly surveilled, and is denied the right to rent an apartment in his name. The situation is more a symptom of political friction rather than the inconsistencies of law.

Jan explains, "His case was an example of how, gradually, European countries tried to lower the level of protection for refugees. They're saying, our only obligation is to not send you back, but that does not mean you can stay with us. If you leave the country, maybe we will not take you back again."

Apart from special permits to attend the peace talks together with the NDFP panel and face the Philippine government, any travel outside the Netherlands posed a significant risk. The Dutch authorities could easily prohibit Joma from re-entering the country, leaving him stranded, stateless, and vulnerable outside of its jurisdiction.

And what of Julie? She found herself in opposite circumstances. The Dutch state granted her permanent residence without asylum because her passport wasn't cancelled by the Philippine government. During Joma's asylum proceedings, she was helping to build relations with parties and movements in Asia and Latin America. She was free to travel, which to the Dutch authorities didn't necessarily warrant a refugee classification. She received her residency papers on humanitarian grounds as a wife and mother eligible for "family reunification." She also acquired an alien passport, which permits travel anywhere in the world except the Philippines.

Throughout their marriage, Julie has been in the puzzling position of being out of the spotlight and yet tightly tethered to one pursued by it. It makes the possibility of her return to the Philippines less noteworthy, yet with the same attendant risks to her life and freedom. It seems the patriarchal undervaluation of Julie as a "threat" — and the implied belief that her status in the revolution must be lower than her husband's — comes with certain advantages to her mobility.

During my interview with Jan, we discuss a recent threat to Joma's current status as a refugee with minimal protections. Interior and Local Government chief Eduardo Año has renewed efforts to bring Joma and Julie back to the Philippines to be prosecuted for his crimes. I ask Jan whether this is permissible under international humanitarian law.

"There is no provision in international law which builds a bridge between refugee law and extradition law. Most countries in Europe essentially say that refugee law supersedes extradition law. Which means that some people could go through the whole extradition proceedings, but the courts can then decide otherwise and consider that person a refugee," says Jan, crossing his arms.

The charges stem from a series of alleged purges in the Communist Party's ranks in 1985.[5] "I can imagine that when the Dutch

---

5 Former NDFP man Nathan Quimpo wrote about alleged purges within the communist movement's ranks prior to the 1986 uprising. The cleansing was directed with poor judgement against those who were perceived to be "deep penetration agents." Rosca notes how CPP officials from 1985–86 circulated documents and publications criticizing the "basic principles of the CPP and iron rules of NPA discipline" and thus led to their violations. This period of disorientation was more than anything a crisis of ideological guidance and understanding among the cadres and revolutionaries. Rosca

see the file on Joma by the Filipino authorities, they would probably want to avoid a trial because they don't want to make a fool of themselves," Jan says, referring to Joma's incarceration while the supposed crimes were committed.[6] "Of course other things depend on diplomatic pressure, the Americans, etc. There could be an attempt," he adds.

In August 2002, Colin Powell, then US Secretary of State to President George W. Bush, came to the Philippines to promote his government's global anti-terror campaign. Part of the agenda was to coordinate the placement of Joma on the US terror list, which was announced by the US State Department ten days after Powell's visit. In addition, the Communist Party of the Philippines (CPP) and the New People's Army (NPA) were also terror-listed. Two days after the US deemed him a terrorist, the Dutch government followed suit. The EU did likewise in October 2002. Only the categorization by the Americans holds to this day.

Neither lawyer nor comrade broke the news to Joma that he'd been labelled a terrorist. Instead, Joma's dentist inadvertently tipped him off.

The dentist called to follow up on a payment from a recent appointment. Impossible, thought Joma. The funds must have transferred. He checked with the bank on the same day and learned his assets had been frozen. Jan guesses that maybe the authorities thought he had millions. They didn't know the senior citizen only had a few hundred euros to his name, the entirety of what little savings he had from his remaining social benefits. Later, Joma was ordered by the Dutch government to pay back in a series of monthly installments the entirety of the pension they'd afforded him as he was now considered a terrorist.

---

also notes how this made Joma feel like he was made to "wallow in crap" after learning of these transgressions (Quimpo and Quimpo 2012, 418–19). See also Rosca and Sison (2004).

6 Joma was in jail when these internal party conflicts occurred creating casualties among their ranks. However the state continues to pin the blame on him. After his release, the CPP pledged all its efforts toward rectification, ensuring that such mistakes, rooted in poor ideological consolidation, should never happen again.

By May 2006, Joma appealed to the European Court of Justice in Luxembourg to be removed from the terrorist list. Jan, his primary counsel, argued there was no Statement of Reasons given by his accusers, the Dutch and EU governments in the form of the Council of the European Union, for duplicating the decision made by the US.[7] Jan was adamant, after the initial damage was done four years ago — assets frozen, message sent — a plausible manifest for declaring him a terrorist had to be given. They waited for another year. In 2007, the Council came up with what Jan bemoans as "a sort of Statement of Reasons."

The Council exhibited a half-page document, stating the Raad van State had approved the decision of the Dutch government to reject Joma's asylum application because of his involvement in violent terrorist action.

The Raad van State didn't side with the Dutch state in refusing Joma asylum because asylum or refugee proceedings do not intersect at all with those of persecuting a perceived terrorist. Furthermore, the question of anti-government activity in the State Council's accounts does not make terrorism implicit. Jan dismisses the contention as "two different logics and legal frameworks. One has nothing to do with the other."

The much bigger problem was that a crucial bit of the "sort of Statement of Reasons" wasn't entirely true according to Jan. The State Council didn't approve the decision to reject Joma's asylum application.

"We wrote a letter to the twenty-seven European Ministers of Foreign Affairs, saying 'take care, because if in the council you approve the new decision to include him again in the list, you're making a serious mistake because the Statement of Reasons submitted to you is wrong, completely incompatible and in

---

[7] The case background states, "in so far as it concerned the applicant, on the grounds that no statement of reasons had been given for the decision, that it had been adopted in the course of a procedure during which the applicant's rights of defence had not been observed and that the Court of First Instance itself was not in a position to undertake the judicial review of the lawfulness of that decision." *Sison v. Council of the European Union* 2009, §2.

complete contradiction to the truth,'" Jan stresses. He reiterates this same thought to me at various points throughout the interview, ensuring I understand his unequivocal message. "There's nothing to interpret there, they said the opposite of what actually happened." And yet —

"They must have done something to correct that?" I ask.

"Nothing happened. They ignored it and still renewed the decision for him to be one the terror list, basing it on the wrong Statement of Reasons," answers Jan.

Jan was incredulous at the proceedings. At one point he attended a meeting of the Committee of the Council of Ministers in the European court. He recognized one of the men present, a high-ranking Belgian civil servant at the table. He sat down next to him and struck up a conversation.

Jan introduced himself. "I'm on the Sison case."

"Yes, I know," replied the man.

"Did you get our letter? Did you see that the Statement of Reasons is totally incompatible with what the State Council actually said?" asked Jan.

"Yes, we saw it." An admission, no recognition of wrongdoing and avoidant of a follow up.

"What do you mean you saw it? And then nevertheless took the decision to talk nonsense, to say, well, whatever?" Jan said.

The man shifted in his seat, and started to school Jan as if he were a naive practitioner. "But you know it doesn't work that way. Every country brings their own list, with a suggested Statement of Reasons. We don't discuss that. We just don't. Because if we start discussing the Dutch proposals then the Dutch will start discussing our proposals. So we just staple it together and it's fine."

"Even if you know it's bluntly wrong?"

"Yes, we don't discuss. Of course we know it's wrong, everybody saw it. But that's what the Dutch wanted. So we approved it," he said, inured to the absurdity of the connivance.

Joma's counsel had to reconfigure their tactics. The second round of proceedings began on more "substantive" grounds. The court questioned how the Dutch government managed to put him on the list in the first place. By law, that required at least an investigation at the national level into supposed terrorist activity. The EU only need to know if such an investigation exists, not even if it was concluded. For their part, Dutch officials claimed the decision in the asylum proceedings was the equivalent of an investigation into, or a court ruling on the implications of a terrorist offense. They tried to establish an equivalence between what was meant to be a criminal investigation and a political one.

However, those parallels didn't work. An accusation doesn't equal an investigation, or even grounds to begin any sort of investigation. In the end, the EU court resolved that an actual direct investigation into terrorist activity had to have taken place. Since there was none to speak of, Joma was not a terrorist as far as the EU was concerned.

The European Court of First Instance ruled in September 2009 that Joma was never proven to have engaged in an act of terrorism and that Dutch court findings were actually favorable to his pleas for asylum. It also lifted the freezing of his bank account.

It took seven years to accomplish this, but it was a major victory for Jan and Joma. They had secured a final recognition from the court that Joma had the right to be duly informed of any charge before being sanctioned with measures such as freezing his bank accounts or violating his right to representation by legal counsel and the right to avail of judicial review.

That an entire bureaucracy persisted with an accusation built on faulty information for years is bewildering. To harass Joma like that must have required much malice. The Dutch government saw Joma as a "pain in the ass" and wanted to show him what it felt like. His exclusion from the terrorist list in Europe sent a clear message to the United States: revolution is not terrorism.

According to Jan, the Dutch government, with US backing, tried to pressure the EU to hear an appeal on the decision. A majority of the countries in the EU said no. He says, "there was no enthusiasm at all to take it to an appeal level."

The complications of seeking asylum and being terror-listed endured by Joma and Julie are part of a political agenda of containment. The two are examples and exceptions to many of the rules and disorders of contemporary politics. Today, Julie is a rejected asylum seeker with residency papers and her husband is a refugee and a terrorist depending on which government you ask.

I believe there is a special kind of pleasure derived from the recognition given by a powerful enemy. Praise from comrades, friends, and the masses warms the heart. But when a great imperialist power like the US government is alarmed by your existence, exhausts an arsenal of legal resources to malign and restrain you further in the hopes you never return home, it's also quite a compliment. It might be regarded with a grim, albeit candid, satisfaction.

Mangoes and Escape Plans

An inviting warmth keeps me company this morning. I can't tell how long it's been with me. The sunlight filters through the third-floor window of my sleeping quarters at the NDFP offices. I'm sweating more than I have in weeks. I kick off my blankets to savor the heat. I'm dreaming of the sun.

When I wake up, I'm clutching my knees. My entire body shivers beneath a thick cotton comforter. Fetal position. The clock says 7:00 a.m. The light won't arrive for another two hours. My subconscious has been mocking me. What I mistook for warmth was actually the cold searing my flesh. Sometimes the sun doesn't emerge until 10:30 a.m., then begins sinking at past three in the afternoon. I miss it. It's almost two weeks since my arrival, and my homesickness has arrived.

After lunch, I head over to Joma and Julie's residence. I'd already visited a few times by bus, but Julie recommended a forty-minute route by foot to Kanaleneiland, and I welcomed the chance to be outside at high noon when the dogged frosty weather was away. Aside from the Pinoys, the only slivers of warmth I gather are from the sky, on those rare instances when it isn't a downbeat gray. The red-brick and cream-colored houses begin blurring together in my vision. A few medium-rise buildings with wide glass windows crack the dreariness of brick.

Pigeons and crows fly low, almost swiping my head, blithely unafraid of humans.

Kanaleneiland, Joma and Julie's neighbourhood, is much like other parts of Utrecht but more compact and pressed together. Wide, four-story housing edifices with dozens of apartment units, uniform in brick or plain white panels, line the streets. The sidewalks grow narrower with scraggly and unkempt bushes. Laundry hangs outside apartment windows.

The shift in the demographics is also striking. No more pale Dutch giants strolling and biking across Utrecht's capacious outdoors. Here, I find migrants whose skin tones come in varying shades of brown: Turks, Moroccans, Indonesians, and a sprinkling of Filipinos. The locals say this is the city's "immigrant ghetto." The more diplomatic Dutch Caucasian will describe the area as "diverse." Residents on the sidewalk wear headscarves, turbans. A couple of street vendors peddle designer knockoff clothes and bags out of the trunk of their cars.

I'm told Kanaleneiland has one of the highest poverty and crime rates in the country. Some pizza places won't even deliver to this area for fear of muggings. I pass by the only affordable restaurant I've seen in Utrecht, at the garage shack of a Turkish cook.

"Yalandino!" yells my newfound friend, the jolly shawarma-selling Turk around the corner, as if to tap into some connection with the Pinoys known to be residing in the area. "Jalandoni," I correct him. But no, I add, I'm not here to meet with any of the Jalandonis, another well-known revolutionary couple in exile.

Their notoriety may not carry the same weight in the neighborhood as it does among compatriots, but the Turkish locals I've spoken to know of Filipino refugees living nearby. Joma and Julie's home was listed on the in-flight magazine over here as a tourist spot. They aren't hard to find.

I'm almost alone in the streets for the duration of my walk. You can travel kilometers here and not chance upon a single soul. Any pedestrian is polite but avoidant, sharing the gloom of the gray overcast. Any movement is obvious on a vacant Utrecht afternoon. I'm sure a lot of people love it here, but the stillness of it all is dampening my enthusiasm. Manila, by contrast, is chaos crossed with amphetamines, so the sudden slowdown of life is odd to me.

Joma and Julie live beside the shimmering Amsterdam–Rhine Canal, a lengthy stretch of water curving southeast from Amsterdam into Utrecht and central Netherlands. Long barges carrying neatly stacked cargo on their decks are seen sailing along.

I climb the building's stairs. I reckon this must be a small but recurring obstacle for the couple, who are both in their eighties. I enter a thin corridor littered with books. When Julie greets me, I raise a concern about them having to hike two flights of stairs. She responds with a grin and a correction: "Two and a half."

I can't repress my curiosity. I find the actual living conditions smoke-screened by the Philippine government's accusations of Joma and Julie's hypocrisy and extravagance. In 2018, presidential spokesperson Salvador Panelo commented that the pair were "living in comfort and luxury while his comrades die for a lost cause" (Romero 2018). This isn't the lavish suite which comes to mind when one hears such claims. Joma and Julie reside in one of the poorest neighborhoods of one of the richest countries on Earth.

Unlike most Dutch households, their heater is off for the month of November, to save on electricity bills. Like the couple, I keep wearing my jacket, sweater, and gloves for the duration of my stay. The house smells of the remnants of simmering tea. Julie leads us past the kitchen, where pots and pans are clumped together with unwashed coffee mugs in the sink. Joma used to smoke beside a small alcove by the kitchen cabinet. But he has been nicotine-free since 2001, when a doctor found his lungs to be severely weakened.

We sit on the couch in their living room. More bookshelves than actual wall is visible in the seventy-five-square-meter apartment. Their personal library includes a variety of communist literature from various parts of the globe; biographies of different world leaders (with a deliberate focus on Philippine presidents); tomes on old and new economic theories; writings by anti-Left authors slandering the CPP; and a few CD cases containing Frank Sinatra, Rey Valera, and a collection of kundiman classics. About half of their living room is taken up by a workstation. Two computers stand back-to-back—three monitors for Julie and two for Joma. This set-up is ideal for multitasking, according to them. In front of the sofa is a battered old television set with protruding plastic sheets and wires. They've also stashed a collection of teas, sugars, and coffee packets in a cardboard box under the coffee table.

Almost everything occupying their waking hours is here in the cluttered living room. Julie apologizes for the mess. By Dutch standards, this apartment and the community are distinctly lower class. To me, however, they've made it nice and cozy, neither a palace nor a shack in the slums.

I forgot to bring mangoes—that often-mentioned craving, the subject of one of Joma's most well-known poems, his eternal yearning (Sison 1994). When I broach the topic of homesickness, he reacts by mourning the fact that he'll never again stand before an abundance of mangoes. "I wrote a poem about it!" an eager Joma informs me, before reclining back into his chair.

After a moment of thought, he backpedals a bit, assuring me there's a proper time and place for cravings. They are fleeting, though, and should never be given too much attention. There are no mango stands in Utrecht, after all. Joma says he is "at home in the world being a proletarian internationalist." That immediate reflex, to dwell on principle over sentiment, helps him regain composure. It's as though he went outside into the cold and came back to fetch his jacket.

Joma and Julie have been stuck in the Netherlands since the Philippine government under then President Corazon Aquino cancelled Joma's passport in September 1988 while the pair were abroad attending speaking engagements. A new charge of subversion was made against him.[1] When the couple received word of this, they stayed for a few months in the home of NDFP cadres

---

[1] The subversion charges, though later dropped when the anti-subversion law was repealed in 1992, stem from supposed claims by intelligence assets

Luis Jalandoni and Coni Ledesma, fellow grandparents of the Philippine revolution.

They didn't take the news lightly. They weighed their options, considered the slim chance of returning to the Philippines in their desperation, only if they could successfully evade the state's ire and punishment. "I had to try," mutters Joma, remembering. "I had to try to come back home." The rebel-filled countryside could provide some much-needed cover for the pair. Except just reaching Philippine soil has its own set of challenges.

They considered a plan to get past the borders of Europe and slip back into the Philippines in secrecy. It involved the help of Irish comrades who volunteered to commandeer a boat for them in Hong Kong to take them back home. Many Irish missionaries had spent time in the Philippines under the Marcos dictatorship and had friendly relations with the resistance movement.

They were supposed to take a plane to Hong Kong and, from there, reach the Philippines discreetly by sea. The airplane trip itself, however, posed too many complications. The pair were under constant surveillance and slipping out of Dutch borders was sure to alarm the authorities. By their estimates, any route through international waters had also been compromised. So they put off their plans and instead sought political asylum.

Even then, Julie toyed with the idea of still somehow finding their way back. She vowed to keep growing her hair until she stepped foot on her homeland. Two years later, on her husband's fiftieth birthday, she snipped her waist-long black locks with a long sigh of resignation. Escaping back into the country was impossible. In the presence of friends and comrades she cut a faint smile, convincing everyone and herself that the matter must be put to rest. There would be better days.

After all, they thought to themselves and with good reason, even if by some miracle they managed to elude all the obstacles preventing their return, the domestic threats were far more

---

of the state that Joma had resumed his post as chairman of the CPP. See *PDI* (1988).

lethal. Even after Martial Law, the state continued to torment and murder scores of activists and revolutionaries.

In the past three decades, the NDFP has uncovered several active assassination attempts against Joma. The couple were, and remain, targets. Coming closer to the crosshairs only endangered them further along with those closest to them.

"Better to be abroad than to be in a cell or in the grave," Joma laughs, wiping his forehead. Yet there is an undeniable ache, ever-present, when he talks about the suddenness of the events that stranded him and Julie in Europe.

Cory Aquino's purported revival of Philippine democracy was upstaged by the continuation of the status quo before and even during Marcos's reign. Human rights violations, massacres of the poor by state forces, numerous coups, and continuing economic downfall overturned what was thought by many to be a drastic new age following the collapse of the dictatorship. The facade crumbled; the charade went awry. State forces assassinated public figures of the mass movement, including the celebrated labor leader Rolando Olalia on November 1986 and fiery mass leader Leandro Alejandro on September 1987. More of the same followed. In hindsight, Joma and Julie believe that had they succumbed to the powerful urge to attend the tributes for their fallen comrades, they too would have met the same fate.

By 1997 the couple attained an unprecedented watered-down form of refugee status. A reluctant state had granted Joma asylum without residence and Julie residence without asylum. Through some manipulation of the legal system, the Dutch government also denied them a host of welfare benefits. Throughout their stay, North American and European governments have been determined to brand the pair and the entire Philippine revolution as terrorist actors in a bid to diminish their protection from extradition. Despite the close scrapes with death in the past, the constant intimidation from numerous governments, and Joma's detention again in 2007, their conditions here are much safer compared to the certain death, and perhaps torture, awaiting them in the Philippines.

Imprisonment is a recurring theme in our conversation. When discussing his prolonged exile, Joma cannot resist bringing up memories of his incarceration during Martial Law. His years abroad and his years in jail have become intertwined in his memory, existing together as twin contemplations of his containment.

Understandably, Joma chooses the prison metaphor for living in the Netherlands. Ever since his inclusion in global terrorist lists in 2001 and despite his removal from the European lists in 2009, the Dutch government has barred him from ever leaving the country. Prior to this, they permitted Joma several trips to adjoining countries to attend speaking appointments, which carried risks of their own. Those in power, with full knowledge of Joma's increasing age and decreasing mobility, have chosen to keep him here. Caught between an assured demise and an uncertain political status, he edges closer to his own mortality, reflecting on his confinement in Utrecht, which has now lasted for over thirty years.

To many Filipinos, Utrecht probably seems like paradise. In my brief stay, it hasn't been, but I understand the appeal. The security of living in safety, meeting your basic needs, and building up some savings, is an excellent selling point to people who have spent their whole lives in fraught, poverty-stricken conditions. Kanaleneiland, for example was the fanciest, cleanest, and quietest "ghetto" I'd ever seen. But Joma and Julie didn't choose this. They are trapped here in a collection of red brick houses, bike lanes, and empty sidewalks. Utrecht is their cell even if it is also their fort, the Netherlands is their prison, and the reactionaries conspiring to worsen their predicament act as implacable wardens.

"Freedom is the recognition of necessity. My best talent was never participating in (armed) skirmishes with the enemy. I just do the best I can with what I can," says Joma, not wanting to linger in his own longing.

In their internment, though, at least Joma and Julie have managed to craft a niche for themselves. The capacity to participate in the revolutionary struggle is their cornerstone, the engine which keeps them going.

"We are proletarian internationalists," Joma repeats, and Julie gently nods. But in their fugitive thoughts, there are daydreams of mangoes and long-ago getaway plans.

Family of Exiles

I'm off to party with a communist. A group of Filipino migrants is hosting a Halloween get-together, and Joma has invited me to attend.

It's 5:00 p.m. The sun has been gone for almost two hours. I've just finished another interview with the couple at their home. Julie isn't joining us. Clad in layers of wool cardigans on top of her duster, she heads straight for her workstation right as our session ends. The light of three computer screens gleams on her glasses as she refocuses her attention. Joma is getting ready, putting on a hat as we wait for his main escort from the NDFP staff to fetch us.

Dennis arrives moments later. A little over six feet, he towers in the lobby, wearing a dark brown jacket which drapes over his body without creasing. The breeze from the canopy over the door plays with his thin silver hair. We wait for our driver, Gary.

Dennis screens the doorway. The streetlamps outside are few and far apart. The three of us stand by the door inside the lobby in a pool of yellow light, surrounded by the darkness beyond the exit. I feel a moment of vulnerability. We are exposed here, easy targets. I can't help but be reminded of the threats Joma has faced throughout his life. But Dennis is with us — a sobering presence, his steadiness assuring me all this is routine.

I hear a snicker from Joma beside me, who seems to have remembered something as we wait behind Dennis. Smirking, he reaches into the breast pocket of his shirt (over which he is wearing his favorite red cardigan). *"May costume din ako ha, naihabol ko pa* (I have a costume, I managed to get it in time)," he pulls out an eyepatch and puts it on his left eye. The Pirate Comrade is ready to have a good time. Gary stops in front shortly after, and upon Dennis's signal, we hurry across the dark sidewalk and into the waiting vehicle.

The party is at an NGO-owned bungalow called Emma House tucked in an Utrecht suburb. We head straight for the spacious main hall, decorated with banderitas, where exiles and migrants alike are mingling and dancing. A party game of Trip to Jerusalem (the colloquial name for musical chairs in the Philippines) begins. Tiny ghouls, witches, vampires, skeletons and others costumed children chase each other across the dance floor.

Joma makes the rounds, switching between his public persona and private character without skipping a beat. He chats with other guests, dancing here and there, then sits alone against the wall to catch his breath. The disco lights flashing on his face helps me keep track of him as the lights flicker.

Dennis sits near the exit, arms crossed, motionless. It's hard to say if he's sleeping — he appears too rigid to actually be at rest. I have a hunch that through the narrow slits of his eyes, which a casual onlooker might take to be closed, he scans the premises.

Halloween is not among the traditional holidays celebrated in the Philippines. The Dutch don't seem to make a big deal out of it either. Whatever importance the holiday has for either of the nations, this occasion is an opportunity to assemble, an attempt to revive homesick spirits. The guests are clutching at some piece of home, reminding themselves of fiestas frozen in memory.

The opening of the buffet table begins with a prayer by the host, followed by anonymous urges every five minutes: *"Kain pa* (Eat some more)!" I haven't seen anyone touch the only Dutch dish on the table, *bitterballen* or Dutch balls of deep-fried meatstew. The main attractions on the table are adobo, sinigang, bistek Tagalog, and relleno, all of which are halfway gone by the time I scoop some white rice onto my paper plate.

The party was put together by the local migrant organization 3K, which stands for Kababayan, Kaibigan, Kaisa (Compatriot, Friend, Unity). 3K has been at the core of most Filipino-related public gatherings in Utrecht through parties, donation drives, and solidarity campaigns for marginalized compatriots. I've been expecting to see an organization more or less akin to activist groups back home, whose activities are primarily political, but 3K is a little different. They try to give more attention to the community's alienation in a foreign land. Like on every other occasion, they opened doors to anyone regardless of ideology.

I've only been in Europe for over two weeks. It's the longest time I've been away from the Philippines. Though incomparable to the ordeals of the rest of the people here at the party, I wonder if my time here offers a hint of what the early part of exile might be like. Until tonight I haven't realized how much I've been craving the comfort of Filipino company. The evening's DJ plays his handpicked set, old Pinoy hits like VST and Company and contemporary crowd favorites like Bruno Mars. But his playlist is eclipsed when one of the guests requests a particular YouTube dance mix. "Budots Two Hours Non-Stop" blasts from the speakers, and a frenzy of PG-13 proportions breaks out on the dance floor. Seeing the commotion, Joma places himself in a ring of boogying migrants to swing his hips and twist his outstretched arms.

I spot a slender vampire zipping around the party. It's Douglas, a member of 3K, whom I recognize from the day I arrived at the NDFP office. Like he did during our first meeting, he races through the hall to greet everyone in a dizzying display of geniality. Somehow he's part of every group conversation and has laughed at every joke throughout the evening.

The 35-year-old Masbate native started working abroad as an IT consultant in 2012. First based in Ireland, he moved elsewhere in the UK, then his company sent him to Indonesia and Singapore before he settled in Utrecht. Douglas befriended one of the NDFP staff around the same time he settled in the Netherlands. His outgoing personality draws many Filipinos to him, since there aren't many of his kind around. When he was invited to visit the NDFP office, he accepted without hesitation — where there are Pinoys, he would be too.

"I'm familiar with the NDF, and the group of Ka [Comrade] Joma and the group of the *aktibista*. Personally, it doesn't mean if you're involved with this group that you're already someone fighting with the government," he tells me. "*Sinasabi nila na may ipinaglalaban sila. Sa akin,* most of the time they are against the government, but I do respect that, *sila iyon at paniniwala nila iyon. Para sa akin, kung na-involve man ako sa kanila,* I'm treating them as my friend (They tell me that they're fighting for something. To me, most of the time they are against the government, but I do respect that; that's them and that's their belief. For me, if I'm involved with them, I'm treating them as my friend)."

I found this perplexing. The big bad NDFP has often been maligned in our homeland, cast as villains in the Philippines' decades-long civil war. The Philippine government considers the NDFP a terrorist organization, accusing it of everything from snatching children from their parents to standing in the way of economic stability. In other words, the NDFP has been subjected to one of the longest and most systematic smear campaigns in the country's history. One might then assume that any mention of the revolutionaries dissuaded people from all interaction. Instead, an invitation to visit the NDFP headquarters draws the same reaction as a party invitation.

"*Hindi ako ilang o takot* (I'm not uneasy or afraid)," preempts Douglas. "*Tinitingnan ko lang sila bilang tao* (I just see them as people)." He is even unfazed by the presence of Joma Sison, chief antagonist in the state's eyes. He treats Joma as a friend, as he does everyone else here tonight.

In the Philippines, where the risk of persecution for having Leftist links is dangerous, these same people might go out of their way to avoid any hint of an association with Joma. Yet the rules here are different. Migrants have fostered an impulse to seek each other out. Over the years, the NDFP has built their base in Europe into something akin to a community center for

Pinoys. The downstairs room at a national liberation headquarters also functions like a multi-purpose hall in one of Manila's barangays. The office hosts a variety of civilian socials, from birthday parties to baptisms to weddings. The New Year's Eve party is a notable hit among migrant workers, the party guests tell me.

"Si Joma Sison ay rebelde, so curious ako, although parang lolo lang siya dito. He is just a normal person here, kagaya ng lahat ng Pilipino dito. Hindi ko masyado nakikita si Tita Julie, 'di masyadong sociable, but I respect them both (Joma Sison is a rebel, so I'm curious, but here he's just like a grandfather. He's just a normal person here, like every other Filipino. I don't see Auntie Julie much, she's not as sociable, but I respect them both)," says Douglas.

I wonder whether other 3K members feel the same way Douglas does. It surprises me to learn that one of the guests tonight, Anna, is a self-proclaimed Diehard Duterte Supporter or DDS. She's dressed as a witch, complete with a pointy black hat and broomstick, running after her three-year-old daughter onto the dancehall. She has been a caretaker and house cleaner for nine years in the Netherlands. She led the 3K preparation committee for this Halloween party.

Someone who supports one of the most rabid anti-communist administrations in Philippine history organized a social event with the NDFP and Joma Sison himself in attendance. I might be the only person here who finds that a bit strange.

Anna shares, *"Ako, nag-campaign pa nga ako dito no'ng eleksyon, e. Pero ngayon 'di na ako active. Busy na ako, e. Less stress ba. Hindi na nga nakakanood ng balita. Bahala si Duterte at Joma, away nila 'yon* (I campaigned here during the recent elections. But I'm no longer active since I've become busy. It's less stressful this way. I don't have time to watch the news anymore. I leave it to Duterte and Joma, it's their fight, not mine)." Her family occupies most of her time, and the NDFP's divergent viewpoint isn't a problem for her.

When I ask for her thoughts on Joma, casually she answers, *"Dito ko na lang siya nakilala. May picture pa nga kami, e* (I just met him here [in the Netherlands]. We even have a picture together)."

She also recalls, shrinking with some guilt, her role in a bit of controversy involving Joma. A couple of years ago, Anna posted on the 3K Facebook page a picture of Joma dancing beside people at a party, one of whom was a young girl. Some DDS social media groups saw it and circulated the image online, accusing the communist leader of being a dirty old man staying in Europe to sate an appetite for impressionable young women.

Anna put a hand on her hips, *"wala naman masama e, 'yong tao lang nagpapasama.* (There was nothing bad about it, there are just some who make it look bad)."

Distressed by the gossip, for a time the young woman in the photo avoided other 3K members and the NDFP. But tonight she's here, having already moved on from the abuse she endured online. I resist the urge to ask her a few questions; she doesn't need to be reminded of bad memories.

Douglas attests that 3K is exactly what people here need. *"Pinakamahirap 'yong malayo sa pamilya, pero na-overcome ang homesickness because of the Filipino circle* (It's very hard to be so far from our families, but we overcome our homesickness because of the Filipino circle)," he says. *"Sina Tita Luningning at Tito Jun parang nanay, tatay ko. Pamilya* (Tita [Aunt] Luningning and Tito [Uncle] Jun are like a mother and father to me. Family)."

Family. All the Filipinos I've interviewed here at the party have uttered the word at some point. I almost suspect they've rehearsed it. They do look like a boisterous, expanded clan gathered here tonight. They are stuck here with each other, might as well get along.

Douglas and Anna are typical Overseas Filipino Workers (OFWs), forced to leave the Philippines in search of a better life. The powers overseeing global capitalism brought them here and they have no immediate prospects of returning home. In a way they are not unlike Joma and Julie, who have been chased out of the Philippines by the same forces. Exile, whether economic or political, is imprisonment by displacement. It is when people are condemned to leave their lands dressed in invisible chains.

The guests here tonight are compatriots whose tethers to home soil have been maliciously severed. It is in many cases a permanent tear of the body from a land whose borders are either shut or a danger to them. It is a horrible fate of constantly longing. Thankfully, exiles are also somewhat magnetized to each other. They throw great parties too.

* * *

The following Sunday, from the NDFP office I slip into a nearby Utrecht chapel to attend noontime mass with the Filipino community. The chapel is run by the Sister Servants of the Holy Spirit of Perpetual Adoration, more commonly known as the Pink Sisters, because of their unique pink habits. I'm late and alone, as Joma and Julie are not the most avid churchgoers. But I'm keen on learning what the congregating Filipinos had to say about their exiled communist neighbors.

Here I meet the cheerful Carmen, a proper parishioner dressed in a dark green blouse, black skirt, pointed shoes, and a silver scapular around her neck. She volunteers to share her thoughts on the Sisons, whom she has considered close friends of the family for most of her twenty-seven-year stay in the Netherlands.

Carmen met Joma in 1999, at a party thrown by Filipino migrants in the Netherlands. Not one to ever shy away from social events, Joma was circling the venue and struck up a conversation with her. They became fast friends. Carmen can almost match Joma's penchant for ceaseless chatting.

She tells me, "When I'm with Tito Jo, we don't talk about politics if you don't like politics. We just talk about normal life." They regularly talk about life in the Philippines, news in the migrant community, and even entertainment gossip. *"Gusto daw niya sana na isapelikula ang buhay niya, tapos gaganap si Vilma Santos at Christopher De Leon* (He says he wants someone to make his biopic, starring Vilma Santos and Christopher De

Leon)." She looks giddy at the prospect of seeing her friend's life on film.

Joma has had countless dinners at Carmen's home. He stays for karaoke, sometimes until three in the morning. They have spent many birthdays and holidays with each other's families. Carmen is also a frequent guest at the NDFP office, dropping by for afternoon coffees.

Even Anna's relatives back in the Philippines have become somewhat adoptive and supportive of their Tito Jo's work. They'd be seen attending his book launches in Manila and one time, even arrived dressed in shirts custom printed with I LOVE JOMA SISON.

"'*Di na nila inisip that it can be very dangerous* (They don't consider that it can be very dangerous)," says Carmen, sneering at their blooper. I imagine the family looking like an overenthusiastic bunch cheering on their uncle at a local basketball game. Carmen is right. Considering the long animosity of the state towards Joma, it could have been construed as a dangerous gesture.

Carmen discloses the backstory to an infamous moment which made headlines back in 2007. She was at first hesitant to add to the controversy constantly following her polarizing friend. In a hushed voice, she proceeds to divulge slowly, to avoid any misinterpretation. This is the closest I'd ever come to reporting about the entertainment industry. I'm intrigued. The tip of my pen is already poised on paper.

In December 2006, Carmen invited Joma to a holiday concert featuring Filipino singer Janno Gibbs and the popular actress Ara Mina. Carmen recounts, *"Pinilit ko siya sumama. Sabi ko, 'Halika, punta ka doon. Isayaw mo siya, dali!' Siyempre sumayaw siya talaga. 'Di alam ni Ara Mina na this is Joma Sison. Inilagay pa niya kasi sa website niya kasi masaya naman siya sa okasyon. Tapos naging laman naman siya ng diyaryo* (I begged him to join us. I said, 'Go over there, dance with Ara Mina, hurry!' Of course, he really danced with her. Ara Mina didn't know that this is Joma Sison. He even posted it on his website because he did have a good time. Then it got reported in the papers)."

Military generals pounced on the opportunity to lambast Joma, and news outlets in the Philippines reported the communist leader had been caught partying with a scantily clad sexy actress. In a press conference, then armed forces spokesman Lt. Colonel Bartolome Bacarro took the opportunity to reiterate a familiar jibe: *"Nagpapakarasarap si Joma sa Netherlands habang nabubulok itong mga komunistang rebelde sa Pilipinas* (Joma is enjoying himself in the Netherlands while communist rebels are rotting in the Philippines)" (Laude 2007).

Carmen swears there was nothing malicious about the pictures of Joma and Ara Mina. They were at a party; people dance. Nor was Joma affected by the military's obvious attempt to blow the incident out of proportion, spoiling what little recreation he had in exile.

Whether reluctant or unable to return home, Filipinos abroad—like most other nationalities, I assume—tend to gravitate toward each other. Religion and ideology may create chasms among people, but here, from what I've seen in my brief visit, that isn't the case.

* * *

A few days later, I got a hold of Coni and Louie at the NDFP offices to ask them about their ties with the migrant community. They tell me it hadn't always been this way.

Throughout the 1970s and '80s, when the NDFP was starting out in Europe, other comrades were branching out through a solidarity movement that put them in regular contact with compatriots. However, the movement had agreed to a policy of keeping the NDFP's work and the solidarity movement separate. This meant Coni and Louie or anyone directly associated with the NDFP avoided any major assemblies where migrants were also attending. *"Ang mga ibang kasama pa ang natatakot na baka ma-identify masyado ang pagtitipon sa CPP, kaya excluded kami. Pero ang ibang mga migranteng Pilipino dito sa Utrecht pa ang nagsasabi na 'Punta kayo sa party namin.' Kaya minsan 10:00 p.m. na kami pumupunta para 'di makita masyado* (Some comrades would be the ones afraid of the gatherings being linked with the CPP so we would be excluded. It was the other migrant Filipinos here in Utrecht who would tell us, 'Come to our party.' So sometimes we would come in late, at 10:00 p.m., just to minimize our visibility)," Coni shares.

In the mid-1990s, following a period of ideological reexamination for the Philippine revolutionary movement,[1] the policy was deemed a mistake. *"Kaya ngayon, nakakasama na namin mas madalas ang mga Pilipino. Tuwang-tuwa kami lahat. Kasamang kumakanta, kwentuhan, piktyuran* (So now, we often join gatherings with other Filipinos. It makes us all very happy. We get together to sing, talk, and take pictures)," Coni said.

With that adjustment, Coni, Louie, Joma, Julie, and the rest grew more acquainted with other displaced Filipinos. The NDFP's initial apprehensions faded for the better. Their political work laced together with the whole of the community, all of whom want something better for their loved ones and to be a little closer to home, a family to fill in the gaps and distances created by the diaspora.

---

[1] In December 1991, the CPP Central Committee published "Reaffirm our Basic Principles and Rectify our Errors," which became one of the central documents relating to the party's criticism of its excesses and mistakes during the 1980s. The document was also one of the heavily referenced material for its "Second Great Rectification Movement" in the 1990s to supposedly correct its methods by emphasizing integration with the masses and study alongside them.

Superstar

The NDFP office in the Netherlands is a small, bland, three-story building, wedged between a line of cafes and groceries. The unremarkable structure has an exterior of gray panels, accented with white. There is no signboard or anything to indicate the nature of the space inside. There is a storefront window where one might peek at the interiors of the conference room through some blinds. Apart from that, the rest of the office has a set of living quarters and a kitchen.

Late at night, on the top floor of the office, I meet Luningning, a staff member and migrant organizer. I switch on the table lamp in the dim room. *"Parang interrogation naman* (It's like an interrogation)," she giggles. She apologizes for the hour, having traveled from Amsterdam where she joined migrant workers for a house-cleaning job.

For Filipino migrants in the Netherlands, cleaning houses is a common source of income. When one is undocumented, it's great to have a job which delivers cash payments after each day's work. *"Marami kasi sa mga Dutch, tamad maglinis kahit madali lang naman para sa atin* (Many of the Dutch people don't like cleaning, but for us it's easy)," remarked one of the migrant workers I spoke with the other day.

Cleaners are given their employer's house keys and payment of up to 100 euro in advance. A Dutch family leaves for the day and expects their household to be spotless by the time they get back. Homeowners pay close attention to the work of their hired help: most will run an index finger over and under tables and shelves, inspecting the surfaces for any trace of grime or dust.

The thought of picking up some cleaning jobs between interviews for some extra pocket money did present itself. But I was a newcomer to Utrecht, and I wasn't staying for long — any client would be wary of leaving a complete stranger alone in their home.

Trust is a big part of obtaining prospective customers and among cleaners themselves. They build relationships over time, with recommendations an important factor in their job networks.

Luningning tells me that securing as many jobs as possible was a source of pride among Filipino migrants. Many of them walk heads held high while a heavy set of house keys hangs from their belts or jingles in their coat pockets.

Sometime around 2014, cleaners made a habit of gathering after work shifts at the Filipino Migrants Center in Amsterdam. Luningning and her husband Jun remember noticing the sound of metal clinking as migrants shuffled into the center, a room at a building's basement. Visitors removed their coats before revealing the keys in their keeping. They'd lay them down on the table and compare to see who had the most. Jun and Luningning had been exiled in the Netherlands for almost a decade by then. They were both experienced organizers in the Philippines, but as they looked down at the rows of keys, this source of harmless rivalry was foreign to them. There was still much to learn about the lives of their compatriots.

In the same year, Luningning decided to work as a cleaner for a living and forge stronger bonds with the rest of the Filipinos. Today, she is an ever-present helping hand to the cleaners, and by association, every Filipino in Utrecht. She babysat Anna's toddler during one of our interviews. Douglas overcame his homesickness through the help of Jun and Luningning. At the Pink Sisters chapel, she jostled me around, introducing each parishioner.

Luningning acquainted herself with Filipinos in the Netherlands while attending a mandatory Dutch language school for aspiring citizens. There sprang the idea of building a Filipino friendship and solidarity group. Together with some schoolmates, many of whom were cleaners, they founded 3K.

Luningning had been told of Filipinos coming together for dinners. They'd meet at KFC, pushing several tables together to eat side by side. Since KFCs in Utrecht didn't serve white rice, it was cooked beforehand to pass around with the tubs of chicken. Luningning craved moments like these, nursing a persistent longing for community. Thankfully, the good thing about organizing is there's always company to be around, and to be found. Sometimes we need our political tasks as much as it needs us.

Before coming to Europe, Luningning was a cultural worker and trained thespian — a regular at street protest performances. She also landed some roles in local telenovelas in the early 2000s, a stint she relishes because it allowed her to support her family. You can count on the activist's flair for theatrics to make its way into her everyday expression. She likes to mimic her idol, Nora Aunor, whom she considers the ultimate authority on all things dramatic. Since childhood, she has badly wanted to meet the superstar.

I tell Luningning about Nora gracing a 2016 demonstration in Manila to support the rights of OFWs. Luningning was already a refugee in Europe by then. In a playful display, she acts out her emotions with movement, mourning the missed opportunity to meet her idol. She presses her backhand to her forehead, her fingers curled upwards, then she plunges an imaginary dagger into her chest.

Luningning is the type who perceives the passing of time in scenes and sequences instead of hours or days. She proceeds to review the events that led to her exile as if she were describing passages from a play.

* * *

In 2003, Jun went to the Netherlands to speak on the situation of activists in the Philippines' Southern Tagalog region. At the time, it was under siege by the notorious General Jovito Palparan, whose murderous counterinsurgency program claimed the lives of over two hundred farmers and community organizers. Local media labelled him as *berdugo* (the butcher), a term Jun often repeated when speaking of the local situation.

Jun's two-week trip turned into something indefinite. The worsening repression in the region made it unsafe for him to return. He was forced to apply for political asylum and join the band of exiles. He broke the news to his family, who were also at risk by association.

Jun and Luningning had four children: three were in their teens and the youngest was eight. Luningning felt her throat cramp with a big lump lodged when learning of the sudden change of plans. Nobody knew when they'd be together again. She huffs from her seat and places her palms on her cheeks thinking of this period.

Luningning and the children began frequenting an internet café across the street from their Quezon City home to communicate with Jun. She says, *"Sa net café kasi mabilis ang internet, e. Isa iyon sa mga difficulties, sisiguraduhin mo na okay lahat ng anak mo, mula umaga hanggang matulog at mag-isa lang akong magulang nila sa bahay. Pero kahit papaano nakakatawag si Jun para makausap mga bata* (In the internet café, the connection is fast. It's just one of the many difficulties, trying to ensure all the children were okay, from morning till night, while I was the only parent at home. Good thing Jun was able to make the calls so he could talk to them)."

Asylum seeking is lengthy. Jun had to complete the process alone before applying for the Family Reunification program allowing him to bring over Luningning and the kids. But Luningning was unsure of this plan. The complete overhaul of their family life took time to sink in; she admits grappling with it even now. This wasn't just a role in a play. The dangers posed by the state, leaving the entire life she'd known in the Philippines and the people she'd sworn to serve, was a reality that felt grimmer than anything she had to portray in the theater.

"*Hindi pa ako kumbinsido no'ng una. Baka may paraan pa para makauwi, mag-antay lang nang kaunti, ganoon. Pero sina Tita Coni, every time na umuuwi sila, nagpapaliwanag sila. Sa huli, mas matimbang nga ang kaligtasan namin at mabuo din ang pamilya* (I wasn't convinced at first. I thought there might be a way for Jun to come home; we could just wait for him. But Tita Coni, every time she and the others came home to the Philippines, they'd explain the situation to me. In the end, it was indeed more important to ensure our safety, and for all of us to be together again)," Luningning tells me.

At the time, acting jobs and other sources of income were scarce for Luningning. She had taken on more responsibilities as a cultural organizer. With Jun abroad, she was practically a solo parent to their children. To help out, Jun saved buckets of copper European cents from the modest allowance the asylum center handed him. His family sometimes used the remittances for Jollibee dinners and going to the theater to try and regain some normalcy in their lives.

By 2006, Luningning and three of their children finally moved to Europe. For the first time in three years, they met a long-haired Jun at the airport. He had vowed not to visit a barber until their family was reunited. However, their eldest remained in the Philippines finishing the school year. Jun's haircut had to wait a little longer.

They moved into an apartment on the stretch of housing complexes in Kanaleneiland. They settled in a top flat, four doors down from Joma and Julie. On their first day there, Jun suggested to Luningning they go and meet their famous neighbors.

Luningning is a brisk talker, often taking detours from her statements mid-way, as though she is commentating on herself. "*Pagdating namin kina Joma, parang natural talaga, kasi nung time na iyon, parang ganoon lang, wala lang. Ay, hindi wala lang... Special din, kasi nag-ayos-ayos pa nga ako, e.* (When we got to Joma's place, it felt very natural. Because at that time, it was just like that. Just nothing. I mean not nothing… it was special because, well, I even fixed myself up)."

During their visit, Joma said, "*O, 'di papano iyan, mag-a-apply na kayo ng asylum. Mga five years at least bago kayo makauwi, kung kakayanin ng sitwasyon* (So, it looks like you'll be applying for asylum. It will be at least five years before you can return home, if the situation permits)."

Luningning strained to keep her composure. She assumed she'd be back in the Philippines within a month or so, to fetch her eldest and more of their belongings. Five years was too long. She had imagined living in Europe for some time, but what Joma described — a permanent stay abroad, with very limited chances to travel back — wasn't something she signed up for. She bowed her head at the memory, "*siyempre tahimik lang ako, nagtitimpi talaga ako* (Of course I didn't say anything, but inside I was angry)."

Luningning hoped it wasn't the case, but the security situation showed no signs of improving. Joma had explained this to ease her confusion of being torn from the Philippines. The news hit hard. She calls it the phantom pain of an invisible limb. Back at their new apartment, Luningning reminisces staring out the window, silent and alone. It was raining. She began to weep. It is a painful memory. In hindsight, she says it was also quite cinematic.

"*Talagang nandoon ako sa may bintana, parang dramatic, umuulan pa! Hindi na pala ako makakauwi. Kinausap ako ni Jun, naisip na nga daw niya na posibleng 'di kami makakaalis* (I was really there by the window while it rained — it was quite dramatic! Apparently I wouldn't be able to come home. Jun talked to me and said he had considered the possibility that we wouldn't be able to go back)."

Their reunion in the Netherlands had to be delayed just a little bit more; they'd have to go to the asylum center if they were to stay in Europe for good. Luningning relocated with her three daughters to the Ter Apel Asylum Center, almost two hours away from Utrecht by train. They lived there for a month, the length required for the immediate family of the applying refugee.

"Parang refugee camp talaga doon, iba't ibang amoy, ugali (It was really like a refugee camp there, with different smells and behaviors)," says Luningning, looking away as though speaking to an imaginary audience on the other side of the room.

At the center, everyone slept in one big hall. Luningning thought their bed sheets were strange, made of a thin, gauze-like disposable paper instead of cloth. She felt like a prisoner. Leaving the premises required permission from the supervisors and a thorough frisking. It became too troublesome that Luningning opted to stay indoors most of the time.

And yet, she adds, it was also one of the most peaceful experiences she can remember. She had a lot of time to herself while her children kept themselves busy at the in-house library.

She smiles and her voice brightens. *"Pero nag-enjoy ako do'n kahit lahat ng makakausap mo doon hindi nag-enjoy. Ako kasi 'yong tipo ng tao na sinasabing walang 'me time,' parang laging dire-diretso ako, walang break. 'Yong 'me time' na tambay-tambay lang, nagkakape tapos nagbabasa, doon ko nagawa* (But I enjoyed myself even though everyone I talked to was having a hard time. That's because I'm the type of person who doesn't really have 'me time.' I am always busy, I don't take breaks. But that kind of 'me time' where you relax and drink coffee while reading, I was able to do that at the asylum center)."

When her eldest son arrived, he was still a minor. The law required a parent to accompany him at the asylum center. Luningning volunteered to go back inside. *"So nandoon na naman ako, nag-enjoy na naman ako, nakapagbasa at sulat* (So I was there again, and I enjoyed myself again, just reading and writing)." Jun, meanwhile, gifted himself a long-awaited haircut.

* * *

On many late nights at the apartment complex in Kanaleneiland, you'd see two lit windows on the whole block, like a glowing pair of eyes wide awake. It was comforting somehow: two households weren't alone in exile. Joma and Julie are absorbed in their work, eschewing early bedtimes even in their old age. Two stories up, the lights beam from Jun and Luningning's apartment. Luningning often spends evenings on house chores or preparing for her children's activities the next day. Several times, I saw her in the kitchen of the NDFP office past midnight, chatting with whoever was awake.

"*Nag-aalala nga ako bakit 'di ako napapagod, e, kahit na-diagnose ako ng breast cancer no'ng 2010. Nag-chemotherapy ako hanggang 2012. Stage 2 na, e* (I sometimes worry why I don't get tired, even when I was diagnosed with breast cancer in 2010. I had to undergo chemotherapy until 2012, because it was in Stage 2)," she says, flapping her hands on her lap.

She was 51 when doctors diagnosed her. Despite this, her active lifestyle was unaffected. During the worst moments of fatigue, she visited her neighbors and fellow refugees, finding rest in the company of others.

Luningning grew comfortable with Joma and Julie, whom she saw often. "Like family," she says. Over time, they became each other's support groups. Luningning relied on their advice during the tough transition to life in the Netherlands.

Small gestures of kindness also soothed her wistful stay, "*Minsan, may palitan kami ng luto. Favorite ni Julie ang dinuguan, o kaya bulalo. Minsan din 'pag sobra mga pasalubong kina Julie—mga tuyo, ganiyan—at alam niyang hanggang dito lang ang para sa kanila, hahatiin na niya iyan at ibibigay sa amin—thoughtfulness na very Filipino. Kahit simpleng sibuyas nag-aabutan 'pag may kulang ka* (We cook for each other sometimes. Julie loves dinuguan and bulalo. Sometimes, when Julie receives a lot of food from visitors, like tuyo and other stuff, and she already knows just how much she and Joma can eat, she'll give the rest to me and Jun. It's a very Filipino thoughtfulness. We'd also hand each other onions should one run out)."

In Luningning and Jun's youngest, who was eight when they moved to Holland, Julie found a surrogate grandchild. At the request of her neighbors, the child called them Tita Julie and Kuya Joma, not *Ka* (comrade).

Often, Luningning brought her neighbors essential oils and ointments. Julie affectionately named the gifts "Luningning drug." Whenever Joma needed to visit the hospital, his first request after seeing his doctor would be this favorite salve from his neighbors.

* * *

In the years since she moved to Europe, Luningning's passion for theater hasn't waned. She and Jun were buoyed by the prospect of establishing pockets of progressive theater among Filipinos. There wasn't much enthusiasm for the idea at first among OFWs and comrades, but the couple persevered.

Joma and Julie were big supporters of Luningning and Jun's artistic endeavors. *"Agree sila sa pagkakaroon ng cultural arm sa bawat organisasyon. Kaya labs na labs ko si Joma at Julie. Nung 2009, nabuo namin ang Willem Geertman Cultural Brigade* (They agreed to the idea that each organization have a cultural arm. That's why I love Joma and Julie so much. In 2009, we formed the Willem Geertman Cultural Brigade)." Geertman was a Dutch environmentalist and peasant activist who spent more than forty years in the rural areas of Central Luzon. He was murdered by the military in 2012. For Luningning and Jun, he embodied the spirit of Filipino–Dutch solidarity.

Luningning breaks from her story with a surprised expression, her arms unfolded but her mouth silent as though caught in the middle of a sudden recollection. She looks to her sides. She cups her face with one hand, drops her shoulders, leaning in to share a proud moment she'd been meaning to disclose. She whispers, *"Nagkaroon ng isang panahon, milestone ng rebolusyon* (There was a time when the revolution reached a milestone)."

I can't resist interrupting her. *"OK lang po siguro sabihin ang rebolusyon, nasa NDF office naman tayo* (I think it's okay to say *revolution* aloud, we're in the NDF office after all.)" Luningning springs upright as if to salute or broadcast to the neighbors. She yells, "Revolution!"

Towards the end of 2018, Joma, Julie, and the rest of the exiles were frustrated because a cultural production they had been planning for quite some time would be delayed until the following year. It was fifty years since the CPP was founded, and they hoped to showcase five decades of revolutionary arts and culture from the Philippines for Filipino and European audiences.

But Jun was determined. He offered to make a last-ditch effort to save the date. He was confident they could still mark the golden occasion before the end of the year in a space that would open its doors to revolutionaries free of charge. He got in touch with Utrecht's eccentric and progressive art gallery BAK (Basis voor Actuele Kunst). Sure enough, the politically incautious management agreed, maybe partly out of curiosity.

Jun and Luningning were now in charge of mounting a two-hour program in less than a month. For help, they turned to their friends among the migrant cleaners, many of whom were members of 3K.

From holding cook-outs to basketball games and Halloween parties, the 3K members had gelled and attached themselves to the rest of the Filipino community in the Netherlands. Typically they'd be more than willing to help Luningning and Jun. But this was different — this was participating, even aiding a celebration of the revolution. The event itself included individuals and groups that many of their friends and family back in the Philippines might have regarded as terrorists.

To get them involved, Luningning dropped by the homes of Filipino friends, including 3K members to speak with their families honestly about the how they became cultural workers and refugees. She explained that many others whom the migrants had gotten to know, including Joma, Julie, Louie, Coni, Fidel, and the others, had dedicated their lives to the cause of overhauling a socioeconomic system which spawned poverty and oppression in the Philippines. And because of that, the Philippine government had effectively banished them. I don't know if Luningning wowed them with a heartfelt appeal, or if it was all those times cleaning and getting to know each other that bore fruit. Nevertheless, Luningning and Jun asked for their help, and in the end, they obliged.

The 3K members and other members of the Filipino community took time off their jobs to help with preparations for the celebration. They crafted decorations, organized the schedule, and rehearsed performances. They put on a show, a celebration, with Filipino, as well as Belgian, British, and Dutch revolutionaries in attendance at the packed auditorium. Jun and Luningning even got the Kurdistan liberation fighters to sing as a choir.

The crowd calmed Luningning's nagging homesickness, even for just a night. She was glad the migrant workers played a vital part in the event and had gained a better understanding of the Philippine revolution. She was proud to have staged her first major production in Holland. She was finding her place in exile after all. I can tell that night was a rousing success from the way she spoke about it. She's had quite a few more since.

Still, she repeats her niggling wish to return home for good.

Channeling her most melodramatic Nora Aunor voice, she cries, *"Not a single day without wishing! Totoo 'yan, from the heart. Minsan makakaamoy ka lang ng isang bagay na magpapaalala sa Pilipinas, 'yon na* (Not a single day without wishing! That's true, it's from the heart. Sometimes, just the scent of something will remind me of the Philippines, and that's it)...."

The Sentinel

Dennis doesn't talk much. But I have a hunch that he has a lot to say on the subject of exile. After all, he has lived in the Netherlands as a refugee for almost as long as Joma and Julie. I just need to sit down with him. I've asked to interview him twice. Both times, he said he was too busy.

He keeps to himself at the office with an eye on anything that might disturb the order. When he catches me in the kitchen with my unwashed plate, I'm immediately prompted to do the dishes. If he walks in when my laptop and its appendages lie in shambles in the conference room, I scramble to fix them up. His mere presence is an admonition.

One evening, I join him to pick Joma up from their house. We arrive early and decide to have dinner first at the garage eatery of Kanaleneiland's Turkish cook. I watch with fascination as he cuts up his food into even portions, divides them into quadrants, and then scoops them up one by one.

Kim tells me his housemates once urged Dennis to take it easy, to not carry the load of managing the office all on his own. At three in the morning following the conversation, they caught him rewashing dishes and resweeping the floors. It couldn't be helped: this was Dennis's way, and in a sense, this particular trait is also what makes him so valuable to the NDFP. His meticulousness about all things security, his attention to detail, and his painstaking nature were all part of the safety net everyone relied on.

He does have his light-hearted moments, a warmth reserved for his family and closest comrades. I've seen him laugh with Joma, just the one *ha* before fading out. On a train ride back to Utrecht, an exhausted Kim leaned her head on his arms to rest. I could tell Dennis appreciated the tenderness of the gesture, like a big brother fond of caring for others.

* * *

After a month, I ask Dennis a third time for an interview, and he finally obliges. I reckon he'd rather be doing other tasks. But he also knows I'm nearing the end of my trip, and that the entire NDFP agreed to open itself to documentation, and that includes him.

For the interview, we meet at a park of his choosing and head toward one of the wooden tables there. He walks as though he counted in advance how many paces he'd need to take before settling down on a bench. He selected the outdoors over the office for our meetup — the only other people here are at least a kilometer away, visible but well out of earshot. He also has a near 360-degree view of the perimeter. There are no surveillance bugs here that's for sure. Better this way, so he can speak without too much concern about security.

Even with these precautions in place, it takes some badgering to get Dennis to elaborate on his accounts. Mid-story, he pauses, squints at the nearby benches, and then resumes talking. Never the type to "go with the flow," Dennis will scout, plan ahead, and check all exits and entrances before deciding if indeed it is a "go." He views his prolonged stay in the Netherlands as his duty, more like a veteran deployed to a new assignment rather than a comrade making the most of his exile. Maybe it's a coping mechanism. In a woeful tone, he begins by counting the 25 years since he left the Philippines.

* * *

Dennis used to be a fighter for the NPA during the Marcos dictatorship and in the early years of Corazon Aquino's presidency. In 1988, he was captured during combat but released the next year on bail. In 1992, Dennis, along with Satur Ocampo, Romulo Kintanar, and other political prisoners, was granted amnesty by former President Fidel Ramos.[1] Dennis thought it was a self-serving move by the Ramos administration. After all, the charges against him — illegal possession of firearms in the furtherance of rebellion — had already been dropped prior to the amnesty declaration. He stresses that his release along with the others had more to do with the diligence of their lawyers rather than an executive order. Ramos just wanted to play the hero.

Upon his release, Dennis found himself adrift. After years of fighting he suddenly didn't belong anywhere, to any group, collective, or squad so his political involvement halted altogether. It was a time of many changes for the revolutionary movement, adjusting to the landscape of the post-Marcos Philippines. Meanwhile, in Europe, the NDFP needed volunteers — specifically cadres willing to take on the extensive international organizing. In 1992, Dennis jumped at the chance to get away from their political dormancy, whatever the task. *"Tapos sinabi sa akin na dito na made-deploy sa Netherlands* (Then they told me I would be deployed here in the Netherlands)," says Dennis, his hands clasped on the park table.

* * *

Despite the government's granting of amnesty, Dennis is still listed — along with several of his aliases — in the military's order of battle, giving him more reason for leaving the country. A homecoming remains dangerous and nearly impossible. Under Duterte, it has become common practice to arrest inactive revo-

---

[1] The order granted amnesty to "all individuals who of their own free will have returned or will return to the folds of the law after having committed an act or acts in violation of existing laws in furtherance of their political beliefs" (Office of the President of the Philippines, 1992).

lutionaries who were once considered notorious or priority targets for state forces. According to Dennis no name is crossed off the list unless they're dead or in jail. Not even the passage of decades can deter his would-be hunters.

By 1994, Dennis, the single parent, arrived in Holland with his toddlers. In the beginning he pursued studies in engineering while juggling duties as part of the NDFP staff. For his thesis, Dennis was able to make a brief trip to the Philippines in 1995. It is the last time he was home, an anomalous worry-free visit, made possible by the peace talks between the NDFP and the Ramos administration.

However, his student visa expired in 2000, coinciding with Estrada's cancellation of the peace negotiations. The chances of a homecoming turned bleak. The state was out to arrest peace consultants, NDFP staffers, and even those protected by international humanitarian law by virtue of the Joint Agreement on Safety and Immunity Guarantees (JASIG) signed by the Philippine government and the revolutionaries. Without a visa or the prospect of safe passage home, Dennis with his children applied for political asylum at the turn of the century.

The main application center for political asylum at Zevenaar, in the east of the Netherlands, was equipped to service only a couple of dozen people at a time. Dennis had ill-fated timing. He found the center swamped with over two hundred applicants a day.

Asylum procedures adapt to morphing diplomatic and international allegiances. In the early 2000s, when Dennis applied to be a refugee, the Middle East was in uproar. The aftermath of Cold War conflicts in the region, along with Eastern Europe, produced a tsunami of asylum seekers.

Dennis and his children spent five days at the application center. They weren't permitted to leave the premises until the initial process was completed. Guards temporarily confiscated all personal belongings, even small items like ballpens. Anyone leaving the premises underwent a routine body check upon return.

Refugees from Somalia, Afghanistan, Kosovo, and Iraq joined Dennis and his family, who were the only Filipinos there. After the offices had closed for the day, asylum hopefuls had dinner at the canteen before resting at a small dormitory. Because the sleeping quarters couldn't accommodate the hundreds coming in, Dennis and his children spent the night on blankets spread on the corridor floors for most their stay. He remembers his fellow applicants were anxious, castaway souls praying for deliverance from the eruption of war.

Next on their stop was slated to be the reception center, where state officials would rule whether their asylum was granted. Unfortunately, Dennis was told all reception centers were also crammed with weary applicants, most of whom faced life-threatening circumstances in their home countries. So the state put up a "pre-reception" center where one waited another step before admission. Dennis and the kids were held at pre-reception for a month, lodged in a residence in the middle of the sparsely populated rural town of Zierikzee, southwest of Amsterdam. Then they were dragged further south to undergo reception at Opvangcentrum Prinsenbosch, a former military camp converted into a reception center in the southern province of Brabant, bordering Belgium. There, they stayed for another three months, waiting out the desolate cold of December in the Netherlands inside overcrowded rooms. More than a thousand others joined them — the stateless, the homeless, and the endangered.

* * *

In 2000, a few days before Christmas, Dennis and his kids were at last brought to the Asylum Center in the town of Duiven, eastern Netherlands. They remained there for the next three years as the state deliberated on their application among the many others.

Dennis explains, *"Dahil kasama ko mga anak ko, required ang mga bata sa eskwelahan. Sagot ng administrator ang education nila. Kaya kung saan ang asylum center, doon din banda ang schooling nila, sa vicinity. Hindi p'wedeng lumayo. May arrangement din sa local government* (Because I was with my children, they were required to attend school, and the administrator would pay for their education. So their school was located in the vicinity of the asylum center. We couldn't move away. We had an arrangement with the local government)."

It wasn't easy. Dennis squints again, then shakes his head at the mention of the unruliness inside. Hundreds of asylum hopefuls crammed together with accumulated irritations simmering in proximity. Sometimes they argued and tussled over small household disagreements brought on by a general lack of understanding among themselves and the fear of rejection hanging over them. The guards, only two to four at a time, scrambled to monitor the whole premises.

Residents were assigned to housing units, each with four rooms, and a basic kitchen and bathroom. Dennis and his kids occupied two rooms in one such unit. They had four other cohabitants. Dennis avoided most confrontations and would only rebuke anything untoward with his stony presence. He behaved, kept to his kids and stuck to his tasks. His circumstances were not like most, and he didn't want to jeopardize his chances either.

The whole family met hiccups throughout the process, as initially their asylum application was denied in the aftermath of the War on Terror. All over Europe, border security tightened, and greater restrictions were placed on the immigrant influx. Global displacement drove governments to make their doors that much harder to open for those outside the developed world. Wartimes are unkind times. Dennis could not have picked a worse period to be an asylum seeker. Thankfully, with the help of the NDFP's lawyers, they won an appeal, and he got another shot at residency.

The upheaval happening in the Middle East was a long way from the Philippines. He fought against a government that has long been backed by the same powers stirring up trouble with the War on Terror. Dennis and his family weren't escaping a new war of aggression; they were blacklisted by an old one. Because bureaucracies struggle to cope with consequences of conflict, asylum processes turned longer and more grueling.

Dennis and his children relocated again in 2003 as the state shifted its resources and dependents around during the global exodus. At the northern village of Egmond aan den Hoef, they spent another two years in identical conditions.

As I interview Dennis, I struggle to jot down the names of these places, and stutter embarrassingly while pronouncing them. These five-syllable words sound completely alien to me. Try saying "Egmond aan den Hoef" a few times and you might feel the same. Dennis guides me with the effortlessness of a native speaker. More than most, he felt the pressure of impressing the Dutch officials. He never said it, but I trace his quick learning of the language to that impetus. Among the NDFP staff, I don't think I've heard anyone speak Dutch as fluently as him.

Even while living at the center, Dennis traveled to the NDFP office in Utrecht three to four times a week to work with the rest of the staff, always making it back for bedtime with the children. He has an intimate knowledge of the procedural and day-to-day office functions. He knows how to secure the more vulnerable and targeted members of the organization, and the engineering graduate is inclined to work on technical tasks. For instance, activists in the Philippines are familiar with videos of Joma or Julie made to mark certain events or to lecture on particular topics. Dennis is often behind them. He also designs content for the organization's website. He also does a bunch of things he'd rather not mention.

Dennis and his family spent a final year at the Asylum Center in Leek, Groningen. It had been half a decade of staggering through the application process, of sleeping on office floors, long train rides to and from Utrecht, changing homes and schools, getting rejected, and getting along with an array of cultures and banished citizens. At their lowest points, Dennis grappled with the possibility of being sent back to the Philippines to face arrest, and who knows what else.

When they officially achieved asylum status, he didn't celebrate. Without fanfare, the family moved to an apartment close to the NDFP office, ready to reacquaint himself with a quiet he hadn't known in years. These days, his kids are quite independent, and Dennis often just stays in the office overnight to save on transportation expenses.

I'm fairly sure that at no point during the interview do we ever make eye contact. Dennis squints again. I suspect that lingering in the back of his mind are thoughts of the life he left in the Philippines — the mountain ranges he trekked as a guerrilla, and the crowded slum communities where he used to stay. He avoided saying much about those days, but there are lulls in conversation, changes in topic, and swings in tone that offer glimpses of it. He only says he misses places where a man won "hearts and minds."

Knockin' on Heaven's Door

Toward the end of 1976, the NDFP sent out an ex-priest and a former nun from Negros Island to Europe in the hopes of kick-starting a global solidarity movement. Like missionaries of old, Coni Ledesma and Louie Jalandoni were entrusted to journey abroad and preach a deliverance from dictatorship.

The years since Martial Law began in 1972 had been a blur to the couple, whose lives were upended by the Marcos regime. They'd spent a year in prison, left their vocations in the church, gotten married, gone underground, had a son, and fully committed themselves to the revolution.

Marcos blocked off the Philippines from the world. He implemented a travel ban and sanitized the reportage on his government's abuses. On September 22, a day after Martial Law was declared, the dictator in his Letter of Instruction No. 5 decreed that no Filipino was to leave on any seafaring vessel or aircraft to "prevent the escape from the country of persons who are known to be actively engaged or suspected to be actively engaged in a criminal conspiracy to seize political and state power in the Philippines and to take over the Government."

"Very few outside the Philippines knew what was really going on," describes Coni. Likewise, the couple knew very little of the European landscape. She and Louie might as well have been visiting from another planet. "Our main task was to tell the world the truth of the situation in the Philippines and generate support for the resistance."

Through their connections with the Church, the couple and their newborn son Pendong sidestepped the authorities and joined missionaries traveling back to their home countries in Europe.

They wound up in Utrecht to link with the support network Filippijnengroep Nederland (Filipino Group Netherlands) or FGN. Very few Dutch spoke English in those days, but thankfully the FGN members did. The network reconnected the couple with Father Ruttenberg, a quiet priest in his late fifties who had met Coni and Louie in the Philippines a few years back while on a service tour for impoverished communities.

Ruttenberg adopted the small family, and like the good book says, gave them meat when they were hungry, drink when they were thirsty, and took them into his apartment even if they were still strangers to some degree.

"*Mabait si Father. Actually malaking bagay iyon na nag-host siya sa amin. Hindi normal ang ganiyan sa mga Dutch, e. Nahihiya pa nga ako kasi halata kong naiingayan siya tuwing umiiyak ang bata. Sanay kasi siyang mag-isa* (He is very nice. Actually it was no small matter for him to host us. That kind of gesture isn't normal for the Dutch. I was uncomfortable because I could tell he was bothered by the crying of our baby. He was used to living alone)," says Coni.

Ruttenberg and the FGN convinced Coni and Louie to apply for political asylum to begin life as the first Filipino refugees in the Netherlands. Amazingly, it was pretty easy. In those days, arriving refugees were an unfamiliar sight. There weren't even procedures for the state to ensure residency, livelihood, and the other basic forms of welfare available to applicants today.

Louie needed to merely visit the local police station with Father Ruttenberg as his escort to initiate the application process. Cops questioned the pair as to how and why they'd arrived seeking asylum from a country with a travel ban in place.

"Your passports are not in your real names? How can that be?" barked the examining police officers. Father Ruttenberg calmed them by invoking some recent history. "Do you remember the Second World War, when many of us went around with different names?" The cops relented. Most Dutch folk had never met Filipinos before, and were unfamiliar with the plight of political refugees escaping the Marcos dictatorship.

Three months later, the state granted Coni and Louie permission to stay in the country for humanitarian reasons. But the FGN encouraged them to appeal the decision to achieve "A Status," which would afford them recognition by the United Nations. While there wasn't much difference by way of the benefits, A Status represented firmer acknowledgment of the persecution that activists and revolutionaries in the Philippines endured. For the NDFP pair seeking to stamp their message across the world, it meant a great deal.

By 1977, Coni and Louie had obtained their A Status. Coni recalls, *"Halos lahat ng sumunod na dumating na Pinoy hanggang after ni Marcos, nabigyan ng A Status* (Almost all the Filipinos who arrived here even after Marcos, were given A Status)." She is proud of the precedent she and her husband set. Joma and Julie were two notable exceptions to be deprived of the same privileges.

"Si Julie, for humanitarian reasons meron. Kadalasan, pag mayroon ang isa, automatic na kasama ang partner. Pero no'ng si Julie binigyan ng residence, may sulatin pang kasama na sinasabing hindi kasama ang kaniyang asawa. Talagang gusto ma-isolate si Joma. Wala siya dito status at all. He is not undocumented, but he does not exist (Julie is here for humanitarian reasons. Usually, when one partner has papers, the other partner is automatically approved. But when Julie was given residence, it was accompanied by a letter saying explicitly that her husband would not be given the same treatment. They really wanted to isolate Joma. He has no clear status. He is not undocumented, but he does not exist)," Coni adds.

Acquiring asylum papers cemented Coni and Louie's decision to stay long term in the Netherlands. However Coni was unsettled in the early years of their life abroad. When a friend of hers advised her to prepare herself for her son Pendong finishing high school in the Netherlands, Coni automatically retorted, *"Anong hanggang high school* (What do you mean until high school)?"

Cut off from her loved ones and most comrades, Coni and her husband fended for themselves. The enormity of Europe magnified their sense of separation from the homeland, stretching the distance further and making them feel that much smaller. She remembers the helplessness gripping her whenever she heard news of a comrade arrested or murdered. Coni is a fast talker, and her pause at the memory of her lost comrades, felt twice as long.

Amid pursuing contacts and touching base with networks for the NDFP, FGN had found the couple an apartment and a modest job for Louie. Coni stayed at home to raise Pendong. "The first months were the hardest. Especially the winter, I could never have imagined that kind of cold," she says, shivering in recollection.

Dutch activists demonstrated a special affection for refugees in general, and the first Filipino family were among those who often received it.

"Parang nagkaroon kami ng community dahil sa pakikiisa ng mga Dutch. Lumaki ang aming circle. May isang family na may anak na kasing-edad ni Pendong, at iyong mga lumang damit binibigay sa amin (We were adopted into a sort of community because of solidarity from some of the Dutch. Our circle grew. One family who had a son the same age as Pendong even gave us some spare children's clothes)," Coni says, clutching both hands together.

A few winters later, the family of three were featured on local television as part of a holiday program. They were depicted as a holy family, fleeing tyranny, not unlike Jesus and his parents. The cover page of a magazine followed. Coni only has vague memories of it, having never seen the program nor kept a copy of the publication.

Coni worried that explaining the conditions leading to their exile might be too complex for their toddler. So while he was young, she and Louie settled on educating Pendong about the home that would not have them.

"*Sa gabi bago siya matulog, kinukwentuhan namin siya tungkol sa Pilipinas. Dapat niyang malaman na ang ugat niya ay Pilipino. Sa amin kasi, panay Dutch ang bata. Pero buti naman later on, dahil sa mga dumadalaw dito na mga kasama, ang tingin niya sa sarili niya ay Pilipino na nakatira sa Holland* (At night before he slept, we'd tell him about the Philippines. He should learn his roots. In our neighbourhood, there are only Dutch kids. Good thing later on, because we were able to have visitors, Pendong learned more about his country. He sees himself as a Filipino living in the Netherlands)," describes Coni.

Coni barely stopped to consider the outcome of her unexpected exile. And for her it was probably for the best. If she had known she'd end up living away from the country for so long, "*baka hindi kami natuloy umalis* (Maybe we wouldn't have left)." She laughs ruefully at her own admission.

"*Ang sa akin noon, ang protracted people's war, iniisip ko mga ten years. Kaya akala namin na after a few years makakabalik kami* (For me in those days, when we'd say *protracted people's war*, I might think it'd take ten years. I thought after a few years we'd be able to go back for good)." Although on some level, Coni muses, she had a gut feeling that it might take longer; after all, there was no way of anticipating what lay ahead. The volatility of the Philippines' political situation has thwarted many well-laid plans.

Coni couldn't quite grasp the weight of their mission, nor envision the vastness of the political wilderness in which they were supposed to operate. She mostly remembers the nagging feeling of "having been dropped in the ocean."

Unlike the exiles that followed the couple as victims of circumstance, Coni and Louie voluntarily left. No other Filipino revolutionary movement had ever attempted to establish a base of operations abroad before.

Coni credits her time as a political prisoner for solidifying her commitment and somehow preparing her for exile. After her arrest in 1973, she was brought to the Ipil Reception Center inside Fort Bonifacio, joining dozens of other detainees of the Marcos regime. Despite many of her fellow inmates being activists, Coni was shy around her comrades. She had been an organizer for some time and stood alongside farmers against despotic landlords, but in this instance she remarks, *"Doon na meet ko ang mga aktibista, mga taga-Maynila* (That's when I met the activists, the ones from Manila)."

She didn't count herself among them at first. *"Ako taga-probinsiya, iba ang kultura. Galing pa ako sa religious sector, sila mga taga KM [Kabataang Makabayan] na sanay sa mga demo. Daladala ko pa sa isip ko iyong pag-iwas sa mga KM no'ng hindi pa ako mulat* (I'm from the provinces, it's a different culture. I'm also from the religious sector; they're with KM and used to joining demonstrations. I still carried some of the thinking I had before I became politically conscious, like avoiding those from KM)."

Coni's curiosity got the better of her. She took a liking to the stories and ideas of Raquel Tiglao, Wilma Austria, and Judy Taguiwalo—those among the women of that era who had threatened Marcos's power. Later, Coni witnessed the arrival of four new inmates that elicited the same reaction one might expect from seeing a celebrity or dignitary. The women whispered among themselves and gasped at the sight of one of the new prisoners. *"Si Lorie* (it's Lorie)!" said a muffled voice next to Coni. *"Malay ko naman kung sino iyon? Kaya tinanong ko* (How was I supposed to know who that was? So I asked)."

Lorena Barros, or Lorie, was the founder of the Malayang Kilusan ng Bagong Kababaihan (Free Movement of New Women) or MAKIBAKA. She was 25 years old when she was imprisoned and was already one of the most important figures, if not the most important of that era, to the women's movement. Lorie, the NPA guerrilla, was captured by soldiers in Sorsogon, Bicol.

Prison bars didn't dampen the women's spirits—it only spurred them to find new methods of continuing political work. Dodging the eyes of their jail guards, the activists organized themselves into small collectives. Straight away Coni immersed herself in one of the groups formed to undertake political education among the female inmates. Lorie was their team leader. In between mandatory jail activities such as gardening, exercise, sewing, and cleaning, Lorie facilitated their secret meetings.

"*Napakarami naming napag-aralan tungkol sa pakikibaka. Tine-train pa kami ni Lorie paano umakyat ng bundok at kung paano mag crawling! Hinahanda niya kami para sa buhay sa kanayunan* (We studied so much about our struggle. Lorie would also train us how to climb mountains and how to do crawlings! She was trying to prepare us for life in the countryside)."

The collectives also supported each other during particularly difficult moments of imprisonment. Coni remembers Lorie possessing a seismic faith in her beliefs and love for those dearest to her.

"*Mahal na mahal ni Lorie ang anak niya. Pero may resentment ang bata sa kaniya, hindi maunawaan kung bakit wala ang nanay niya. Nahihirapan din si Lorie. Hindi madaling unawain kung bakit mas malapit ang anak mo sa iba kaysa sa sarili niyang ina. Madalas naabutan naming si Lorie na umiiyak. Sinusubukan naming i-comfort at sabihing baka naman nagtampo lang iyan* (Lorie loved her son so much. But the boy held resentment toward her, he couldn't understand why she wasn't with him. It was hard for Lorie. It's not easy to comprehend why one's child is closer to others than his own mother. We often found Lorie crying. We'd try to comfort her by saying the kid is just having a tantrum)," recounts Coni.

"*Mahal na mahal din niya ang asawa niya* (She also loved her husband very much)," shares Coni. But Lorie's husband surrendered to the military. He took soldiers to the guerrilla zones and fed them information on his former comrades. In response, the heartbroken Lorie vowed to take her husband's place. Lorie's giant heart kept her loving a son who rejected her and helped her carry a responsibility her husband abandoned.

After Coni's release, she and Louie were on parole and obliged to report back to the army in Camp Crame regularly. During one visit, they heard mumbles of six Ipil detainees escaping, and learned one of them was Lorie. Coni trembled with joy in front of her former captors. Sadly, Lorie met a martyr's fate a few years later, just months before Coni and Louie departed the Philippines. She was caught in 1976 after an encounter in Mauban, Quezon. The military demanded information from her. She refused and was shot in the nape.

When NDFP established a base in Europe, Coni became MAKIBAKA's International Spokesperson, inspired by the memory of her friend.

Since then, Coni has been reaching to women all over the continent. *"Abante ang pagtingin natin pagdating sa kababaihan at gender. Nagsusulong na tayo ng same-sex marriage no'ng kalagitnaan ng nineties bago pa ito napag-uusapan ng mga bansa sa Europa. Marxist-Leninist ang standpoint. Hindi ito lalaki laban sa babae, kundi paninindigan ng kababaihan ng uring inaapi* (Our views on women and gender are advanced, I would say. We were pushing for same-sex marriages in the mid-1990s before it was discussed in European parliaments. Our standpoint is Marxist–Leninist. It's not about men versus women, but about standing with women of oppressed classes)."

On the back of the sacrifices their comrades made, Coni and Louie pressed on. With a whole continent to explore, they naturally began with folks they were already familiar with.

"Nagsimula kaming kumalap ng suporta dito sa Holland dahil sa FGN. Nakilala din namin sa Pilipinas ang mga pari na nadeport dahil tumutulong sa urban poor, kaya nakarating kami sa Italy. May isa pang Irish priest na misyonaryo sa Pilipinas at nagsettle sa London (We started gathering support here in Holland because of FGN. We had also met priests in the Philippines who were deported back after serving the urban poor, so we found ourselves in Italy. Then there was another Irish priest who was a missionary in the Philippines then settled in London)," says Coni.

By the start of the eighties, more and more Filipinos were migrating and taking on jobs in Europe. More organizers for the NDFP arrived as well.

Coni and Louie went up and down the continent in search of any bit of support, by political or material means, for the Philippine struggle. They put together solidarity teams in Stockholm, Antwerp, and Zurich. Ahead of the 1986 People Power uprising the NDFP convened the Permanent People's Tribunal on the Philippines, establishing a firm foothold among the ranks of European movements.

The fall of Marcos evoked a brief spell of jubilation and hope within Coni. If the peace talks went smoothly, they might relocate back home. Unfortunately, the negotiations with President Corazon Aquino collapsed, and so did every iteration with each succeeding president.

"Iba ang aming direksyon at objectives. Sa amin, klaro na ang Hague Joint Declaration ang susundin para sa just and lasting peace. E, ewan ko ba sa kanila. Sinabi na nga namin sa kanila na 'ang gusto niyo lang sa amin ay mag-surrender,' e, hindi naman mangyayari iyon (We have diverging directions and objectives. For us, it's clear that we must follow the The Hague Joint Declaration to achieve a just and lasting peace. But I don't know about them. We've already told them that 'all you want is our surrender' and that's not going to happen)," scoffs Coni.

However, in the short periods during peace talks when there were diplomatic relations between the NDFP and the Philippine government, Coni and the family made the most of each opportunity.

After the EDSA uprising of 1986, the couple sent then ten-year-old Pendong to stay with relatives back in the Philippines. *"Tuwang-tuwa ang bata pero umiyak na no'ng pauwi na. Matapos ang ilang buwan, may ceasefire naman no'ng November, nakadalaw kami ni Louie kasama ulit siya* (He was so happy but was in tears when he had to come back to us. Then after a few months, there was a ceasefire in November. We were all able to return home for a while)."

During the Ramos administration, the prospect of traveling the Philippines to hold peace consultations excited Coni. Every now and then she and Louie joined a Sunday mass, something they didn't do often in Europe because "it's something that's part of home."

Coni's time with the Church is also something that has come to characterize her public persona. Ever since Coni stepped into the public eye as an activist and then political detainee, she's been pegged as the real-life inspiration behind the popular film *Sister Stella L*. She brushes off the assumption, saying she never even met the scriptwriter.[1]

Beginning in 1959, she spent thirteen years as a nun with the Good Shepherd Congregation. She likes to say the experience taught her patience, along with many of the other values she brings to negotiation tables during peace talks. "The teachers at the congregation had asked me why I chose to get involved in politics. I told them it's still part of my beliefs as a sister. We are trained to address social problems, especially of women. Except now I see society has basic and root problems that are behind these social problems. Fighting those problems are my vocation," she explains.

The Second Vatican Council in the 1960s also had a lasting impact on Coni as it spurred many of her generation to direct action. *"Panawagan para sa religious na sumanib sa masa, malaki naging epekto nito sa pagmumulat sa amin* (It was a call for the religious to integrate with the masses. It had a great effect in raising our social consciousness)," she recalls.

In 1972, a few months before Martial Law, Coni was in Negros helping wanted activists evade the authorities. Her congregation contacted her from Metro Manila, asking her to come back and keep safe. She declined. It was too risky for everyone involved. After that, she began to question whether her place really was with the convent. During the first Christmas period under Martial Law, Coni made a break for Metro Manila to tender her resignation from Good Shepherd.

"I was very happy as a nun. But since I became more involved in activism, I wanted to do more. Personally, it was Martial Law that pushed me to leave the religious life. I wanted to be free of

---

[1] During the COVID-19 pandemic lockdown, Coni and Louie finally had time to see the movie. She says it's definitely not based on her—maybe an amalgamation of religious folk joining the struggle.

the binds or boundaries of being a nun. It was a whole process," remarks Coni. It was quite an easy decision in the end.

My initial approach to our interview was to probe the reasoning and thought process behind her faith. But Coni tells me that's not how faith works.

"To tell you frankly, I don't think much about my faith. I am deeply involved in the national democratic struggle, but I don't try to analyze my faith. I just do what I do and that's helping people," she says, imploring me to do the same.

Memories of Socialism

Gillian Peralta didn't tell her mother she was leaving the country. In 1971, she joined fourteen other people on a study trip organized by the China Friendship Association to learn about socialism.

What was meant to be a three-week stay lasted for ten years.

Gillian tells me how she was twice exiled as we sit in the kitchen of the NDFP office over some late-night tea and toast. She speaks to me warmly, but I can sense her cautiousness about divulging intimate details of her life to a near-stranger. When I ask for permission to record, she fixes her eyes on her cup and straightens up in her seat.

Gillian was twenty-one when she left for China, and one of the leaders of the militant Kabataang Makabayan (Patriotic Youth) or KM. The group looked at Mao Zedong's China as a blueprint for what the Philippines could be. When Gillian was invited to see first-hand how a socialist society was being built, she jumped at the chance.

Gillian kept her trip a secret, knowing her family would try to stop her. The red-scare hysteria of the 1970s had stoked the apprehensions of Gillian's relatives toward anything that might be labeled subversive. Her family feared for her safety — being a political activist in the Philippines, then and now, remains a perilous vocation.

She boarded a plane for Beijing on August 21, 1971. On the same day, the Liberal Party was holding a political rally at Plaza Miranda in Manila. During the event, a grenade exploded, killing nine civilians and injuring most of the party's leadership.

The infamous Plaza Miranda bombing caused an uproar for a suspect to be named. Activists blamed political opponent and soon-to-be dictator President Ferdinand Marcos. But Marcos himself blamed the CPP, which was then led by Joma.[1] Marcos secretly suspended the writ of habeas corpus hours after the explosion, using the attack as a pretext to crack down on critics and order raids on opposition groups. It was a taste of what was to come — in 1972, the dictator declared Martial Law, remaining in power for the next fourteen years.

Gillian and her companions weren't sure how long this political strife would last. She rests her head in her palm trying to remember. "It took some days for us to receive the news. When we got wind of it, we thought it might be temporary and we could go home. But the suspension of the writ really worsened the situation. Thankfully, the China Friendship Association was keen to ensure our safety and invited us to stay a bit longer."

A month later, Gillian received a news clipping from her comrades in the Philippines. The Marcos government had accused her and the delegation of masterminding the bombing, branding the unfortunate timing of their China trip as an escape plan.

On November 13, 1971, Gillian was charged, together with fifty-five others, with violating the Anti-Subversion Law. The Marcos government labelled KM as a front organization for the

---

[1] Primitivo Mijares, the former Marcos press officer, spoke of a comprehensive plan by Marcos involving "fabricating incidents or exacerbating crises" so that the public "accept as an only viable alternative to nationwide anarchy, the imposition of martial law." He mentioned the Plaza Miranda bombing as part of this plot, including the decision to immediately name the communists as the culprits. Mijares revealed that the actual orders for the bombing came from "a special unit of the then expanding Presidential Security Command" (Mijares 1976, 118, 126–27, 130).

CPP and a threat to national security. An arrest warrant awaited the 21-year-old upon her return to the Philippines.

Gillian's voice raises a little and she looks directly at me. "We were shocked. At the same time, we found it absurd. How could we, a bunch of student leaders so far away, instigate something like that?"

She worried about the uncertainty of their future. Still, despite the sudden change in plans and her turbulent situation, Gillian couldn't help but also feel excited by what she found in China. Gillian's eyes glimmered behind her small glasses. "We were young. We were students and activists. We went to China because we wanted to see socialism for ourselves. We couldn't restrain our elation even though we knew we were stranded."

Because China was largely isolated from the world at the time — especially from American allies like the Philippines — communication was difficult. There was no business between the postal services of both countries. Letters had to be sent through Hong Kong and were often delayed. A year passed before Gillian and her mother began receiving letters they'd sent to each other.

"I tried to explain to her everything, from the time I left the Philippines to my stay in China. I wanted her to know that this was part of my conviction. I apologized and told her that I had to do this. She wrote to me that it felt like she'd lost one of her children," says Gillian.

Meanwhile, Gillian and her Filipino comrades joined delegations from the US, Laos, and Cambodia to study and learn about China's route to revolutionary victory. It was the time of the Cultural Revolution.[2] Mao was campaigning to keep the country faithful to socialist ideals amid moves by those he called "capitalist roaders." The Filipino delegation adored the Chairman,

---

[2] Pugh describes Hinton's time and take on the Cultural Revolution and says of the period that, "All over China, tens of thousands of revolutionary committees in factories, farms, and schools were built. Inspired by Mao's vision, people developed other socialist new things that revolutionized society, such as barefoot doctors in the countryside, and cultural works based on the rich life experiences of China's workers and peasants" (2005).

awestruck by the chance to throw themselves into a grand festival of revolutionary activity. The group traveled cross country to understand its transformation into an economic powerhouse under socialism.[3]

Gillian explains, "At the time, Mao's foreign policy stood for supporting the people's struggles all over the world. They believed countries want independence, nations want liberation, and the people want revolution."

In 1973, at the rural Dayudao village in Shandong province, Gillian and her group began work at a factory, staying there for a year. This effort was part of the Cultural Revolution's drive to industrialize the countryside and improve agricultural outputs.

"This was happening in many villages throughout the country, and the standards of living increased. We saw it for ourselves. We produced modern fishing and farm tools that were being used in the fields. I thought about how wonderful it would be to transpose the same practice to the Philippines," she says, growing more enthusiastic at the memory. It's past midnight. This is not a planned interview; Gillian has just attended a meeting downstairs in the conference hall and was about to go home when we began talking. Weary at first, but with her memories all greased up, Gillian sweeps through the details of this period. She paces the room then leans on the kitchen sink while sipping from her tea cup. Socialist China faced an economic embargo from Western countries, making industrialization a more challenging goal. Villagers who'd never thought of having a factory on their land carried this responsibility with pride. Gillian saw locals scavenge for toothpaste tubes and discarded metals to recycle in the furnaces.

---

3   *Encyclopedia Britannica*, s.v. "The Transition to Socialism, 1953–57," https://www.britannica.com/place/China/The-transition-to-socialism-1953-57. According to the *Britannica*, China's first decade of socialism was a period of "rapid industrialization […] still regarded as having been enormously successful." This laid the foundation for the future of the Chinese economy, with collectivization of agriculture and the construction of many factories being helped along.

"We were assigned a buddy at the factory. The males were given a chance to handle machinery. I was hammering away at metal. Most days were partly spent working in the factory. The rest of the time we studied about the Cultural Revolution and learned of domestic and international news with other villagers," adds Gillian.

After leaving the factory, they lived in a commune for another year to learn farming as part of a Production Brigade. The local party secretariat made them responsible for making a plot of land productive. Through their collective efforts, they were expected to till the land, fertilize the soil, plant crops, and design an irrigation system.

Several villages working together comprised one commune. Each individual commune member earned Work Points, which were exchanged for income. Work Points were monitored by the local party's formation-based output in the fields.

However, Gillian remembers how more value was placed on political attitudes and the ability to work in a collective setting. The most crucial aspect of production was recognizing collectivization as a political act. It wasn't just about harvesting crops, but planting the ideas of socialist culture. This amazed Gillian. Despite the language barrier, she closely observed the interactions and work in the fields, hoping to emulate it someday in the barrios of the Philippines.

By 1974, ten of the fifteen people in Gillian's delegation were able to return to the Philippines. The five remaining Filipinos all had standing warrants. Gillian was the only woman left among them.

Wanting to make the most of their indefinite stay, the remaining members decided to each take a different university course in the hopes of sharing their socialist curriculums one day in the Philippines. Gillian began with two years of mandatory language lessons at the Beijing Yuyan Xueyuan (Beijing Languages Institute), before pursuing a a medical degree at the Bei Yi Xue Yuan (Beijing Medical College).

Since the 1949 revolutionary victory, the state passed laws guaranteeing equal rights for women, including access to education. The Cultural Revolution, Gillian says, encouraged this attitude further as most of her classmates were women with blue-collar roots.

She mentions that "in schools, factories, or communes, people flocked to study sessions. They talked about what the party directives were and what was going on in the country as far as promoting the Cultural Revolution." Gillian lived in China at a time when people in her age group had grown up with socialism and Maoism. They had never seen the warlords of the past, the invasion of the Japanese, or the pestilence of the old society. These children were born into a new world, and they defended socialism fiercely.

Gillian was at her dormitory in September 1976 when loudspeakers on campus broke the news at sundown of Mao Zedong's passing.

Students sat motionless outside their dorm rooms in the afternoon, staring into the distance, while others wept quietly. Thousands of youths were dazed by the loss of the only leader they'd ever known. It is one of Gillian's gloomiest memories of her time in China.

Funeral music played for hours as Gillian sat among the listening students. She hardly noticed the day turn into night. Mao's death signaled the end of the Cultural Revolution. The next day in Beijing, everyone wore black armbands, expressing their grief.

"Mao," she says, drawing a deep breath, "was considered to be the father of the Chinese people and the Party, and they really looked up to him. We were just speechless outside the dorm."

Gillian acknowledges that mistakes were made under Mao but rues how they were singled out by his detractors to vilify his contributions to socialism. She'd heard of cadres dragged into the streets to be publicly criticized for their mistakes. The more harmful mistake in her eyes, was magnifying those excesses for political gain.

Gillian growls. Her voice grows coarse as though something is suddenly blocking her throat. She looks up at the kitchen light and the sight of her eyes is obscured by the gleam on her glasses. She begins telling me about Mao's successor, Deng Xiaoping.

"I didn't know it then, but trouble was already brewing behind the scenes in the Communist Party of China (CPC)."

She remembers how state propaganda turned against the Cultural Revolution, convincing the public its excesses were inherent to the socialist system and therefore major reforms had to be pursued. "Deng Xiaoping looked in awe at the Western model of capitalism. He believed it to be a superior system that had to be emulated. The revisionist successors call it socialism with Chinese characteristics," she explains.

By early 1977, "the authorities were already telling us that we ought to look for ways to leave because the foreign policy is changing," she says regretfully.

Gillian worked as an assisting physician in Hunan for a year during the late 1970s. She never thought of China as a permanent home, rather it was an extended stopover in her journey back to the Filipino people. She wished to be a doctor in the barrios, and her obstacles led to severe bouts of homesickness.

"Prolonged exile took a toll on my physical, mental, and spiritual health. I was separated from my loved ones — my mother, sisters, family, friends, and classmates. I was uprooted from my home and country. I felt lost. I was torn away from everything familiar and separated from people close to me," she says.

In the rapidly changing China after Mao's death, with the country beset by upheavals on the road to capitalist restoration, Gillian felt increasingly unwelcome. "This is not a place for us anymore," she thought.

A decade after her arrival, Gillian applied for asylum in the Netherlands, becoming an exile twice over and evading the arrest warrant still waiting for her on home shores.[4] Her place was wherever she might get as close she could to the Philippine struggle, so she joined the solidarity efforts in Europe.

---

[4] With Marcos Jr. now in power, Gillian holds fears of the government reviving the case and it affecting her life in some way.

In the Netherlands Gillian met Joma and Julie, who she says were like distant relatives. It was the first time the communist leader and the student of socialism — supposed coconspirators in the Plaza Miranda bombing — had ever met in person.

Not long after the 1971 blast, it became commonplace for the government to name Joma as the main perpetrator. There were even exposes published, such as a 1989 article in *The Washington Post* stating that unnamed former cadres had come forward to name Joma as some kind of architect of destruction.

Joma dismisses the longstanding allegations. Often he wonders: if the military was so sure of his culpability and had irrefutable evidence, why did they never charge him for the crime even when he spent nearly a decade in their custody?

After decades of friendship, Gillian still cannot imagine Joma orchestrating "a terrorist event" like the bombing. She firmly believes that such a needless and indiscriminate act of violence was enacted by the military, and not by protesters. "Revolution is Joma's worldview, and terrorism is not to be condoned within this."

Following the downfall of Marcos in 1986, Gillian returned to the Philippines and reunited with her mother. Everyone from her delegation came back, including Chito Sta. Romana (who went on to become Philippine ambassador to China) and Jaime Flor Cruz (who later took a position as a Beijing-based reporter for the magazines *Time* and *Newsweek*).

Today, China is unrecognizable from Gillian's memories, when socialist construction was at its peak. Transformed into Asia's capitalist powerhouse, China is accused of everything from severe labor rights violations to flooding the markets of its neighboring territories to weaken their economies. Meanwhile, Filipinos have been especially outraged by China's incursions into contested maritime territories.

Gillian has "an emotional attachment to China. I had very positive experiences. And then these things happen. It's hard. Who can avoid the conclusion that the Philippines is being harmed by China's aggression under Xi Jinping?"

The years she spent in exile in China, though marred by her precarious situation, strengthened her resolve. "Socialism cannot remain a dream for Filipinos. We must forge our own path," she says firmly.[5]

---

[5] An earlier version of this chapter was first published in *Al Jazeera* (Beltran 2021).

Yet Again

In 2006, Dennis noticed something odd. Something that didn't need to be there. Something that looked ordinary yet tripped an alarm in his mind.

After over a decade living in Kanaleneiland, he'd rarely seen window washers come to their ghetto. That year, however, they showed up four times at the apartment complex where Joma and Julie lived. Even more peculiar, Dennis thought, was the disproportionate number of hours they seemed to spend cleaning the windows on the side of one particular apartment building. After working hours, the cleaners would leave, abandoning their crane for days. They'd return to retrieve it, then put it back in the same spot after another few days and leave it sitting there unused. Its long beam was crouched so the platform hung across Joma and Julie's living room, as though it were peering inside.

After the third time the washers left the crane idle, Dennis took it upon himself to call the cleaning company and ask it to move its equipment. They did. They pulled the crane a few feet back.

"*Pucha, nakatutok pa din* (Damn, it was still pointed at the house)!" Dennis winces in remembered frustration.

He operated under the assumption that Joma and Julie were under constant surveillance. They were targets — stationary ones — the most difficult to protect. In 2001, the couple and the staff members had uncovered a plan to eliminate Joma, hatched within the top echelons of the Philippine government. While the regime had changed since then, living in exile taught them that threats can outlast their masterminds.

* * *

In 2000, under former President Joseph Estrada, an assassination attempt on Joma almost succeeded. Fidel V. Agcaoili, the NDFP's chief negotiator, was crossing the street to enter their office with Joma when he saw a man near the office doors who stood as if waiting for someone. The man was motionless, but his eyes were unquestionably fixed on Joma and Fidel. When the two old communists reached the other side of the road, the man opened his coat and reached into his inner pocket for what looked like a knife.

Joma and Fidel were not alone. They were escorting a child, one of the NDFP staff members' children, who sometimes ran errands with them. Seeing the threat, Fidel rushed his companions into the office. The man's hands remained inside his coat pockets, clutching his blade. Fidel and the others later hypothesized that the assailant had hesitated because the child presented an unwanted complication. Months later they would learn that the attempt was part of a standing state directive.

In January 2001, longtime radio anchor Mike Enriquez announced a scoop on his morning show. Barely a week after the ouster of Estrada by the second People Power uprising, Enriquez said there was an existing directive by the Philippine government to liquidate Joma. During an interview with Colonel Reynaldo Berroya, the officer revealed that two teams had been designated, under orders from Estrada's Police Chief Panfilo Lacson, to carry out the task.[1]

---

1 Former *Pinoy Weekly* editor Kenneth Guda (2007) in an independent report published on his website shared that, "The leader of the team, it was later revealed, was Romulo Kintanar, former head of the New People's Army who in 1992 became an intelligence agent for the military. Along with Arturo Tabara and Nilo dela Cruz, Kintanar went to the Netherlands

At the time of Enriquez's exposé, Estrada, Lacson, and others in the former president's inner circle had been removed from their government posts. More scandals of the old regime came to light as new officials assumed power. Berroya blew the whistle in a bid to distance himself from his former bosses. He traveled to the Netherlands in February 2001 to present information to the Dutch police. Joma then filed a formal report stating his life had been endangered by Philippine law enforcers.[2]

There was minimal progress on the complaint for the next five years. It wasn't until 2006, when the cleaners left Kanaleneiland for the last time, that the police summoned Joma to their station to discuss the case.

Over the phone, the cops informed him that they wished to discuss new developments regarding the attempts on his life. However, they wanted to meet Joma at a different police station from where he filed it. Joma thought this was unusual; the new venue stood on the other side of Utrecht. Joma nevertheless agreed to show up at 9:30 a.m. on August 28, at the behest of a certain "Mr. Bird Vogel."

That morning, Joma, Louie, and NDFP staffer Ricky headed to the station together. One of their group, Turkish lawyer Dundar Gürses, was running late and said he'd catch up at the station. The three Filipinos walked into the precinct's reception area. The people who waited inside, curiously, seemed to be there alone, loitering.

It was only 9:20 a.m. They were early. Joma approached the wooden reception desk, manned by a sole police officer, and informed him of his appointment with Mr. Bird Vogel. The officer had to suppress a laugh — he found the name comical. The Dutch word *Vogel*, pronounced as "fogel," means *bird*.

---

to carry out the (assassination) plan. It was botched, according to Sison, when a 'backup triggerman' was arrested by the Dutch police in an earlier separate incident." See also Cantos and Rongalerios (2001).

2   GMA NewsAmita Legaspi (2017) reported on the NDFP's assertion of the assassination plot and Berroya's cooperation in sharing evidence with Dutch authorities. The report was made in relation to an alleged plot still within the military to assassinate Joma.

"All right. Please sit down. Would you like coffee or tea?" said the officer. The trio were surprised by the hospitality. Later, they surmised that because they'd arrived earlier than expected, the cops needed to stall and disarm them into complacency.

Dundar arrived five minutes later. "I'm sorry, but I can't stay long," he said, hurrying into the reception area. "I have another appointment at 11:30 a.m."

At 9:30 a.m., the agreed-upon time, Louie stood from the bench. Glancing through a small window behind the reception desk, he noticed the cops inside the precinct were clustering over a telephone, as if quietly receiving instructions.

Moments later, two officers appeared at the door opposite the bench. One of them motioned for Joma and the group to join him inside.

It was 9:38 a.m. Joma walked up to the door, Dundar behind him, as Ricky and Louie trailed after them. As soon as Joma entered the room, the officer interrupted the others' passage. "No, it's only for Mr. Sison," he said, and shut the door without waiting for an answer.

"Nakakapagtaka (Makes one wonder)," said Louie to himself in a low voice as he retreated to the bench.

Julie was at home, in the bathroom. Coni was in her own home too, preparing breakfast. Dennis sat in front of the computer at the ground floor of the NDFP office, working. He was alone; they all were.

All three of them heard a knock on their doors.

A platoon of armed policemen broke down the door to Julie and Joma's house, charging into their living room, startling Julie. At that precise moment, the same thing was happening to Coni in her home. Dennis, meanwhile, heard the doorbell ring. He assumed someone was delivering a package. He opened the door, whereupon a group of policemen barged in and grabbed him, forcing him to take a seat.

Coni stared at the armed men who forced their way into her home. "Why are you here? What is going on? Do you have a warrant?" she demanded.

"The judge is still in Kanaleneiland," someone answered. Coni came to the frightening conclusion that the judge was with Julie.

Julie was held down in Joma's favorite chair, the one facing the same window through which they had been watched for the past year. She sighed with exasperation. "Not again," she thought, but refused to show any fear, keeping an eye on her captors.

"Where is your warrant?" she asked flatly over and over. They ignored her. Eventually, a judge entered the apartment with a search warrant. They were looking for weapons — guns, ammunition, anything of the sort.

Julie, Coni, and Dennis were unaware of the scale of the operation. The simultaneous raids were designed to subdue each staff member and apprehend Joma.

"This is part of an ongoing murder investigation," an officer told Coni.

"You go to Malacañang, she's the one killing people," Coni snapped back, unable to conceal her anger. Her jibe was a reference to then President Gloria Macapagal-Arroyo, whose administration racked up more than 1,200 victims of extrajudicial killings.

Coni wanted to use the bathroom. "I have not taken a bath," she huffed.

"I can accompany you inside the bathroom," offered one of the officers.

"Ay, hindi, ha (No way)!" howled Coni, inadvertently switching to Filipino because of the audacious suggestion.

"I want to call my lawyer," she said. But the officers denied this request too. They said they'd make the call for her. Fine. Coni dialed the number. The secretary answered and told the police that Coni's lawyer was in a meeting. "Allow me to talk to the secretary," she said, grabbing the phone from one of the cops. Before they could react, she said, "Linda, the police are here raiding the house! Please ask Bernard to come!"

On the morning of the raids, lawyer Bernard Tomlow was in a conference with his coworkers inside his firm's spacious office building, located in the wealthier part of Utrecht. Around the borders of the lot, several Chinese banners hang from wooden poles, shouting out his name in bold, booming letters. His success as an attorney came alongside his work as counsel to the Filipino revolutionaries, a niche garnering him substantial praise in the legal profession.

Bernard is a bulky, bearded, and bear-like figure who greets friends and clients with heavy hugs and firm handshakes. As soon as news of the raids reached his ears, Bernard rushed to the rescue.

Now, over a decade later, I ask him where this sense of urgency comes from when aiding the NDFP. Bernard flings out his arms and roars, "I'm part of the family!" He assures me that family emergencies come before his responsibilities to the law firm. Indeed, he once pledged to Coni and Louie, "If you have a problem, you come to Papa."

Mid-morning of August 28, 2007, Papa was coming fast. He hopped on his motorcycle and flew past the snail-paced Dutch traffic startling pedestrians as he whizzed through uneventful streets.

At that point, Louie had called for backup, worried either he or Joma might soon be detained. Backup arrived in the form of Wilhelm, Dundar's law partner, who burst through the station doors at 10:05 a.m. Wilhelm and Dundar approached the reception desk, displeased as to why their client had been kept from them for so long.

"Oh, didn't you know? Mr. Sison has been arrested for murder. He is being brought to The Hague."

Wilhelm and Dundar turned to Ricky and Louie, on the bench. "Get out of here as fast as you can."

"But we have to wait for the car," Louie said. Amid all the day's commotion, the police had confiscated Ricky's car and bag with his laptop inside.

The group assembled at the police station learned a vital piece of information from the cops: there was no update on the report filed in 2001. It was a ruse used by the police officers to lure their target in. Once Joma had been isolated from the others, they slapped handcuffs on him and said, "Mr. Sison, you're under arrest, we are now just waiting for the warrant."

Minutes later, police whisked Joma away to a prison complex in the Scheveningen district of The Hague, which had formerly been used as a Nazi prison for Dutch undesirables.

Jose Maria Sison was charged with orchestrating the murder of Romulo Kintanar in 2003, as well as the murders of Arturo Tabara and his companion Stephen Ong in 2004. Kintanar and Tabara were former leading cadres of the CPP during the period of ideological and organizational mistakes and misguided revolutionary actions the movement has since recognized and sought to rectify. The CPP alleges the pair engaged in counterrevolutionary work and collaborated with the Philippine government against the NPA. According to Berroya's public testimony, they were also the involved in the botched assassination attempts on Joma. The former police official added that Kintanar even traveled to the Netherlands, but ultimately abandoned the operation.

Older activists had told me that minutes after Kintanar's death, former NPA spokesperson Ka Roger Rosal called up some of his contacts in the media to own up to the action. The NPA considered it retribution for crimes committed against the revolution and the masses. Rosal's statement read, "The NPA has long been ordered to arrest him and present him before the people's court, but Kintanar was evading arrest and even took countermeasures to avoid facing his criminal accountabilities" (Villa 2003).

Even now, Joma's detractors say he had motive to personally oversee these operations. They paint a picture of a senile leader wasting away in a distant land, wanting to reassert his dominance in the party. They say he was jealous of Kintanar and Tabara's reputation in the movement, and he was paranoid about the possibility of them undermining his ideological authority. In 2007, the Philippine government pitched Joma's guilt to the Department of Justice and the Dutch Embassy.[3]

---

3   In the article, San Juan Jr (2007) reports: "Arroyo's cabal of manipulators are thus the main sponsors of the two widows who filed an affidavit against

Their theory was that, from all the way in the Netherlands — amid dealing with his own troubles concerning asylum, the terror listing, and assassination attempts — Joma had directed a military operation of the NPA. And apparently, the Dutch legal system concurred.

Back in Utrecht, Coni's son Pendong arrived at half past ten in the morning. He was also a lawyer in the same firm as Dundar and Wilhelm. The police searched the house for a cache of weapons to support their suspicion that Joma's accomplices in the Netherlands were armed and ready to fight.

Coni recalls, years after that day, *"Diyos ko, ang gulu-gulo na nga ng bahay namin, lalo pang nagulo. Pati ang bodega namin, binuksan. Halatang may hinahanap sila at aligaga sila* (My god, our house was already messy, and it became even messier after the search. They even barged into our storeroom. It was obvious they were looking for something and they were on edge)." She shudders at the memory.

Pendong intervened in the search and barred the police from overstepping their warrant. It also helped that the police gave up on sifting through the contents of the bodega after taking one look at the volume of clutter inside.

At the station, the cops returned with Ricky's car, now bagless and laptop-less. Ricky and Louie were unsure what would happen with Joma's arrest, but eventually they decided to leave, not the least because Louie also really needed to use the bathroom. They went to a nearby sandwich shop to relieve themselves, eat, and begin planning their next move.

Dundar called Pendong to inform him about what happened at the station; Pendong gave his account of the raid at Coni's home. Pendong called Edre Olalia of the National Union of People's Lawyers in Metro Manila. Louie called Fidel Agcaoili, who

---

Sison with the Philippine Department of Justice. Secretary Raul Gonzalez confessed that his office gave all kinds of assistance to the Dutch National Criminal Investigation Department, including names and data of NDFP personnel. In short, trumped-up charges, connivance of Dutch and Filipino officials, skullduggery and bureaucratic abuses all converged in the August 27 dragnet."

was in Hong Kong. The calls across the globe went on until each bit of information could be pieced together.

A horde of infantry raided the homes of seven NDFP staffers, including the one in Kanaleneiland, plus the office. Each location was ransacked and Joma was arrested.

Everything transpired in less than three hours. In the Netherlands, the entire NDFP was already on alert by 11:00 a.m. By midday, activists were protesting in the Philippines to condemn the raids and arrest. Parallel demonstrations took place in Hong Kong, the United States, and Europe — places with a significant Filipino population and representation in their progressive organizations.

Flexing his political muscle and influence, Bernard convinced the cops to leave the various sites they were searching and cease their operation for there was no evidence to be found. Papa had done good, defusing the situation. Coni, Julie, and the rest gathered allies and friends of the NDFP in Europe, to prepare their next steps. That evening, Pendong, Dundar, and Wilhelm, along with Bernard, convened at their office to deliberate how to best represent Joma. In a room across from them, Julie, Coni, and Louie joined a group of local activists to plan a campaign for Joma's freedom.

The lawyers decided that attorney Michiel Pestman would be the lead counsel for Joma. Joined by Dundar, he raced to The Hague in time to confer with their client before police questioned him. Pestman and Dundar stood on the other side of a one-way mirror, watching the interrogation.

The lawyers gave their client a simple instruction: don't talk. Easy enough.

Across the table from Joma, the investigator asked, "What is your name?"

The suspect launched into an overview of his genealogy, his ancestral roots in Ilocos, and how the Sisons came to be, overwhelming his captor with an avalanche of information that could most charitably be described as tangentially relevant to the question. "Don't talk" was an impossible rule to follow for Joma Sison. He'd built his life on an inability to keep silent. He gave speeches, he conversed with comrades, he chatted to strangers, and indeed most of the books and articles documenting his life described him as a man who spent hours talking to anyone and everyone.

A truthful Joma told his interrogators everything they didn't need to know. Reporting back to the NDFP, Pestman and Dundar said, "We told him not to talk, and he gave them his whole life story."

Joma was sent to solitary confinement, to be reminded of his prolonged and painful detention under Martial Law in the Philippines. The punishment for the man who loved to speak was isolation. Joma compared his new cell in Europe with the one he'd occupied during the Marcos regime. Some physical dimensions had changed. Now he had an iron door and a high ceiling, but the dinginess and even the positioning of the cot and toilet were eerily similar.

He relied on his old tricks to survive solitary confinement. He exercised his self-proclaimed "musical faculties." Every day he sang, relishing how his voice echoed from the high ceiling, mimicking a duet partner. He also called upon his overactive imagination. His guards, who hadn't asked for it, were treated to a descriptive account of his previous detention. *"Binibiro ko nga ang gwardiya na nangyari na 'to sa akin no'ng Martial Law* (I joked with the guards that I'd been through all this before, during Martial Law)," he tells me, beaming at the feat of having beaten prolonged isolation, twice.

Julie was once again at the helm of the campaign for his release. She and her comrades staged continuous protests in front of the courts in The Hague. She worked with the lawyers to design actions aimed at pressuring the Dutch government to release her husband. She condemned her husband's jailors for barring his prescribed medication, the unnecessary use of solitary confinement, and for limiting Joma to a new set of warm clothes once a week.

The response and support they received was heart-warming, recalls Coni. *"No'ng nahuli si Jo, matindi solidarity dito* (When Jo was arrested, the solidarity here was amazing)," she recalls. For instance, because all laptops had been seized during the raid, the next day many of the friends of the NDFP came to give them brand-new laptops.

On the day the court was set to rule on how to proceed with Joma's case, the prosecution handed Pestman the file. It was 9:00 a.m., and the hearing was slated for 1:00 p.m. that day. He quickly read the dense jungle of case files, which pieced together how Joma supposedly planned the two murders from his Utrecht ghetto. He ploughed through the readings like a student cramming for an exam, then reported to Louie and Julie. It was 12:30 p.m. A confident Pestman assured them, "They have no evidence. There is no case."

His assessment proved to be correct. The judge dismissed the charges for lack of sufficient evidence. Not even Joma's detailed account of his life history to the authorities was enough to mount a case against him. For several years after, the Dutch police continued to search for evidence even in the Philippines, hoping to press fresh charges. But in 2010, they closed their investigation for the same reasons as the court: lack of evidence.

The question of Joma's guilt or innocence is certainly a complex one. The NPA claimed to be acting of their own volition when they eliminated Kintanar and Tabara. According to Ka Roger's public statement in 2003, "[Kintanar] didn't choose to live in peace and return to civilian life […]. Instead, as part of the government's military, he chose to fight and wreck the revolutionary movement" (Villa 2003). But the Manila government still presumes all major actions taken by guerrillas in the Philippines are the result, at least in part, of direct orders from Utrecht.

The revolutionary movement is its own living, breathing organism whose cellular structure produces a multiplicity of decisions, victories, and defeats of its own accord. Joma did play a crucial part in what it is today. At the same time, it's also doubtful whether every action can be pinned on the movement's arguably most public figure. In past interviews, Joma maintained that the leadership of the revolution is in the Philippines. Joma, however, is the easiest, most obvious, and most stationary scapegoat.

An exile's safety is limited and transient. In November 2019, as I first hear these stories, the possibility of another arrest looms. Notorious strongman Rodrigo Duterte is in power, and one of his cabinet members, Eduardo Año, has publicly threatened to send over a team to the Netherlands for the express purpose of ensuring Joma's arrest. The same people — Bernard, Dundar, Louie, Coni, and the rest — are prepared to face the same debacle all over again.

"May peligro talaga dito, naka-eye-to-eye ko na nga ang team ni Año (There's real danger here, I've even been eye-to-eye with a member of Año's team). But relatively my security is better here than in the Philippines, especially with the help of comrades," says Joma, hunched in his favorite chair where Julie was pinned on the morning of the raids.

On September 14, 2007, Joma was released after seventeen days in solitary confinement. On the day of his exit, a crowd gathered outside the prison, complete with local TV crews awaiting the appearance of the infamous Filipino. Joma flinched at the blinking camera lights before flashing a smile to cameras. He stepped through the prison gates wearing the same clothes as the day he was arrested. Over his shoulder, he carried the rest of his belongings, thrown together in a garbage bag. "He looked like a homeless Santa Claus," said Coni, smiling. The two-time inmate was welcomed by his family and comrades. He was sixty-eight years old, and had eluded imprisonment for another day.

A Bottle of Wine

A communist party can be a curious and fickle thing. It can usher in great changes but also sabotage itself. Unless its custodians are careful and correct in their analysis and tactics, parties can be undone even by the most unlikely culprits.

The original Partido Komunista ng Pilipinas (Communist Party of the Philippines or PKP) was established on November 7, 1930. It consolidated strength among the Filipino working class over the next decade. They were responsible for the HUKBALAHAP, the guerrilla army which resisted colonial Japan during World War II. By the 1950s, they renamed their Central Luzon-based troops as the Hukbong Mapagpalaya sa Bayan, or HMB, colloquially called the Huks. But with internal disagreements over party policy concerning their participation in armed and parliamentary forms of struggle, their overall strength declined. Some opted for one or the other, and the lack of a coherent strategy resulted in seesawing between the two forms of struggle.[1] This led to the loss of any stable mass base.[2] Fighters, activists,

---

1   The CPP document "Rectify Our Errors and Rebuild the Party" (1968), was first studied by the PKP years earlier as a political report drafted by Joma. Both versions of the document trace how by 1955, the PKP had practically abandoned armed struggle twice.

2   According to political historian David Wurfel (1988, 225–26), from the peak of the Huk strength in the early 1950s, they practically disappeared by

and cadres deserted the PKP, disillusioned with the promise of achieving the same heights as the Soviets.

By 1958, the PKP and its General Secretary Jesus Lava remained active but in hiding. He operated in secret in a bid for self-preservation, but chose to stay in urban centers where he was closer to the enemy's grasp and thus more vulnerable. Directives were issued using the "single-file" policy.[3] This meant he only ever met with a liaison who conveyed his orders to the rest of the party leadership and membership.[4] He was a one-man command machine, cut off from any direct interaction with the world, including the revolution.

In hindsight, it's easy to disparage the old PKP compared to the more enduring Maoist CPP which Joma later founded. In the early sixties, the PKP stood as the vanguard of the proletarian movement in the Philippines, no matter how ragged the party was. Jesus and his brothers Jose and Vicente were the contemporary communist figures of their time. Apart from leading the Huks, they had ventured into mainstream politics with their electoral party, the Democratic Alliance, and influenced scores of trade unions.

In 1961, Joma was 22 and a fresh college graduate. He revered Jesus Lava. The PKP had made unprecedented strides in introducing Marxism to Philippine revolutionary discourse. Joma even penned a poem of praise for the leader. He recites it to me from memory, titled "Jesus Walks the Land":

Jesus walks the land,
The Incarnation

---

the early 1960s. Part of the dissolution resulted from tension between Jesus Lava and Huk commander Luis Taruc, who surrendered to the Magsaysay government in 1954.

3 Bart Pasion shares that the difficulties in receiving transmissions made communications sparse. Many PKP forces were acting without guidance from their leadership (Tadem 2019, 114).

4 Since 1958, Jesus Lava moved around Metro Manila, staying indoors for months or even years at a time. He drafted books, articles and many of his political transmissions or instructions to PKP forces (Dalisay, Jr. 1999, 140–42).

> Spreading the word,
> Bringing hope to the masses,
> Using his healing powers,
> Angering the Romans,
> The merchants,
> The pharisees,
> The politicians, the lackeys
> Of imperialism.

The recognition was warranted then and remains so even now. *"Hindi ako antipatiko sa kanila, as a matter of fact, impressed ako sa pamilyang yan. Si [Teodoro] Agoncillo nga, papuri niya sa mga Lava, intellectuals who gave their abilities to the revolutionary movement* (I am not discourteous toward them, as a matter of fact, I am impressed by their family. Teodoro Agoncillo even praises the Lavas as intellectuals who gave their abilities to the revolutionary movement)," attests Joma, citing the well-known nationalist historian. But like shadows in the noontime sun, something grew alongside Joma's admiration: a sharp criticism of what he perceived as isolation and indolence in the party's leadership. Looking back, Julie remembers the PKP leader more like "Jesus pacing in his robe," referring to his time spent quarantined from much of the direct political work.

According to Joma and Julie, Vicente "Buddy" Lava, Jr. served as an alternate to his invisible uncle Jesus. Both Lavas took note of Joma's writings in the *Philippine Collegian,* the student publication of the University of the Philippines (UP), which criticized American interventionism and neocolonialism in the country. From their campus base, Joma and Julie had established the Student Cultural Association in UP (SCAUP), an activist collective working in study circles for radical theory and political organizing. Joma was its founding chairperson. The Lavas heard the noise from the SCAUP kids who led a 1961 march against the McCarthyist hearings of the Committee on Anti-Filipino Activities. This was work which the PKP should have been doing, but wasn't. The Lavas did the next best thing and absorbed the students who were already fulfilling in practice the Lava's revolutionary ambitions. Jesus wanted a piece of the action.

In early 1962, they approved a recommendation by Buddy to touch base with 23-year-old Joma Sison.[5] Buddy asked his wife Josefa for contacts. As a UP professor, she got a hold of literary critic Petronilo "Pete" Daroy, a good friend of the couple behind SCAUP. Pete delivered the message to Julie, and she informed him that Joma was and would be abroad for some time. For the majority of 1962, Joma was based in Indonesia, where he studied the neighboring country's revolution, which was proceeding ahead of everyone else in the region.

On his return to the Philippines, he soon ran into Pete. Both still frequented campus hangouts during late afternoons. *"Maski wala na si Joma sa UP, pumupunta pa rin siya sa campus. Istambay sa Vinzons Hall* (Even though Joma wasn't at UP anymore, he still frequented the campus. He'd hang out at Vinzons Hall)," says Julie. Thrilled at the news of the proposed collaboration, Joma met with Buddy in December 1962 to begin forming the Executive Committee of the PKP under Jesus's instruction.

Buddy had never been preoccupied by working-class organizing. He spent most of his time as a well-paid executive in the Philippine branch of Colgate-Palmolive. Despite corporate comforts, he strived to fulfil the wishes of the uncle who had shaped his worldview. As his nickname suggested, the tall Buddy was amiable. Julie describes him as "charming" and *"macariño* (affectionate)." She still remembers the rare guyabano-flavored liquor he gifted the couple many years before, at the onset of their comradeship.

---

[5] In his autobiography, the former secretary general shares that from isolation, he sent out Political Transmission 17 which "called on Party cadres to break isolation from the masses" in light of young activists fulfilling their "catalytic" role in the revolution (Lava 2002, 286–87). He was referring to the movement headed by Joma and Julie from UP. And having conferred with Buddy, who was with the PKP Finance Department, Jesus approved the proposal to have Joma inside the PKP. He later comments though that he was surprised at the decision to split from the PKP.

Buddy convened the meetings of the PKP's Executive Committee on Saturdays or Sundays at his home on Manigo Street in Teacher's Village, not far from the UP campus. The accessible upper-middle class house was two stories high and stood on elevated ground. It also had its own basement, an unusual feature in the Philippines. This Western architectural affectation denoted some level of affluence, more so since Buddy used it as his personal study. Neither Buddy's family, nor the housemaid who tended to them, paid any attention to the Communist bunch that arrived at the house every weekend.

Along with several other cadres who came from professional backgrounds, the enthusiastic Joma attended with Julie, who took on the role of committee secretary. In addition, Joma brought along labor leader Ignacio Lacsina, president of the National Association of Trade Unions (NATU). Buddy also invited cousin and Court of Appeals lawyer Francisco "Paco" Lava, Jr. Like him, Paco had practically inherited party leadership by blood.[6] Joma also remembers Ching Maramag of the *Manila Times* joining their group.[7]

From 1962 to 1964, they held regular meetings in the living room of Buddy's home. Joma and Julie's memories of these gatherings are unremarkable. They were quick and stale. The consultations consisted of running down developments in the direct political work of those who had done any. There was a dearth of any in-depth discussion on how best to advance the revolution.

Joma had his reservations about the direction of the collective at large. He, Julie, and Lacsina spent their days setting up mass organizations of youth, workers, and other professionals. In contrast, Buddy, Paco, Ching, and the others mostly carried on with their professions save for their weekend sympathies.

---

[6] Jesus Lava (2002, 289, 292) shares that Paco was involved in youth organizing before he had met Joma. Jesus even named him "Secretary for Intellectuals." Before forming the executive committee, Paco had told Jesus he considered Joma and his lot "exceptionally talented, dedicated and capable activists."

[7] Rosca's account also says the Executive Committee had five members in the beginning (Rosca and Sison 2004, 13).

Should they be faulted for pursuing careers?[8] Perhaps not. But claiming to lead the revolution without taking an active part in organizing is problematic to say the least. And yet, they all got along fine in the beginning. Joma and Julie retained their optimism that the collective could still achieve more.

After two years, and with barely any help from the Lavas,[9] Joma and Julie formed the militant youth group Kabataang Makabayan (KM, Patriotic Youth) in 1964. It spread through campuses and communities, introducing a new generation of youths to national-democratic politics and anti-imperialism. Meanwhile, Lacsina had become a frontline leader for the new, albeit short-lived, Lapiang Manggagawa (Worker's Party) by 1963. All of them made progress in the mass movement as the Lavas were content to learn of updates during meetings.

It was also in 1964 when Lacsina's distrust in the committee was sown. Joma recounts, "Paco wanted to add Cipriano ['Cony/Jun'] Robielos. *Pumalag si Lacsina pero sa akin lang sinabi* (Lacsina opposed this, but only told me)." Cony was a friend who had grown up in the same areas as the Lava family. He worked as a registrar for the Commission on Elections. His primary contribution was to acquire information from a brother, Sid, who had contacts with military intelligence at the time.[10] The committee sought strategic information such as the

---

8 Former PKP cadre Bart Pasion reveals he lambasted Paco Lava and the rest of his comrades for maintaining their day jobs and not stepping back from their class origins to be closer to the "vanguard." This was sticky issue among the PKP leadership. This happened shortly after Joma and the others split from the PKP (Tadem 2019, 122–23).

9 Jesus Lava (2002, 291) claims that right before his arrest he sent out two final orders in the form of Political Transmissions 18 and 19. He says those orders suggested the creation of Kabataang Makabayan and the approval of Joma as its founding chairman. Jesus may assert that the landmark group was his idea, but it was a product of the surging youth movement that would eventually form the backbone of the national democratic struggle.

10 Jesus Lava (2002, 291) shares that Sid was a personal contact of Defense Secretary Macario Peralta and he was pressured by the military to reveal where the Secretary-General was hiding. According to Jesus, Sid fed the state wrong information to misdirect a raid.

conduct of surveillance on those the government suspected as communist conspirators.

But Lacsina's previous clashes with Cony had caused some lingering friction. He told Joma, *"Walang kwentang tao iyan. Pinakilala sa akin 'yan no'ng tumakbo akong congressman. Susuporta daw sa akin. Sa campaign rally, dumating isang jeep, lasing siya, tatlo o apat lang sila* (He is a worthless person. He was introduced to me when I ran for congress. He was supposed to lend support. At a campaign rally, he arrived in one jeep, drunk with only three or four with him)." Neither Lacsina nor Joma said anything to the group, preferring to be cautiously optimistic on the dealings with Cony who joined in some meetings. However, Joma observed the emergent rift, one Paco would later widen.

Paco didn't possess the striking demeanor and confidence of his cousins. In contrast to his slender relatives, he was heavyset and diminutive, and maybe a little insecure.[11] Julie remembers him having a sour attitude. Paco didn't say much, but was quick to snarl at threats to his standing.

Sometime between late 1963 and the first half of 1964, Joma recalls learning of Paco, Buddy, and another Lava, Horatio, going for a night out that went awry. Their soiree set into motion a sequence which planted the seeds of spite. The three men got a table at the fancy Café en Barion (or was it Café Italiana? Joma is uncertain) in Cubao, Quezon City. None of my sources could describe the café, but for my own sake I imagine it to have a murky interior, with maroon leather couches and divided booths. Maybe there was a brick wall and orange neon signage inside.

At any rate, somewhere in the café were two women who supposedly caught the attention of the three Lavas. They weren't

---

[11] Bart Pasion tells the author that he thought Paco "lacked self-confidence" and that this was especially evident when he presided over meetings. He was also furious at Pasion for insinuating he didn't spend enough time engaged in revolutionary work (Tadem 2019, 123).

strangers and had some ties to the Marcos regime. The Lavas knew this.

It didn't stop Buddy from ordering that fateful bottle of wine and sending it over to the table of the ladies with a smile. The two women were flattered and responded to this overture by joining their tables together. One of the women took a liking to Buddy, and later became his mistress. The other began a relationship with Paco.

With their absence from the mass movement, doggedness on leading the party from a position of privilege, and their failure to grasp, let alone embody, correct ideological understanding, one could say the Lavas might have unknowingly cemented the PKP's doom that night. They did it with a bottle of wine. There are only rumors of what had happened and there aren't many living sources to corroborate. However, being such public figures in the revolutionary circles, it was difficult to escape scrutiny from their contemporaries. In any event, what followed among the Lavas represents where their revolution was heading: away from masses and toward capitulation.

It wasn't the drinking itself that was disastrous, nor the adultery—nothing so Biblical or moralistic. Rather, it was what followed: squabbles and bickering, an antagonism they soon embraced more than they had ever grasped their duties as party leaders.

Paco's new flame soon abandoned him for his married cousin Horacio. In retaliation, he exposed the affair to Horacio's family, starting a feud. He didn't stop there. The vindictive Paco also snitched on Buddy to Josefa, leading to yet another family dispute. Paco and Buddy were cousins as well as comrades, and combining those two relationships presented its own complications. Their dispute soon turned volatile, with their personal, even petty concerns, taking precedence over their politics.

Julie sighs during our interview, pitying the state of cadres who descended into soap opera theatrics rather than rise to common man heroics. She shrugs, *"Mga taong walang ginagawa para sa masa* (These people who are not doing anything for the masses)."

Bruised egos disturbed the already complex matters faced by the committee in guiding the mass movement. Due to the infighting among the Lava cousins, Joma says the frequency of their meetings dwindled from weekly to monthly throughout 1964, and then just occasionally beyond that. To make matters worse, in May of 1964 Jesus Lava was arrested in Sampaloc, Manila. The government of then President Diosdado Macapagal celebrated his capture and did what all administrations tend to do when bagging an influential rebel leader: foretell the imminent demise of the communists.[12]

With Jesus imprisoned, Paco angled for the position of Secretary-General while Joma was named Secretary for Youth and Lacsina was appointed Secretary for Labor. However, Paco's ambitions were stalled. Shortly before Jesus's arrest, he had appointed his old colleague Pedro Taruc as his deputy for peasant struggles — and as his putative successor.[13] This was the same Pedro Taruc who, with cousin Luis, surrendered the HMB over to the government in 1954, claiming they did it in the name of national reconciliation.[14] The act decimated the guerrilla movement, with the burden of leadership falling on the shoulders of an isolation-bound Jesus. Taruc's ascension to a position of leadership didn't help soothe the contradictions in the committee.

Without any tangible ties to sectoral movements, nor the blessing of his uncle to assume a leadership role, Paco remained an ordinary member of the committee. The stocky Lava's pride was wounded further.

---

12 In President Macapagal's fourth State of the Nation Address (SONA) on January 25, 1965, he hailed the arrest as a "crippling blow." In his SONA a couple of years earlier on January 28, 1963, he also declared how "the communist enemy is being pushed into retreat and defeat."

13 In Tantingco's (2012, 179–80) article bridging the split in the PKP, he says that Pedro Taruc had close ties with Kumander Sumulong, a gangster and extortionist Huk leader. They led a clique of the Huks who fell "subservient to local politicians, US Imperialism and the fascist policies of the Marcos regime."

14 *Time Magazine* (1964) noted Pedro Taruc's ascension to power and that he was likely to continue the Huk's wayward activities, causing trouble in far-flung barrios.

By then, there were also new additions to the group. Experienced peasant organizer Godofredo Mallari and Marxist academic Francisco "Dodong" Nemenzo, Jr. joined their meetings sometime between 1963 and 1964.[15]

These changes mattered little in terms of pushing the party forward. There was still no clear direction for the collective, besides scattered organizing efforts. Joma says Taruc never showed up at any committee meeting.

Personal quarrels over recognition of authority, bitterness over lost lovers, and a feeble connection with expansion on the ground left the Lava cousins in disarray.[16] The arrest of Jesus seemed to paralyze them further. Without their uncle's guidance, the rifts between them afflicted the committee. Meetings stopped altogether.

Macapagal's prediction proved to be partly correct as the committee's existence teetered on tokenism. On the other hand, SCAUP, KM, and Lapiang Manggagawa gained momentum, aided by fresh batches of cadres. An initiative by labor leader Felixberto Olalia also led to the creation of the peasant group Malayang Samahan ng Magsasaka or MASAKA. Joma admits that in this project, at least, Buddy contributed a little bit more. The young members of the peasant class also became core units for KM as the youth organization expanded beyond the capital to the countryside.

Paco and Lacsina's relationship continued to deteriorate. To assert his dominance, Paco issued handwritten memos, barking orders on sheets of yellow pad paper bluntly labelled FROM HO (referring to the "Higher Organ" of the Party). Tony "Ngiwi"

---

[15] Nemenzo stayed with the PKP after Joma broke from the executive committee. At Joma's funeral tribute, Nemenzo admitted to being on the wrong side of history. Later in life he rekindled his friendship with Joma. The pair celebrated birthdays together as they were one day apart in February.

[16] Lacara (1988, 124), another party cadre who witnessed the height of Huk strength in the 1950s to the 1968 reestablishment of the CPP says that even during the late 1940s, many comrades had observed how the Lava and Taruc families monopolized power in the PKP and Huks. This he says and the in-fighting that came with it was a weakness the leadership never corrected.

Santos, the crooked-jawed staff member who had a reputation for being quite the ladies' man, delivered Paco's commands to other party formations. But Lacsina was defiant. He said, *"Ano'ng authority niyang mag-issue ng memo na iyan? 'Di nga ako susunod* (On what authority is he issuing this memo? I won't abide by it)."

The aspiring secretary-general, however, wouldn't tolerate disobedience. He told Joma, *"Bibigyan ko ng warning iyan si Lacsina* (I will give that Lacsina a warning)."

"'Pag tinuloy mo, lalaban lang iyan (If you do, he will fight you)," Joma cautioned.

Paco, it turned out, was also unhappy with Joma. Among labor and activist circles, Paco claimed that Joma pressed for a policy to disallow membership to the party if one did not possess a high school diploma.[17] He sought to paint Joma as *matapobre,* an elitist.

Joma and Lacsina, leaders of the youth and labor movements, held a deep mutual respect and were often on the same wavelength. When Lacsina learned of the slander spread by Paco against Joma, his friction with the committee became even more heated.

"'Yan daw ang sabi ni Salamin (That's according to Glasses)," Joma says, recalling how Paco referred to him behind his back. He sits up in his seat and places a hand on his chin. Just now during our conversation does it occur to him to ask, *"Bakit kaya iyon ang tawag niya sa akin? May salamin din naman siya* (I wonder why he called me that? He wore glasses too)."

By the end of an eventful 1964, Lacsina had severed any connection to all members of the committee besides Joma and Julie. His parting words to Ngiwi, to be relayed back to Paco, were biting: *"Sabihin mo sa putang-inang iyan magbarilan na lang kami* (Tell that son of a whore we can shoot it out)."

---

17 Bart Pasion echoed this sentiment. But Tadem (2019, 120, 138) also notes an interview with Dodong Nemenzo, who comes from the same group. Nemenzo clarified the conflict arose more from Joma's draft on the PKP's history which criticized the party's errors and thus angered Paco Lava.

In April 1965, with Lacsina gone, Paco called for a rare meeting and moved for an election of officers. "*Election* niya (*His* election)," quips a snarky Julie, as Paco appointed himself Secretary-General. He claimed such an appointment was the wish of party elders Jose and Jesus. There was no actual voting; it was more of a preordained coronation with Paco as the heir apparent. Buddy wasn't present — his relationship with Paco remained fractured. The only people who attended were Joma and newcomers Godofredo and Dodong, whom Paco appointed as his second-liners for organization and education, respectively.

Joma stops the story and asks for warm water. We take a break, sipping tea gathered from the boxes Julie keeps under the living room coffee table. While the pair can narrate their memories in great detail, it takes some difficulty to recall the correct sequence in which these events occurred. Joma asks for a moment of silence, his feet pattering, his eyes closed. Julie delights in her tea.

"Ah!" Joma raises an index finger, realizing an answer to a question he posed to himself. "By December 1965, *naatasan na akong magsulat ng political report* (I was tasked with writing a political report)!"[18] It was Joma's idea and the committee approved it. He wanted to haul his comrades back into some semblance of operationality.

In fairness to the committee, one of its main accomplishments in this period was laying the groundwork for the Movement for the Advancement of Nationalism (MAN), a broad alliance of progressives in the 1960s. But Joma believed there was great value in going beyond yellow-pad memos. He pressed for determining the strengths and weaknesses of the party from its founding up until that point. The young intellectual was honored to be given the task of de-constructing the history of the movement to find answers on how to move forward. Joma had

---

[18] By 1966, the PKP had also set up the National Organizing Committee where cadres, along with Joma and Julie, were tasked with researching the PKP history and developing new programs, structures, and basis for action (Tadem 2019, 118–19).

some difficulty in tracing everything since the late 1950s. Most written accounts of the party were comprised of Jesus's political transmissions. Nevertheless, it was a sorely needed undertaking given the succession of mishaps the PKP had gone through. Joma decided only Julie could be his partner for the surgical dissection needed to produce the document.

When he submitted the draft to his comrades in the middle of the following year, it was met with a less-than-enthusiastic response. Joma and Julie presented a scathing examination of the PKP's setbacks with the uncles and nephews of the Lavas and Tarucs at the helm. They described how the old PKP suspended the insurrection in the immediate postwar period to focus on their congressional bid under the Democratic Alliance banner. In 1946, the government of Manuel Roxas and traditional ruling families prevented them from ever stepping foot in Congress. Having been kicked out of the political mainstream, they reoperationalized the HMB from the underground in 1948. However, a loose and underdeveloped mass base — the result of indecisive strategies — led to numerous defeats by the military. Huk Commander Luis Taruc surrendered to President Ramon Magsaysay in 1954. The Philippine government used rebel-returnee Huks as a propaganda tool to discourage mass struggles and future uprisings. Jesus went into hiding. Guerrilla troops shrunk and fragmented further.[19] Recognizing past mistakes could have galvanized the committee. Instead, its members dismissed the findings in the document. Later the draft would be reworked and renamed "Rectify our Errors and Rebuild the Party," the theoretical basis for the reestablishment of the Communist Party of the Philippines in 1968 under Marxism–Leninism and Mao Zedong Thought.

The assessment demanded immediate and comprehensive action and spoke of ideas to which none of the PKP leaders

---

[19] According to *Singsing Magazine* (2012, 171) on Central Luzon history, in 1965, the Huk split into factions: one supported incumbent President Macapagal while the other backed Ferdinand E. Marcos. Both factions eventually embroiled themselves in violent attacks against each other as a result.

had ever paid any serious attention. For instance, the "Rectify" document posited that the legal democratic movement and the armed struggle shouldn't cancel each other out. It wasn't a choice between one or the other; both were pursued as complimentary, mutually dependent elements with the same aim. Armed warfare is given primacy, but both are distinct and not separate forms of waging the revolution.

Paco was uninterested in these proposals. Joma remembers hearing him say, *"Ah, memorandum lang iyan. Ako susulat ng final* (Ah that's just another memorandum. I will write the final version)."

"After that I just kept quiet. *Intrigero talaga siya* (He keeps sowing intrigue)," says Joma with slumped shoulders. After the "election" and the dismissal of the merits of the report, Joma and Julie felt their time with the group had come to an end. The committee was reluctant to move forward or take an honest look back at itself. Paco's attempts at consolidating the group through a power-grab and hijacking the report were damning actions, considering he held no political leverage. Joma says there wasn't a single party branch to command, no leading organs and no Political Bureau. The party had only a few isolated members and a few mass organizations among the youth, labor, and peasant forces from the the earlier efforts of Joma, Julie, and Lacsina.

The memorandum Paco egregiously volunteered to rewrite, an addition to his collection of unpopular yellow-pad orders, was given to Julie for editing. He summarized the entire political report into two pages but nullified the criticisms within it. Three times Paco modified the two-page write-up and handed it to Julie. Julie never finished reworking and typing the memo. To her, it wasn't worth the effort anyhow. *"Bagsak. Doon pa lang sa introduction, bagsak na siya* (A failure. Just looking at the introduction, he already messed it up)," she says.

Disheartened at what had become of the group, like a child meeting the irreverent actors playing one's favorite heroes, Joma looked elsewhere for support. He shared his dismay and consulted with other youth cadres managing KM. *"Iba na ang takbo ng utak ng mga ito* (Their heads are running on a different frequency)," he confessed to them. The Lavas seemed only interested in inheriting party power and nothing more.

The KM crowd agreed to shift away from the Lavas. They helped Joma and Julie establish the provisional bureau for the new CPP in 1967, thereby formally denouncing the "Lava Revisionist Renegades." In their eyes, what was left of the PKP's Executive Committee had disintegrated.

"We informed them of our intentions. They expelled us, and we expelled them," scoffs Joma. Accounts of the PKP trail off by the 1970s. There aren't many archived news articles about them, and few historians can point to any activity thereafter. It is hard to say whether they continued to exist outside a name and a memory.

The most notable decision they made was entering a "Political Settlement" with the Marcos government in November 1974 for the release of Jose and Jesus Lava and others from prison.[20] In their eyes, Marcos was a possible ally in the fight against imperialism: their greater enemy. It was a convenient excuse for surrendering the Huk's armory, renouncing armed struggle, and assisting the Marcos government in fighting the CPP–NPA.[21] The PKP claims to have done this to continue its struggle in legal spheres, but there is barely an existence to speak of. Since the settlement, they have stayed ineffectual and irrelevant. These days, there are still rare occasions when I catch a glimpse of some spray-painted graffiti in obscure corners of the city — a bus station bench, or behind a 7-11 branch — of the old PKP's logo. The image doesn't evoke any sort of pride, more like a cautionary tale to those who know it. Its hastily drawn hammer resembles

---

[20] Both Manoling Lava and Paquito (Paco's father and Jesus's brother) even in the mid-1960s had already expressed a willingness, even an inclination to side with Marcos. Even during Martial Law, Buddy Lava noted that Marcos was capable of nationalistic sentiments. Jesus maintains the settlement was not a surrender but a just transition to aboveground work (Dalisay, Jr. 1999, 153, 156).

[21] According to Pasion, negotiations with the PKP had started as early as 1972 and there wasn't much consultation among the ranks of the Lava-led party. Pasion says the PKP could not resist siding with Marcos (Tadem 2019, 134).

a slanted T and the sickle an incomplete P, then it's signed PKP –1930 at the bottom. I was honestly surprised to find they still have a semi-functioning website.

Writer and social critic Jose "Butch" Dalisay, Jr. wrote in "The Lavas Brothers, Blood and Politics" (1998) that they left an undeniable mark in the first half of the twentieth century. They were forerunners in rattling the system, radicalizing middle-class circles, and connecting with the working masses. They inspired countless Filipinos, Joma included, to search for revolutionary alternatives. Or, as Dalisay put it, "to fill the void in critical and nationalist inquiry that half a century of American rule had managed to create in the hearts and minds of the people" (1998, 111).

Was Joma the undoing of the party that the Lavas had worked so hard to maintain, as some loyalists of the old PKP say? Did their rift supplant what could have been a stronger anti-imperialist front in the Philippines? I'd answer no to both questions. After many years of mishaps, it didn't take much in the end for the PKP to stagnate and then capitulate. It was bound to happen, one way or another.

Fighting Makes You Stronger

At the end of 1968, the still-unarmed young guns of the reestablished CPP had rigorous work ahead of them. Their daunting tasks — building a party from the ground up, founding a revolutionary army, establishing a reliable underground network safe from state forces and even the ire of the contemptuous Lavas, expanding their mass base and laying the theoretical basis for a protracted people's war, among others — were mostly achieved in just four frenetic years. Joma and Julie believed conditions were ripe for a revolution, but not without its challenges.

In 1972, the CPP and the NPA had scant numbers, but enough of a presence for the Marcos government to count it as their biggest threat and thus respond by imposing Martial Law.

Right before the reestablishment of the CPP, Joma and Julie were enjoying the relative comforts of aboveground or legal democratic political activism. They worked with KM and a host of other trade unions — organizations somewhat tolerated by the state. They maintained day jobs which paid the bills and served as satellite centers for their respective duties in the mass movement. Julie took on a slew of librarian jobs, which in those days were in high demand. Universities, law firms, and all manner of business required archiving professionals. Most of the time, she was left to herself or with a minimal staff, which allowed her time to edit propaganda documents. After office hours, she'd board a jeepney for a brief visit home to shed any unnecessary items for her next destination. Then she'd make a quick survey of the house and the street outside before taking off again to one of several apartments which doubled as a press and printing office, carrying some office supplies the library didn't seem to mind losing. *"Kailangan bantayan mo talaga ang bahay kasi may mga naga-attempt na pasukin, o na mag-misrepresent tapos manghihingi ng kung anong material. Hindi naman ubra iyan sa katulong* (You really need to guard your house because there are those who attempt to break in, or misrepresent themselves while asking for some political materials. That can't be entrusted to a helper)," she says, content with not having busied herself among the crowded rallies of activists but being industrious all the same. She took charge of producing the literature for KM and the soon to be reestablished CPP, and their respective newsletters.

Joma taught English at the Lyceum of the University of the Philippines where he daydreamed of pursuing an academic's life. Ironically, politicizing his classroom drew him further away from the rewards of the academe.

He says, *"Masaya iyong nakakapagturo sa kabataan, precisely dahil diyan napapadulas ang organizing* (I was happy teaching young people, precisely because it helped to make organizing smoother)."

I ask what attracted him to the academic life.

Joma looks out the window and says, *"One of the best kinds of life. Tahimik, though it has its own gains and turbulence. Pero napasubo na, no'ng pinasok ang rebolusyon. Kung gusto mo mahinahon, academic life. Pero gusto mo pakikibaka, e siyempre ano, that falls as a priority. As a general possibility for people who can teach at walang ambisyong magpayaman, maganda ang academic life* (One of the best kinds of life. It's quiet, though it has its own gains and turbulence. But I had too much on my plate when I started with revolution. If you want something calm, that's academic life. But if you want the struggle, well of course, that falls as a priority. As a general possibility for people who can teach and have no ambition to get rich, the academe is a good choice)."

Like UP, the well-known base for radicals, Lyceum was spawning its own batch of militants. *"Pero maingat ako sa Lyceum, hindi ako iyong mismo nagre-recruit. Ayaw ko din naman na mag-KM kung gusto lang makapasa sa klase ko. 'Pag may prospect, sasabihan ko ang ibang mga KM na estudyante, sila ang lalapit* (But I was careful in Lyceum, I never actually recruited anyone. I also didn't want students to join KM just to get ahead in my class. When there was a prospect, I would tell other KM students and they would approach)," Joma shares.

After classes, he spent late afternoons at the offices of the National Association of Trade Unions (NATU) along T.M. Kalaw to hold consultations with workers who arrived from their shifts. When he got home to the Retiro apartment he shared with Julie, he found KM members and UP contemporaries waiting to engage his views until past midnight.

In addition to heading the KM, Joma was vice-chairperson of the Socialist Party (formerly the Lapiang Manggagawa). On certain days he devoted time to the Movement for the Advancement of Nationalism (MAN), a catch-all alliance chaired by progressive lawmaker Lorenzo Tañada.

The entire National Democratic movement was a rapidly growing entity and required constant attention from its cadres and caretakers. Between his desire for an academic life and his urge to fulfill his political duties, Joma made the latter his priority. Ultimately, he was a willing servant to the blueprints he and Julie outlined for the movement. It was an easier decision than he had made it out to be in those days.

"You have to have a sense of your limits," he says as we discuss the initial stages of their foray into party-building. *"Ako man abante, ang magagawa ko sa umpisa is to have a group to share with ideologically... by its nature maliit iyan* (Consider that I am politically astute, what I can do in the beginning is to have a group to share with ideologically... by its nature it should be small)."

I recall a conversation I had with Joma a few days ago. We were at the NDFP office and I didn't have my notebook or recorder, but I caught one thing he muttered in the middle of one of his stories: "Fighting makes you stronger." I mention that comment now and ask him to elaborate.

Joma lectures "talaga namang line namin ang mapunta na sa armed revolution (Our line was always headed toward armed revolution). What distinguished us from the Lavas is that they had no idea when to make the revolution. For them, the uprising may come after an indefinite period of legal struggle, the end of which you do not know. But if you have enough mass base to start with, you can go ahead. In a semicolonial and semifeudal country like the Philippines, you can start armed revolution if you have enough cadres."

And in the beginning of 1969, they did just that. Joma, Julie, and a handful of cadres from intellectual and middle-class backgrounds sought to light the spark of their prairie fire in the countryside. The party was illegal from the very onset of its existence, since its primary purpose was violently overthrowing the reactionary state ruled by landlords, compradors, and imperialist puppets.

That year marked the founders' complete shift into full-time underground or "UG" work, for the movement. This meant assuming different identities, following one's political duties throughout the country, and trying to evade capture by the authorities. To the government, they were terrorists and brigands — bad seeds that needed to be exterminated before they could sprout roots. To each other, they were evolving renegades, sacrificing their careers and families' aspirations to spearhead what would become the world's longest-running communist insurgency.

In those days, however, they'd spent most of their young adult lives in the cities, buried in books and study circles. The only action they'd ever seen was at demonstrations. Street skirmishes with the police during protests was no preview of the bullet-laden road ahead.

Enter Bernabe Buscayno or "Kumander Dante," a maverick guerrilla who'd fought from the age of seventeen with the Central Luzon-based HMB or Huks. He hailed from a poor family of tenant farmers in Sta. Rita, Capas, Tarlac. The young Dante's reputation and commitment grew, but so too did his frustration with the Huk leadership. His commanders seemed more interested in acting like an army-for-hire rather than defend impoverished farmers.

Faustino Del Mundo or "Kumander Sumulong" was head Huk honcho and the subject of Dante's discontent.[1] Sumulong had supported Marcos's candidacy in the mid-1960s as well as the misdeeds of the Lavas and Tarucs since World War II. He also extorted protection money from businesses and politicians. Huk commanders ordered the rank-and-file to function as mercenaries in local political quarrels, always siding with the highest bidder. Sumulong was reported to have personally collected a million dollars a year from bars and brothels in the American Air Base in Clark, Pampanga (Warner 2012, 176–77).

Even though Dante rose to district commander under Sumulong, he loathed his superior's gangster tactics and refused to participate. He wasn't yet the mythical folk hero whose name people chanted in the streets or the figure to be immortalized in movies, but he was well on his way. He'd heard of Joma Sison the intellectual. He'd heard of KM and the upheavals in Manila. The disillusioned but not disheartened fighter sent word from his own set of contacts to arrange a meeting with Joma. Dante was primed to link up with the unarmed young guns who had also gotten wind of his notoriety.

It takes a while for Joma to get a sense of my questions about Dante and their meeting. For a moment, he looks puzzled and doesn't recognize the name. Finally it clicks. *"Ahhh, si Payat* (Ah, you mean Slim)!" he cries. Julie laughs as they both recall Dante's scrawny and unassuming features which made more of an impression on the couple than his famous alias.

---

[1] Luis Taruc's surrender to the Magsaysay government left a power vacuum that was filled by factions among the Huk. The most prominent was Kumander Sumulong, who used his Huk forces like a mercenary army to influence local politics and set up extortion and protection money rackets from local businesses in Pampanga and the greater Central Luzon area (Sangil 2012, 172–73).

A month before the CPP's birth, Joma travelled to meet "Payat" in the village of Dolores, close to his hometown of Sta. Rita. Dante, the friendly hacienda overseer, led Joma under the shade of a mango tree. They sat and talked for an entire evening. "We became instant comrades as we exchanged information and ideas. It was too late to invite him as a delegate when we met, but he welcomed the reestablishment of the party and understood the reasons for this," remarks Joma.

Payat was decided. Meeting Joma reinforced his plan to break away from Sumulong's forces.[2] He took a handful of equally disgruntled troops from the Huks, and by February of 1969, they were conducting politico-military training with the reestablished CPP in Tarlac. A month later, the NPA was founded on March 29, the anniversary of the Huks. This was a deliberate decision to honor the Huk's revolutionary beginnings as the HUKBALAHAP, the freedom fighters who resisted Japanese colonization during World War II. They were leaving the past without forgetting it. The NPA was the latest iteration of a Filipino guerrilla army fighting for liberation. This time, they fought to rid the country of its neocolonial masters, defeat the reactionary military, and pave the way for socialist construction.

The NPA began with a mere thirty-five rifles, nine of them automatic. Months later, they launched tactical offensives and gained a foothold in the Central Luzon provinces of Tarlac, Pampanga, Zambales, and Nueva Ecija.[3] Ambushes on enemy camps happened so often in Tarlac — three to four each month — that the NPA seized around two hundred automatic rifles in the first year and a half of its existence.

Fighting makes you stronger. Another two hundred might have been snatched had planned ambushes pushed through,

---

[2] Sumulong was later arrested in 1970 and sentenced to *reclusión perpetua*, bringing what remained of the Huks to dissolution.

[3] The astounding rate of growth and expansion was also noted by author Ninotchka Rosca. She reveals: "By 1976, the CPP membership had grown to 5,000 and had spread out among ten regional organizations; the NPA had a thousand rifles and nine regional commands" (Rosca and Sison 2004, 26).

bemoans Joma. But the guerrillas called them off due to insufficient preparation.

The peasant masses of Central Luzon were infatuated with their rebel heroes. They saw folks just like them, who walked like they'd been born in the barrios, but carried new ideas and attitudes — something to aspire to. The NPA relied on the people for their safety and in return sought to redefine how an army, a people's guerrilla unit, treated civilians. They demonstrated a humanity previously unseen in rifle-carrying troops. Stories of Payat's selflessness spread. He never asked for anything and took only some of what was offered to him by NPA supporters. His fellow fighters followed suit, scrubbing floors, ploughing fields, and cleaning dishes whenever they passed through villages. NPA guerrillas were a trusted security force. Locals could leave their belongings and livestock alone knowing everything was protected.[4]

The CPP looked northeast to expand its base, setting eyes on the province of Isabela. Their famous 1970 raid on the Philippine Military Academy armory yielded dozens of rifles which they sent to the Cagayan Valley region in preparation for a new guerrilla front. The dense forest area along the Sierra Madre, filled with dissatisfied farmers, was fertile ground for guerrilla warfare. From there, the NPA deployed expansion teams northward to the Cordilleras beginning with Ifugao province. The more sentries you send, the more chances of winning.

Joma and Julie zigzagged across Luzon lugging portable typewriters. They spent several months in Tarlac, then sped off to their transit point in Baguio, then back to Isabela. Apart from overseeing the party expansion, they also piloted a survey of Northern Luzon feudalism. The pair bounced in and out of peasant communities, finding the time to, write, consult, deliberate in party conferences, and interact with locals.

---

4 Tadem (2006) shared an account by Pampanga local Apung Bising, who knew Dante and his comrades always paid for anything they used as was part of the NPA regulations. When Apung Bising's sister was sick Dante even offered money for the hospital bills but she couldn't accept the gesture.

"*Hectic ang panahon na iyan. Kailangan palaging may time ka din magsulat, time para magpulong* (That was a hectic time. You always needed time to write, and time for meetings)," says Julie, scratching behind her ear.

She holds tender memories of this period, of the work and moments in between. "*Walang oras para maglibang. Kung meron man, chika-chika sa mga taga-baryo. Sa araw nagtatrabaho, sa gabi kakain sa kung kaninong bahay kasi iimbitahin ka. Alam mo iyung delicacy nila na buro? Nalaman ng mga tagabaryo na paborito ko iyon, pero nagsawa nga ako kasi tuwing iimbitahan ako, lagi na lang may buro* (There was no time for recreation. If any, we'd have light conversations with people in the barrio. During the day, we'd work. At night, we never ate at the same house twice because there were so many invitations to visit. Have you tried their delicacy, the *buro*? The locals discovered that it was my favorite, but I got a little sick of it because at every invitation to visit a home, *buro* was prepared)." There is much love encased in moments away from duty, at intervals of levity within struggle.

The government was quick to draw its weapons against the NPA. In 1969, the military initiated operations to maim, and capture the new leaders of the revolution. Joma recalls one raid by soldiers on a CPP conference that year. The communists escaped just in time because the locals warned them.

Soldiers pilfered important papers at a party conference as attendees dashed to safety. Among the stash were records of the founding of the CPP and NPA, as well as the draft of the first issue of the publication *Ang Bayan* (*The People*). The Marcos regime and the military celebrated their loot of key documents by publishing them in the *Philippines Herald*, intending to stir up anti-communist hysteria and celebrate (prematurely, as it turned out) their success in nipping the NPA in the bud through "Oplan Prophylactic."

This emergent period had many close calls and casualties, as the nascent revolution first made strides. From 1969 to 1976, twenty-five members of the Central Committee were either killed or detained in varying circumstances. The authorities arrested cadres who performed non-military duties, while the fatalities resulted from armed clashes. *"Ang tsamba na hindi nakikilala ng kalaban, marami iyan* (There are many instances where you were lucky not be recognized by the enemy)." One night in 1969, Joma, Julie, Magtanggol Roque, and his wife Mila were driving from Pampanga into Tarlac when they came upon a police checkpoint. It was election season and the government was cracking down on illegal gun ownership. Joma was carrying a pistol. There were several vehicles in front of them. In the minutes it took for the police to let one after the other through, Joma debated with himself *"kung magpapahuli o lalaban at may mamamatay sa amin* (if I will surrender or fight at the cost of a casualty among us)." When the cops asked the van in front of them to lower its windows, Joma and the other braced for a confrontation. Luckily, the police discovered a gun inside the van and in the ensuing commotion, they allowed Joma and his comrades through without so much as a knock on the window.

Another incident in 1969 required Joma to capitalize on his background as a son of the Ilocos provincial elite. While crossing provincial borders into Bayombong, Nueva Vizacaya, late one night, Joma, Julie, and two others stopped at a highway gas station. A constabulary captain and his sergeant were manning an outpost beside the gas station. Julie heard the sergeant mumble as he scanned their parked car: *"Tarlac plate. Tangina, NPA ito* (Tarlac plate. Fuck, it's NPA)." Even more troubling, Joma was again carrying a pistol with him. He had already been warned not to bring one, even for protection. After all, the weapon offered little defense against multiple assailants, and was also an implicating item at routine searches.

"Pero ayun, e (But it's like that), you can never tell," shrugs Joma, who preferred to go down fighting with his nine-millimeter handgun should things have taken a turn for the worse.

As Joma confronted the police, he heard the captain's accent, and presented himself as *"taga-Vigan* (from Vigan)." The wayward Ilocano aristocrat assumed a relative's name (not Sison) and proceeded to disarm the captain with references to their shared hometown. He name-dropped respected Ilocanos, hint-ing at a sophisticated upbringing. Impressed, the captain let them through without an inspection.

Another trickier hurdle was handling contradictions among the people without the necessary humility. Joma mentions, "*Sa loob ng NPA noon, if you act dogmatically or bureaucratically, tipong ikaw bossy na commander, delikado ka niyan* (Inside the NPA before, if you act dogmatically or bureaucratically, like you were the bossy commander, it landed you in trouble)."

He recalled a comrade conducting military research for the Central Committee who was deployed to the countryside. He made the dangerous mistake of flaunting his standing in the party to the point of insulting NPA troops with peasant backgrounds especially. His arrogance was what sparked altercations and got him killed by locals he had offended. Arming people was always going to be complicated. Regrettably, some lessons in humility cost lives.

Other recruits couldn't take the constant uncertainty. Squads came under demoralizing spells after unlucky encounters with the enemy. Sessions of criticism and self-criticism (known among cadres as "CSCs"), aimed at constructive assessments among their ranks, also dampened spirits when done incorrectly. Some of these CSC sessions turned harsher than intended, causing some initiates to leave without warning. NPA deserters tended to be found by the enemy or even converted into informants.

The subtleties of learning local languages also posed some difficulties at times. Joma shakes his head. "*Meron pa, iyong wrong phrasing lang magkakagulo na. Halimbawa ang sabi mo, 'pupuksain natin ang pangangalabaw,' pero ang rinig ay para bang 'pupuksain natin ang mangangalabaw'* (Sometimes, the wrong phrasing can cause trouble. For example, you say, 'let's eliminate the grazing of cattle,' but it's misheard as 'let's eliminate the one who grazes cattle')."

Nevertheless, the NPA spread in all directions from the Tarlac front. By 1971, based on Joma's estimates, their total Isabela mass base consisting of both red fighters and barrio-level activists of which the latter was the majority reached 150,000, compared to 80,000 in Tarlac. From 1972 onward, the CPP also deployed teams as far off as Mindanao.[5]

Even into his sixties, battle-tested former Huk Ka Eddie Layug was heading the expansion into the northern regions. He outlined the rough sketch of functions and responsibilities for what became the basic unit of the NPA, the Sandatahang Yunit Pampropaganda (Armed Propaganda Unit) or SYP. As opposed to operating with large formations drawing unwanted attention, the SYP integrated scouting, organizing work, building barrio militias, and waging agrarian campaigns among a small team of no more than five to seven people. A single NPA guerrilla is at once a combatant, barrio organizer, and agricultural aid worker, weaving between defending the poorest peasants and easing the burden of farm labor. A highly mobile unit less than half the size of a squad able to work across several municipalities made economic use of their forces.

In the forest ranges of Isabela, Ka Eddie guided several hundred people through cadre training from 1969 to 1971. Locals christened the grounds as the "People's Republic of Dipogo," after the nearest village and stream.

Ka Eddie may not ring through historical accounts with the same prestige as Payat, but Joma and Julie vouch that his contributions amid the NPA's growing pains cannot be understated. Julie recalls him being *"maalam pero walang yabang, magaan* (knowledgable, but without arrogance, easygoing)." Older, wilier, and grizzlier, the tall veteran was a regimental Huk commander in the early 1950s. He led the August 1950 raid on the military's Camp Macabulos in Tarlac, boosting the Huks' renown.[6] A few years before the CPP's resurgence, state

---

[5] The CPP's official publication *Ang Bayan* (1978) reported that it had established "5 big guerrilla fronts in 12 provinces of Mindanao," effectively covering the three main island groups of the archipelago. It also said that since 1977, "the NPA increased its firepower by 50 percent in that region by launching tactical offensives whenever the conditions are favorable."

[6] It was estimated that around five hundred Huks stormed the military camp. Dalisay, Jr. (1999, 119) notes there were twenty-five military casualties, including a Red Cross nurse.

forces captured and jailed him on charges of rebellion. Upon his release, Ka Eddie was intent on rejoining his comrades.

"*Kinulong, pero fighting spirit paglabas* (They detained him, but he had a fighting spirit when he got out)," remembers Julie.

To move through the Tarlac peasant communities without alerting the enemy, he took a job as an insurance agent. Using his cover, he collected information about his comrades and learned of the disagreements between Payat and Sumulong, siding with the former.

In those early days *"security ang matinding problema* (security was the biggest problem)," says Julie. Many have heard of how the NPA went from a ragtag few dozen to having guerrilla fronts across the country, but what about its infancy? Nothing difficult is ever straightforward, and a lot of lives were lost because of mistakes which today's generation of guerrillas might have found elementary. A large number of the revolutionaries came from the intelligentsia, brave and bold yet inexperienced in strategic warfare. This is where the hardened Huks delivered their biggest contribution, steering the movement to stand on its own two feet.

"*Salamat sa mga unang gerilyero, ang pondo ng kaalaman nila at karanasan, naipasa sa NPA* (Thanks to the first guerrillas, the wealth of knowledge and experience they had was passed unto the NPA)," says Joma.

Fighting units needed to be flexible and develop the habit of mobility. The guerrillas crumpled their toes when skirting downhill to prevent the build-up of unwanted momentum. They kept their backs straight when carrying heavy packs to redistribute weight on the body. During any trek, they planted heels first, lessening the noise of footsteps. One's breathing also needed to be managed when hiking up a slope to avoid overexerting the lungs. Holding a tiny breath right before exhaling and then tapping the rifle's trigger steadied the aim. They learned by doing.

Joma and Payat were both arrested in 1977 and incarcerated for roughly the same duration. Years later, President Corazon Aquino granted the pair amnesty during the whirlwind of transition after Marcos's ouster. Payat, semi-retired, began working with agricultural cooperatives near guerrilla fronts to aid the agrarian campaign efforts. The pair still saw each other often before Joma left for Europe.

Payat would see his old comrades in person for the last time when he joined the 1992 peace negotiations between the government and the NDFP. He repeated the promise he'd made to Joma and Julie right before they left the Philippines for Europe. "*'Di niya daw pinapaputol iyong puno ng mangga kung saan kami unang nag-usap, sa Barrio Dolores* (He said he wouldn't allow the mango tree where we first talked to be cut down)."

Puri and Art

In talking with Joma and Julie separately, two unfamiliar names come up. It's hard to say what might have become of the couple without the unsung feats of many comrades. Puri and Art are reminders that this a struggle of masses, not saviors.

Purificacion "Puri" Pedro was a student activist at the University of the Philippines in the mid-1960s taking up a degree in social work. She befriended longtime activist Judy Taguiwalo, who also spoke with me in the Philippines about her old classmate, although Puri was a year older.

Judy was fond of Puri's sense of humor. She remembers one judo class they took for their physical education requirements. Their instructor, a good-looking young man, initiated an exercise where he'd embrace a student who was tasked to retaliate with a counter-maneuver. Judy shares, "Puri's plan was just to allow the instructor to embrace her and she would embrace him back! I cannot remember if she actually did this but it shows the kind of fun we had during our undergrad years."

Puri graduated in 1969, the same year the NPA was formed, placing tenth on the national board examinations for social workers. She spent the next few years working with the Immaculate Conception Parish to set up day-care centers and cooperatives in Quezon City. In 1972, when massive floods washed out barrios in Central Luzon, Puri led relief efforts of the Church.[1] Martial Law was declared that same year.

Not long after, Puri sought more meaningful integration in remote and rural areas. By 1974, she was organizing full time against the displacement of and violence upon Indigenous peoples due to Marcos's Chico Dam project. Judy joined her on a similar journey and can only laugh at memories of her easygoing comrade mimicking Maria von Trapp from the film *The Sound of Music*. To keep spirits high and amuse her companions Puri would belt out in her out-of-tune voice, "Climb Every Mountain" at Cordillera's summits.

In 1977 she took a clandestine trip to a guerrilla front in Bataan to meet friends of hers who had joined the NPA. She supported her contemporaries who chose armed struggle as the clearest path for continuing resistance against dictatorship. In around the same period, Puri wrote to her family to help them understand the predicaments she'd put herself in. One letter reads:

Hindi lingid sa ating kaalaman ang mga hirap at panganib sa atingn. Subalit marami na akong natutunan ngayon, kung kaya't panatag ang aking kalooban sa lahat ng nangyayari. Ako'y natutuwa't nasisiyahan sa karera kong pinili. Hindi ito dahil sa pananalaping benepisyo na habol ng ibang propesyonal. Higit pa rito ang karanasan kong makipamuhay sa mga tao, ang mga mahihirap at ang mga nakaririwasa... na ang hangarin at pagsisikap ay para sa isang tunay na makataong kaunlaran. Alam kong nag-aalala kayo sa akin, at nagpapasalamat ako sa lahat ng inyong panalangin, subalit huwag kayong mag-alala. Nakatitiyak kayo na aking ginagawa ang sa wari ko'y nararapat, at matibay ang aking paniniwala na lahat

---

[1] Puri practiced her vocation in social work dearly, beginning with out of school impoverished youths, then Indigenous peoples. Her letter to her mother can be found in the Bantayog ng mga Bayani archives (Rodriguez 2015, 165).

ng ito'y para sa kapakanan ng nakararami—ang mga dukha't sinisiil, ang pinaka-aba sa ating mga kapatid.

(We are not unaware of the hardships and perils our activities entail. However, experience and wisdom have mentored me in the way of peace amid turmoil. I am happy and content with the career I have chosen. It deviates from the wealth-seeking path of typical professionals, but its dividends outweigh money: I have lived where people live and have struggled where they struggle — both with the poor and the rich, the full gamut… all the while maintaining a single-minded aim for humane progress. I know you worry about me, and I truly appreciate your prayers, but be at ease. Rest assured that I am fully certain of the justness of my course and that I am doing this for a nobler, greater good—for the poor and the oppressed, the least of our fellow men.)

During the mid-1970s, Joma and Julie circled around Luzon. At each of their stops, they were pursued by soldiers as priority targets of the Marcos regime. For any guerrilla front to host them required additional scouting, surveillance, and security.

In January 1977, Joma and Julie were in Mount Terrano bordering Bataan, Zambales, and Pampanga provinces preparing for a party conference. Despite all their precautions, the enemy had identified their location. Puri was among those in the guerrilla unit who were ambushed while approaching the conference site. She was shot and wounded in the left clavicle. The soldiers succeeded in isolating the bleeding Puri and capturing her, as Joma, Julie, and the guerrillas retreated to safety.

Puri convalesced at the Bataan Provincial Hospital where she was placed under military guard. Relatives watched over her as she feared the worst from her captors.

Other Martial Law veterans told me that when a detainee was subjected to interrogation, often including torture and the threat of death, it was considered ideal to hold out for at least three days before revealing any information. Three days was usually enough for comrades to make security adjustments—it was time for them to regroup, change locations, shift patterns, and secure themselves for future work.

Puri kept quiet for six days before she was murdered. Her silence was a lifesaver for Joma and Julie. She gave no details about the whereabouts of anyone. On January 23, the sixth day after her arrest, an interrogation team from Manila headed by the infamous Colonel Rolando Abadilla barged into her room and forced her sister to leave. Presumably, they tried to squeeze any useful bits of information, including the whereabouts of Joma and Julie. Again, she refused to talk.

After an hour of interrogation, the team strangled Purificacion Pedro in her hospital bathroom with a piece of wire, leaving her body to be discovered by family and the attending nurses. Puri's lifeless and hardened fingers clutched a medal of the Virgin Mary (*Bantayog ng mga Bayani* n.d.).

Joma and Julie were eventually captured in November of the same year. But for the eleven months free from incarceration, they have comrades like Puri to thank.

Maybe, at some point, they caught glimpses of each other, but Joma and Julie were never introduced to Puri. They never had the chance to speak. It seems peculiar to have never met your rescuer, to owe so much to a person who is both a stranger and a guardian. Puri held the line and she died on it. She was 29 years old.

Another whose mere memory caused Joma to weep was Arthur Garcia. He was Joma's former student and friend, and a man whom he trusted dearly. Art was with him throughout so many crucial flashpoints in the revolution's younger years.

Art grew up in the backstreets of Manila's tondo slums. He was a charter member of the Kabataang Makabayan (KM or Patriotic Youth), the first national-democratic mass organization in the country, and was among the founding members of its chapter at his alma mater, the Lyceum of the University of the Philippines. "He was an outstanding student and comrade, daring but calculating in pushing for militant actions in Manila," Joma recalls.

Joma describes Art as a bit shorter than himself, five feet seven, but with a broader, more muscular frame. It came from the slew of part-time blue-collar jobs he took to help pay the family's bills and put himself through school. Art threw himself into political work. He was a campus propagandist at the onset of KM and also reached out to high-school students and urban poor youths in his Tondo neighborhood. A year after KM's founding in 1964, Art spearheaded labor organizing efforts, mobilizing unions and young workers from the US Tobacco Corporation, San Miguel Brewery, and Manila Cordage, among others. *"Maraming nakuhang kadre mula diyan* (A lot of cadres came from there)," confirms Joma.

By 1966, Art had become a public-school teacher at Tondo's Torres High School, a position he used to educate teenagers about imperialism and country's class divide.

Little has been explored about Art's hand in laying the groundwork for the national-democratic revolution. He was instrumental in the militant mid-1960s which paved the way for the First Quarter Storm of 1970—a series of youth-led demonstrations that seemed to make Metro Manila convulse with progressive ideas. Protesters flooded streets and battled cops, while those from the shanties either cheered them on or joined in. Art was there when consultations were held to establish a provisional politburo separate from the "Lava revisionist renegades." Joma makes sure to mention that we have Art to thank for coining the enduring slogan, *"Makibaka! Huwag matakot!* (Struggle! Don't be afraid!)"

In 1968, Joma survived an assassination attempt. He escaped with just a cut on the arm after three men lunged at him inside a jeepney. Since then he often had the pleasure of Art's company for security as the latter was adept at procuring discreet transportation for meet-ups with comrades.

In December of that year, Art arranged the use of a small hut on a modest farm owned by his father-in-law in Barrio Dulacac of Alaminos, Pangasinan province. It was to become the site for the reestablishment of Communist Party of the Philippines, guided by Marxism–Leninism and Mao Zedong Thought. Art was one of the founders and a member of the party's first Central Committee.

From then on, Art stayed as a full-time party worker in Tarlac. He was tasked with organizing and mobilizing peasants while reconnecting with the fragmented old-guard guerrillas of the Hukbong Mapagpalaya sa Bayan (HMB). Joma reflects that in hindsight, the always optimistic Art may have overestimated the capacity of the first batches of guerrilla recruits.

"Nagpasampa ng taga-barrio si Art kahit na may babala ang magulang na 'Mabuti pa at 'wag niyong tanggapin, may nakita kaming diperensya sa anak namin. Kapag nagagalit, walang kinikilala' (Art had recruited someone from the barrio even if that person's parents warned, 'better if you don't accept him, there's something abnormal about our son. When he gets angry, he really loses it')," Joma recalls. But Art persisted, perhaps thinking many parents felt the same way about their adolescent kids and hoping that engagement in the revolution could remold any character flaws.

At a squad session for criticism and self-criticism facilitated by Art, his new recruit received constructive advice from another guerrilla. The ill-tempered recruit incorrectly judged Art to be taking sides against him and walked out of the meeting, retreating to a nearby bamboo hut. Art pleaded with him to come back and resolve the issues he had with comrades. Instead, the new guerrilla fired a bullet through the slits of bamboo, fatally wounding the Tondo native.

"Pinatay si Art no'ng kinukumbinsi ang nabuang na bagong rekluta. Tragic. Magaling na kadre (Art was killed when he was trying to convince the new recruit who was acting crazy. Tragic. He was an excellent cadre)," mourns Julie.

Lessons on handling the armed masses while facing the responsibility of developing rural strongholds, were paid for by the best of cadres, the best of a generation. Art died in Concepcion, Tarlac in November 1969, the same year the NPA was founded.

I wonder how the enthusiastic Art imagined the NPA blossoming in his dreams, heard the sound of courageous tactical offensives across the islands, and felt the fresh air rustling through the holes of his hammock as an ageing guerrilla. Like Puri, he was 29. There are far too many goodbyes in a revolution. Puri and Art bled from the same wounds. Like Joma and Julie, we are still saying goodbye to them, carrying their memories like scars. The dead don't care for our tributes, however. We commemorate because there is something they leave behind for us, for others to carry on.

The Singing Detainee and the Librarian with One Book

Last night, Joma was flailing his arms as he slept. The bed shook beneath him. Soldiers had broken in to drag him away. He opened his mouth but could only muster faint, garbled noises of resistance. Words failed him. He needed his wife, his partner, to know what was happening. He needed to rouse a reaction from her even if it was pointless in the end. He wanted to leave an imprint of the incident before the familiar ordeal of arrest and imprisonment began anew.

In his sleep, he whacked Julie on the shoulder. She awoke, disgruntled but worried. Joma was having nightmares again.

"*Kinuha ako, kinikidnap ako, humilagpos ako* (They were taking me, kidnapping me, I was resisting)," he tells me in his living room with eyebrows twitching, as he sits hunched in his favorite chair. Today he is dressed in long-sleeved polo and his hair is messier than usual. A month earlier, Interior and Local Government secretary Eduardo Año had promised to finally arrest Sison with the assistance of the Interpol. Joma's lawyers say the threat is all talk — empty posturing from another mouthpiece, a tradition of the Philippine bureaucracy. Año made it sound like the Interpol would act on behalf of the Philippine government but the organization only monitors and coordinates police information worldwide. It doesn't make arrests for sovereign nations or compel police forces to follow the Philippine government's wishes.

Joma's scars go a long way back, long before Rodrigo Duterte ever rose to national power in the Philippines to make empty threats of arrest. His night terrors trace their roots to the trauma of 1977. In November of that year, he and Julie were caught by the military. They wouldn't be freed until 1986 and 1982, respectively.[1]

Now, almost fifty years later, the couple can find humor in the lingering aftermath of the miserable experience as they joke about last night's fracas. Julie fires at her husband, *"Noong una naman, kapag nagna-nightmare ka, 'di ka nakakasakit* (Before when you'd have nightmares, you didn't hurt anyone)."

"Baka kunwari lang 'yong nightmare noon (Maybe I was pretending to have a nightmare)," teases Joma.

"Suspetsa ko din, ang sakit no'ng hampas mo, e (That's what I suspected, your hit really hurt)," Julie laughs.

She bends to look through the jumble of packets and boxes under the coffee table. She sits down after pouring tea for the three of us. Last night was the first time in a long while that Joma has had nightmares she tells me.

I ask her how long she was detained, and without skipping a beat she replies, "Four years, four months, twenty-one days." Her prodigious memory is still intact at the age of eighty-one.

When Julie was captured, the military brought her to a big building inside Fort Bonifacio. She was kept far from the other buildings in the army headquarters, surrounded by tall concrete walls, topped by barbed wire coils, and overlooked by a tower manned by three daily shifts of armed guards.

Sometimes, soldiers brought persons under investigation to one of the few jail cells inside, but their stay was always tempo-

---

[1] *Bulletin Today* (1977) reported that Joma, Julie, and three others who were staffers of the Central Committee were captured on November 10, in San Fernando, La Union. Marcos remarked that the seizure of Joma would temporarily cripple the CPP and that their asset would be impossible to replace by the communists.

rary. Once they'd been intimidated and interrogated, the captives were released. Julie was the sole permanent resident of that building. To this day she has no clue as to why her confinement was extra isolated.

Locked up in a prison cell bigger than her current seventy-square meter apartment, she had so much space, yet nothing to do in it. "Walls all around," she muses — the most obvious observation to be made about a cell, yet also the most damning assessment of it. Aside from a toilet and a sleeping mat, the only other object in sight was a broom. Giving the female prisoner a broom might have been a casual decision by her jailors, but also felt like some sort of patriarchal practical joke. What cruel irony, to have a room of one's own, à la Virginia Woolf, yet the room was a cage and the single available activity was to sweep the floors clean, with a broom of one's own. Every morning upon waking, Julie got to work with her broom in repelling any intrusion of dust into her cell.

Julie's guard lived hours away from Fort Bonifacio. To avoid wasting money on the commute, especially given her low-paying security job, the guard spent occasional nights sleeping inside the quarters of her ward. The two women sometimes conversed with one another. "It broke the monotony," Julie says. She was eager to hear stories from the outside world and a voice other than her own. *"Binigyan ako ng papel no'ng roommate ko na gwardya, isang pad pati panulat* (My roommate the guard gave me some paper, one pad, and a pen)."

Armed with these essentials, she got to work. A world of possibility awaited with those two basic items. *"Araw-araw nagpapadala ako ng request sa officer-in-charge sa detention, si Melchor Acosta. Humihingi ako ng dagdag-papel, ballpen, libro. Araw-araw iyan* (Every day I sent a request to the officer-in-charge of our detention, Melchor Acosta. I asked for more paper, pens and books. That was every day)!" Julie recalls, raising her arms in the air. *"Tinatanong ko rin si Acosta kung kamusta si Jo* (I also asked Acosta how Jo was doing)." Each time, Acosta assured her Joma was doing fine.

He was lying. Joma was handcuffed to the frame of his small cot in a three-by-five-meter room throughout the day, barely able to stand inside the chicken coop of a cell. He also had a toilet, but he had to ask the guards to uncuff him every time he needed to use it. He likens the mental torture in solitary confinement to huge blocks of lead pounding on his brain. Comparatively, the beating and waterboarding earlier inflicted on him were mere fraternity hazing.

Even now, the enforced seclusion of that period remains the source of his most wicked nightmares. The tremors of that particular pain — the fear of spending the rest of his life alone in a cell, without anyone to see or speak to — still haunts Joma. Physical torture injures the body, but solitary confinement leaves lasting wounds on the psyche.

He recites an excerpt from his poem "Fragments of a Nightmare," which was composed in prison. His poems documented the ordeal while relieving his mind from prison life's dullness. By force of will, he kept sane, he kept busy.

> The torture does not cease
> But becomes worse a thousand times.
> The seconds, minutes, days, weeks,
> Months and seasons fall
> Like huge blocks of lead

"Like one ton of lead," he interrupts himself.

> On my brain and nerves,
> On my prostrate body on the rack,
> With my left hand and right foot
> Constantly cuffed to a filthy cot
> In a perpetuated process of violence.

All in all, Joma spent over five years in solitary confinement and over three years more in partial isolation. For almost a decade, this extremely ebullient man had just himself to converse with. He pushed himself to flood his mind with thoughts, books, and memories. He played elaborate chess games with himself. He made use of every mental technique he knew to stop himself from imploding.

"*Ako, hindi lang intellectual, kun'di musical resources. Kumanta ako* (It's not just intellectual resources that I have but musical as well. I sing)!" he says with sudden cheer, seizing the chance to remind others, yet again, of how much he loves music. He was less concerned about staying in tune than about focusing on the melody to free himself from bondage with a few moments of reprieve. The singing detainee sang so much that the guards either sang along with him or turned the radio volume up allowing Joma to hear the news. He quite liked either outcome. Joma, the English major, also drew upon his recollections of every book he had ever read. "You cook up plots for novels or recite poems. *Akala no'ng guwardya naloloko na ako. Paulit-ulit mong i-recite hanggang makabisado mo at matuyo na lalamunan mo tapos babagsak ka na sa higaan para matulog* (The guard thought I was going mad. I recited and memorized poetry repeatedly until my throat was dry and I'd fall into my beddings ready to sleep)." He used repetition in lieu of pen and paper to record his thoughts. He declaimed some of his own verses so often until every word and line became stamped onto his mind. "*Kahit iyong guwardya nakabisado na din sinasabi mo* (Even the guard memorized what you were saying)," jibes Julie.

One poem he composed became a favorite because it served a specific, practical purpose. "*Meron akong tula na may pagka-ironic* (I had a poem with a little bit of irony) — 'The Secret of Prayer.' Prayers are repetitive, they lull you and put you to sleep." When he had trouble sleeping, he recited that same poem repeatedly until he was drowsy.

For the entirety of his solitary confinement, Joma's west-facing window was boarded up. Through the slits of old, cracked wood, he saw the sunset and welcomed the faint chill of evening winds. At one point, with the aid of soap, he slipped out of his cuffs, remaining silent through the pain of metal scraping his skin raw. Then he pried open the wooden board covering his cell. He crawled out and managed a few strides on the premises. But he was soon spotted and thrown back into his cell.

That was his first and only escape attempt. Soon after, the guards replaced the boards with iron bars. It made another breakout impossible, but allowed daylight to pour inside his quarters.

After nearly two years of detention, Joma received two pieces of reading material: a copy of the Bible, and the book *Today's Revolution: Democracy* by Ferdinand E. Marcos. These two books comprised the bureaucracy's sorry effort at his reindoctrination, one which he'd already studied, and the other a rationalization of authoritarianism. The unnecessary texts, combined with a prolonged jail sentence, didn't seem to be the best way to convince the country's most wanted communist leader to switch sides. It was almost as if they were meant to blunt his mind rather than realign it. *"Napurga ako sa libro ni Macoy* (I got sick of Macoy's book)," he says.

"*'Pag tinamaan ka ng buryong, dapat nilalabanan* (When boredom strikes, you need to fight it)," continues Joma, his tone falling hushed. "It's not that I'm so strong with the mental weapons to counter it. It's just real to be bored to death. *May matutuluyang masiraan ng ulo. Kagaya no'ng guwardya na tinabi sa selda mo, Julie, 'di ba? Isang linggo lang nagbe-breakdown na, e* (Some go permanently mad. Like the other guard near your cell, right, Julie? After one week, he started breaking down)."

"*Bibliya lang ang tanging libro na binigay sa akin* (A Bible is the only book they gave me)," scoffs Julie. She received the book after three months of detention. Pairing the holy book with her pen and paper, Julie had another activity — and it was something familiar, something she had been doing for years. She began translating the English Bible into her native Irigeño, one of the languages in the Bicol region. Julie the librarian, keeper of so many of the revolution's archives and tasked with rendering their contents into other local languages, had found a way to keep her mind active. For her purposes, a library of one book had to be enough.

"Na-translate ko hanggang Pentateuch, iyong unang limang libro ng Bible, bago ako ilipat. Seven months ako sa solitary. Doon sa dating pinagkulungan kina Osmeña ako nilipat (I was able to translate the Pentateuch, the first five books of the Bible, before I was transferred. I spent seven months in solitary. I was then put in [then-businessman and eventually senator Sergio] Osmeña's old cell)," she tells me, without any hint of pride or satisfaction in her accomplishment. To Julie, translating the Bible was little more than an exercise to ward off restlessness.

Two years after his arrest, Joma was finally given paper and pen as well. He drafted memos, wrote letters, gave advice to his lawyers, and jotted down recommendations to comrades. He made sure to fold and cut each piece of paper into three separate strips to maximize the space for writing. He flushed his notes and unused drafts down the toilet, much to the chagrin of the military's attending personnel — after all, when higher-ranking officers order their subordinates to scavenge for specific documents, even the most unsavory places weren't exempt from the search.

In November 1978, Jose Ma. Sison was charged with rebellion and subversion. By virtue of Presidential Decree 39, Marcos had set up military courts supposedly to try cases and infractions involving his armed forces. But in truth, the military subjected many civilians to these proceedings.[2]

Two years after the declaration of Martial Law, once many of Marcos's political opponents had already been sent to prison, the dictator ordered the return of civilian courts. Some special cases, however, were maintained in military courts — among them, that of military-officer-turned-rebel Lt. Victor Corpus; the landed elite senator turned staunch Marcos critic, Benigno

---

[2] The order reads "the Chief of Staff of the Armed Forces of the Philippines has been empowered to create military tribunals to try and decide cases of military personnel and such other cases as may be referred to them" (Office of the President of the Philippines 1972b). That last bit is broad enough to encompass anyone who the regime felt was enough of a threat to put through military tribunal.

Aquino, Jr.; and of course, the unapologetic leaders of the country's tireless insurgency, Joma Sison and Julie de Lima.

The Marcos government charged Julie, along with three others who were with her and her husband, upon capture. She was sentenced to fourteen years of hard labor.

"Alam mo, siya lang convicted, ako hindi (You know, she was the one convicted, not me)," Joma says with a grin at his wife, snickering at the uselessness of this distinction. In fact, Joma was kept imprisoned for almost twice as long as Julie.

When asked how long Joma was confined, he pauses to think about it. After a few minutes of computation, we arrive at a figure: eight years and five months, give or take a few days.

Their lawyer, Juan T. David, was a titan of the profession. Ironically, he had been Marcos's counsel up until the beginning of his presidency (Matthews and Bernard 1978). When Martial Law was declared, the strongman jailed David's son, a journalist who'd penned some damaging stories about the regime. He became active in the Civil Liberties Union and went on to defend many high-profile activists while famously never taking any money from his clients.

The defense of Joma and Julie in court coincided with the increasing clamor, locally and internationally, against the violations of the rights of political prisoners. The campaign pressured Marcos to issue an order that, in the case of arrested spouses, the wife could be released if she was with child. By 1979, the government permitted the couple conjugal visits, once a week or sometimes once every two weeks. Eventually, Julie got pregnant and gave birth in prison. Because Julie was a nursing mother, it was possible to petition her freedom on humanitarian grounds. Julie's release, four years before her husband, was accompanied by much less fanfare from the public, but it was more meaningful to the couple. After four years, four months, and 21 days in prison, she was free return to a life with a growing family of comrades, loved ones, and a newborn.

Joma sent David many of his missives from prison, those strips of paper which had been filled back-to-back with cramped handwriting. Joma recalls David's thunderous and scene-stealing courtroom speeches only enhanced the seventy-year-old lawyer's already excellent reputation. David and his clients prepared themselves to go to the Supreme Court for as many as twenty times if need be to file habeas corpus petitions. Not long after the third of these petitions, the EDSA "people power" toppled Marcos and political prisoners like Joma were released.

Today, they may be living outside jail cells, but they remain caged by exile. The nightmares are an unwelcome souvenir of what they suffered under the dictatorship. But they've developed ways of coping — methods of "escape," habits developed during detention.

In the Netherlands, where ruling powers have kept them contained in a new prison of sorts, there are at least some comforts. They take heart in their youngest son, conceived in prison, christened amid unrest. Julie the librarian now surrounds herself with shelves overflowing with texts, which she can translate into Irigeño in her free time. Meanwhile, the singing detainee is known to bust open the karaoke machine at the NDFP offices and belt out his rendition of a Frank Sinatra classic. He always makes a stirring finale of the chorus by crooning, "I did it Mao's way!"

Therein Lies the Difference

Joma, wearing his favorite red cardigan, has just finished recording a video message for an event by national democratic youth groups. The old communist leader, who jokes that he'd rather not be called old, still monitors developments in the Filipino youth movement around the world. NDFP staff members say Joma "listens to young people."

"I know my tasks," Joma comments. "You cannot expect me to wage armed struggle from here. My weapon is my pen; my tasks revolve around that."

Joma receives a lot of requests to attend online activities or to write and record messages, especially from young activists. Last-minute demands might annoy him, though. He's fine with requests made a month or so before the event, but he admits that requests made with less than a week's time tend to raise his blood pressure. Still, he usually agrees to such wishes, *"kahit na irritated ako minsan* (even if I get irritated sometimes)."

"Iyong iba (the others), just the day before," Julie adds.

"Ay iyun! Puputok ang buchi ko. Sobra naman ang day before magre-request. P'wede naman akong pumuna eh (Ah yes! I will lose my temper. Requesting something the day before is too much. I can criticize too)," says Joma. Only now has he ever sounded like an old man giving a sermon.

"*Oo! Puputok ang buchi niyan, galit na galit. Pagkatapos, gagawin din niya* (Yes! He loses his temper. After that he does it anyway)," says Julie, raising her eyebrows.

"*Uto-uto ako ng movement, e* (I am gullible when it comes to the movement)," Joma jokes. In a professorial tone, he adds, "Mao says, to serve the people, your head must be bowed like the cattle."

"Like the ox. And it was Lu Xun," Julie corrects. They both giggle.

Smiling, Joma tilts his head toward me, as if to make doubly sure I understand him. "*Basta* (Anyway), the essence is to serve the people. *Kahiya naman maging bugnutin* (I would be embarrassed to act so grumpy). But if even the most ridiculous requests serve the people, then so be it. We have to do the most we can while not being able to go back to the Philippines."

In his video messages, Joma is the veteran statesman. He speaks commandingly, almost rigid in his delivery, as he reads from a TV-sized teleprompter. His accent is a mixture of his Spanish, Chinese, and Filipino lineages, as he articulates his analyses and recommendations for organizing.

This was the Joma I had known for many years, a talking head tucked away in Europe, an elder to a global tribe. If ever his character revealed itself, it was only through statements, books, and interviews about the revolution. He spoke like a living book, its pages increasing with every answer.

To many cadres, Joma and Julie still provide ideological guidance even if they no longer hold any formal positions of central leadership in the party. Because of this, the couple are routinely pitted against and compared to Philippine presidents. However, leaders who work to change the ruling order are different from those who seek to fortify it. Many of those belonging to the higher tiers of society have betrayed the Filipino people, and only a few of them ever betray the interests of their own social class.

Joma and Julie, statesmen for the revolution, have repeatedly brushed against the tragedy that is the seat of power in Malacañang. Joma realizes, "Between us, we've met all presidents since Marcos at one time or another!" From the founding of Kabataang Makabayan in 1964 up until their last months in the Philippines, they met every current or would-be president of the country. Each of these encounters were either by chance, or at crucial junctures in the country's history.

They run through the list, attaching nicknames to each president: the dictator, the general, the daughter of democracy and her son, the action star, the economist, and the brat.

Joma has a remarkable memory. He can map the familial connections tied to one's last name, including their history, origins, whereabouts, and ideological dispositions. It seems that part of the reasons why his life has been so well-documented is that he himself has an intricate catalogue in his mind to keep recollections filed away. He remembers many of his students from his teaching days at the Lyceum of the University of the Philippines from 1964 to 1967. He can still name those who were brilliant, and those, he admits, who were good-looking. The future Philippine President — his student when they met — was neither, according to Joma, which is why he only has the vaguest memories of the unexceptional student in his class.

"*Di ka nagbasa, ano* (You didn't read, am I right)?" Prof. Joma inquired of his student. "*Sir, athletic scholar ako, e* (Sir, it's because I'm an athletic scholar)," Rodrigo Duterte replied.

That single exchange is young Duterte's most notable imprint in the ledgers of Joma's memory.

President Joseph "Erap" Estrada, whom Joma and Julie met in the mid-1960s, is a much more memorable figure to the couple. He was one of the biggest action heroes ever to grace the screen as the star of "Da King" Fernando Poe Jr.'s production house. The Burke building in Escolta, Manila housed both FPJ Films and the office of the National Association of Trade Unions (NATU), then headed by veteran labor leader Ignacio Lacsina. Joma, Julie, and other activists of the era bumped into a host of showbiz heavyweights on site.

Their politics were on constant display at the studio lot. Pamphlets were piled up, streamers and other protest materials were produced in the garage areas, and agitated assemblies were held out front. "Maybe he got his anti-bases inclinations from the placards we were making," jests Joma, referring to Erap's "no" vote in 1991 to renew the treaty that maintained US military bases in the country.[1]

Erap carried himself like there was a fight around the corner, recalls the couple. He never shed the tough-guy persona he projected onscreen. Maybe his craft was more "method" than we give him credit for.

In contrast, Tony Santos was a demure errand man for the old Lava-dominated Partido Komunista ng Pilipinas (PKP), which then had Joma and Julie as members. Despite having the merciless nickname "Ngiwi" because of a slightly askew jaw, his disarming charm earned him favor with the ladies. One such lady happened to be the ticket seller at Erap's favorite cinema, which hosted many of his films' premiere nights. After party meetings, Tony would distribute regular batches of propaganda and progressive reading materials. He delivered some of them to his girl before each primetime screening. On many occasions, she handed out these materials to Erap himself who presumably took some interest in them. That was the closest they ever got to swaying the action star to their cause.

Joma's meetings with presidents Corazon Aquino and Ferdinand Marcos were well-documented and much-publicized. He first met Marcos in 1966 at the presidential palace. Former senator and Movement for the Advancement of Nationalism (MAN) chairman Lorenzo Tañada introduced Joma, who was then his Secretary-General, to Marcos. The three met in a fruitless dialogue with the president. Marcos wouldn't budge on maintaining US influence over Philippine politics.

His second face-to-face encounter with the dictator came after his arrest on November 10, 1977. Cops took Joma, Julie, and three others to the Presidential Security Compound a little before noon. Another future president, General Fidel V. Ramos,

---

[1] In a historic turn of events, the traditionally pro-American Philippine Senate voted "no" to the renewal of American naval bases in the Philippines. Estrada was among the twelve senators who rejected the bases.

was also present. He was treated to a scolding by Julie, who demanded the military account for all their belongings — the typewriters, documents, folders, and personal items that had been confiscated when they were arrested. "I want receipts for all our things!" she yelled. Now, over forty years later, she laughs at the memory, finding humor in the futility of her demand.

Joma had a kinship with Ramos.[2] The military man's middle name was Valdez. His mother came from one of the illustrious families in Ilocos Norte, and the brother of Joma's Serrano grandmother had married a member of the Valdez clan in a union between two landed clans of the north.

In the detention room, Ramos extended a hand to Joma, mentioning that his sister was once a university colleague of the captive. Despite his awareness of their ancestral link, Joma left Ramos's hand hanging. This was an occasion wherein all the manners and politeness of the ruling elite couldn't mask the sufferings the rebels knew they were about to endure.

Several hours later, the guards escorted Joma to the lobby. Marcos sat imperiously, dressed in a *barong tagalog* with twelve generals standing by his side, including Ramos, like praetorian guards flanking an emperor.

Marcos motioned them away. Only four remained: Generals Baltazar Aguirre, Fabian Ver, Benjamin Felix, and Major Rodrigo. Rodrigo was notorious but clandestine. Many Martial Law veterans never knew his first name, only that he was feared. He led the team to apprehend Joma, gaining a promotion to Colonel. His most notable trait, Joma noticed, was a distinctly US English accent, noticeable when he spoke in Ilocano.

The regime's prized catch, Joma was scruffy, somewhat distraught, and trying to keep stoic, wearing slippers and sun-

---

2 Joma mentions that early on he was contemptuous of Ramos taking the military route, being known particularly for his being adept at psychological warfare and a friend to US interests. Toward the 1986 uprising, Joma says he tried to goad and encourage visiting officers to his jail cell to move against Marcos. He doesn't know if his advice ever reached the would-be president. But he also credits Ramos for engaging in peace negotiations with the NDFP during his time in power (Sison 2017, 326–29).

glasses below a shaggy head of hair. Joma grappled with the reality of his capture. Pain and torture awaited him and his wife as soon as they left this room. A subtle verbal duel ensued. Ever the gentleman, Marcos feigned acknowledgment of his counterpart by saying, "I read what you write."

Marcos hinted at the possibility of reconciliation between the two parties. Joma replied there could be no peace without genuine land reform and national industrialization. But there was never any intention to conduct genuine, meaningful negotiation. The dictator only wanted complete surrender.

Marcos closed the two-hour meeting with an understated and ominous warning. "Write to me," he told Joma, "Because I may not see you again." The prophetic threat proved to be true, but not in the way Marcos thought. The dictator died unceremoniously of lupus in 1989, after he was ousted and exiled to Hawai'i by the EDSA uprising of 1986.

Joma endured almost nine years in prison. When he finally saw daylight from outside his jail cell, a new president was seated in the palace.

In the meantime Julie, having been released ahead of her husband, resumed her work amid the changing political scenery of the 1980s.

Julie visited the Quezon City estate of Gloria Macapagal Arroyo to convince the future president, then an economics professor at Assumption College, to join the Association of Philippine–China Understanding and to contribute to the anti-dictatorship campaign. Arroyo's home featured several fancy cars and a pony, much to Julie's bewilderment. As with so many other politicians in history, Arroyo was an ally at some point then a tyrant a few years later.

Julie had also founded the *National Midweek* magazine. She managed the editorial staff and published a column charting the public's growing anti-Marcos sentiments and the increasing detention of activists like her husband. In a confusing gesture, General Ramos visited their offices and applied for two subscriptions. *"Para yata sa AFP iyong isa* (The other one was maybe for the AFP)," she thought, wondering about the military man's intentions.

Post-EDSA, newly installed President Cory Aquino granted amnesty to Joma and Kumander Dante. It was a decision in concurrence with her earlier invalidation of Marcos's proclamation subjecting civilians to military courts. It was well-known that Cory came from a family of wealthy landlords, but she also acted as an important figure in the downfall of the Marcos dictatorship.

Cory's staff brought the two men straight from jail to the Cojuangco building penthouse. It was owned by Cory's family and was the temporary office of the new leader. Doña Aurora Aquino, Cory's mother-in-law, admitted the newly freed political prisoners into her custody. Noynoy Aquino, Cory's son and another future president, was present when the pair introduced themselves. He listened to them talk with his mother and said nothing.

Julie met them at the penthouse. President Aquino was cordial and pleasant to the couple. At this point, she was still campaigning for the rights of those imprisoned by Marcos's regime. "*Tulungan niyo ako, ha* (Help me out, okay)," she implored the communists, who noted her inviting tone.

The prospects of mutual support on certain issues soon deteriorated. Joma scorns Aquino for ultimately chosing to heed her reactionary roots and follow "the advice of the US and her pro-US subordinates to distance herself from me and the movement." He adds, "Anyone who comes un-remolded from an exploiting class and becomes president cannot fully be trusted."

Despite their differences, Joma always considered Cory a personal friend. He remembers sitting on her left, with Ramos on her right, during the 1986 Labor Day demonstration, wondering how the appearance of a giant hammer and sickle amid the singing of The Internationale struck the pair. Nevertheless, Joma was critical of the regime and much of his contempt is also directed against Cory's military advisors who, even after Marcos, harbored a strong desire to annihilate the revolutionaries.[3] The cancellation of passports in 1988 came two days after the military filed subversion charges against Joma.

In the heady period after the Marcos dictatorship, Joma and Julie could've taken up important positions in the Philippine government and become actual statesmen. Indeed, throughout the decades, they were often invited to leave the movement and pursue mainstream political careers. Joma was capable of climbing the political ladder — in another life, the young boy from Ilocos could quite possibly have fulfilled his father's wishes for him to become president.

And yet all their encounters with the country's leaders only drove them further away from that path. Neither Joma nor Julie have any regrets about choosing the revolution over stable careers in the Philippine government. Revolutionaries do not have the luxury of retiring to a mansion after their term in power.

There are so many paths to reactionary power for prominent individuals. However, the mere possibility of revolutionary victory was a far more enticing prospect. Although, if you ask the couple, they'd scoff at the term *possibility* and contend that the triumph of the proletariat is a certainty.

I get the feeling, maybe owing to his beginnings as part of a landlord clan, Joma remains fascinated with the ruling class. And yet his disdain is unmistakable. "I have the lowest regard for the presidency. A president may shine only against a worse counterpart. Like Cory, who looks good compared to Marcos, but she is also a big landlord and a big comprador."

More recently, Joma trades barbs with his one-time student, now notorious for his human-rights violations since he became president in 2016. President Duterte chided the communist leader by boasting of his own meteoric ascent from mayor of

---

3   Cory made many attempts at Amnesty with the CPP-NPA. However, as shown in many news reports during this period, there was intense military pressure to attack what both AFP General Ileto and Ramos designated as "Communist Strongholds." The former threateningly declared to the press, "We'll attack" (*PDI* 1987).

Davao City to the country's chief executive, deriding Joma as an "aging armchair passé rebel" (Corrales 2019). He has argued that the communists have lost the appeal they had during Martial Law, that their flock suffers from the brainwashing of blind devotees and the CPP's credibility survives on the past achievements of a stubborn old man living abroad.

Has Joma, with the help of Julie and the party, nurtured a personality cult like the one around Mao Zedong? Can his actions and ideas be reduced to this? There is considerable debate about whether the former ruler of China was a dictator. I thought to ask someone particularly familiar with communist leaders being both slandered and praised.

Gillian Peralta refutes the charge that the CPP's ideological strength relies on a personality cult. She was exiled in China leading up to Martial Law. For years she studied the Great Proletarian Cultural Revolution during its heyday under Mao. "Emperor worship is strong in Chinese culture," she explains. In the commune where she stayed, people began and ended their sentences by praising then thanking Chairman Mao. *"Talagang nagba-bow sila in front of his picture! Pero kami hindi obligado* (They'd really bow in front of his picture! But we were not obliged to)."

One thing she admired about Mao's time was the party-backed effort to curb these attitudes. "During the Cultural Revolution, one of the campaigns was combating old ideas and customs to achieve a socialist culture instead of a feudal one," she shares. She also raises doubts as to whether a personality cult can be or has ever been adopted by Filipinos. *"Hindi papatok sa atin ang ganoon* (That wouldn't become a trend among us). Although we have an authoritarian streak politically in our elected officials, our culture is very different. *Parang pagbubuo ng barkada sa atin* (It's more like a close group of friends), and it's different especially among comrades who have undergone integration with the masses through the movement. *Pero maaaring sumulpot ang ganoong kultura kung 'di mag-iingat* (But it's possible for that kind of culture to sprout if we aren't careful)."

Gillian was then exiled in the Netherlands after Mao's death. She has since come to know Joma for many years, and observes, *"Makikita mo naman, approachable siya, 'di ka mangingimi na lapitan, kausapin, tanungin. Hindi rin siya magdadalawang-isip. Kahit mag-message ka lang sa Facebook, sasagot siya. Marami kasi siyanggustong i-share, kaya siya madaldal* (You can see, he's approachable. You wouldn't be cautious about meeting, talking, and asking him anything. He wouldn't think twice either. You can just message him on Facebook and he'd answer. He has a lot he wants to share, that's why he's so talkative)." She describes Joma as "like a teacher, with younger people especially, without necessarily acting like an authority figure."

In 2018, Duterte fired and replaced his presidential spokesman, Harry Roque. Gillian was with Joma, and they caught the news on TV. Roque (who had been much derided for his unstinting loyalty to Duterte) had been eyeing a bid for the Senate, but as they watched, the president threw him under the bus, even poking fun at Roque's slim chances of winning an election. Without so much as an explanation, the president, maybe on a whim, cast aside his devoted subordinate like a used rag. With furrowed eyebrows, Joma said, *"Iyan ang hari* (That's a king)!"

The Workhorse

Julie agrees to a one-on-one interview with me. This will be be the first time we speak without Joma present. I still don't have a clear impression of her even after weeks of conversations with the couple. She tells me to let her know when and where would be convenient, and I ask her what messaging app she uses.

"*Mamili ka: Signal. WhatsApp. Viber. Jitsi. Kumpleto ako, pero wala akong Facebook* (You choose: Signal. WhatsApp. Viber. Jitsi. I have them all, except for Facebook)."

"*Wow, techie po pala kayo* (Wow, you're a techie)."

"*Talaga. Matagal na* (Definitely. For a long time now)."

I meet Julie at 2:00 p.m. on a Sunday. She greets me in her usual home-office attire — a duster dress under a thick white cardigan dropping below her knees, a thick knitted scarf around her neck, and wool socks rolled up over her shins. As she opens the door, she warns me not to make too much noise, because Joma is resting with a mild fever and has had to forego his day's itinerary.

But for Julie, the day will be as busy as any other. No weekends for her. As on every other visit, all three of her computer monitors are turned on.

The TV, set to the China Global Television Network (CGTN) channel, is airing a feature on the global market. A few years back, she made some money on the stock market just by monitoring the news. In the 1960s, she had almost finished the coursework for a master's degree in economics from the University of the Philippines when she decided to go underground. These days, she stays updated on China's economic maneuvers in the global market.

Julie is indeed tech-savvy beyond my expectations — she has been customizing entire computer rigs since 1992, assembling them from carefully ordered parts tailored to fit her professional predilections. "I just read the manuals," she says, like anyone could do it.

She also possesses a knack for carpentry, honed by watching her father in her youth. It shows in the apartment. She's crafted small stools by hand and smoothly sealed a crevice on top of their wall-sized window. Quite impressive for an 81-year-old who stands a little under five feet in height. Over the course of their three decades in this apartment, she has fixed doorknobs, tables, chairs, and all manner of mechanisms at one time or another. *"Lahat ng kutingting ng tatay ko, nakuha ko. Paano kumilala ng poisonous na snake, dangerous insects, ituturo niya sa amin, pati mga constellations* (Everything my father worked with, I also learned. How to recognize poisonous snakes, dangerous insects, he would teach us, along with the constellations)," she says, pointing out her handiwork.

Most people who know Julie personally are aware of her flair for woodwork, gadgets, and trading. But "most people" isn't a lot. Despite being a prominent personality for the movement, she is decidedly reserved. To me, Julie is a mystery. She's the significant other of the most venerated individual in the ongoing Philippine revolution, yet she has kept a low profile, going about her work like it's nobody's business.

I always bring a recorder to our sessions, pausing each time a question has been answered to divide the audio files into separate, organized segments. After one of my previous interviews with Joma and Julie, she asked me if I was certain I had recorded everything. I said yes and showed her my handwritten notes as a backup. She nodded and informed me she had a third backup should I need it. She pointed to another recorder, leaning on one of the pitchers on the coffee table, a red light blinking on its side. She had also been recording me while I interviewed them. I was impressed.

During each interview, Julie kept her answers short.

There's a dearth of information about Julie online: a Google search of her name yields more results about a distant blood relation, Senator Leila de Lima. She has no social media accounts and there's not even a Wikipedia blurb. This strikes me as somewhat unjust, although I get the feeling Julie prefers it this way. Maybe. See, I'm still unsure.

When we sit down to begin, her aversion from the spotlight is the first thing we discuss. I ask if she prefers it this way.

"Oo. Mas payapa, more freedom. Dito although you're under surveillance, minsan mo lang ma-notice ang surveillance. Pero gagawin ko ang kinakailangan, if public appearances are what the work demands. Pero sa special circumstances ko nga... (Yes. It's more peaceful, you have more freedom. Here, although you're under surveillance, you won't notice it much. But I'll do what's needed, if public appearances are what the work demands. But because of my special circumstances...)."

"Sikat (Being famous)?"

She brushes off my assumption with a laugh.

Thanks to the anonymity relative to her husband, she has some respite from slander and a degree of protection from security threats. Julie is seldom attacked in the public eye by state officials the way her husband is.

Then there's Joma's rumored dalliances with multiple women, which his enemies are quick to pounce on. Their portrayal of Joma abandoning the Philippines for a life of pleasure and decadence in Europe often include accusations of womanizing: military and state officials sound like tabloid reporters when speaking of blind items and rumors. They took particular interest when Joma was seen dancing with actress Ara Mina at a party in 2007, which then became media fodder in the Philippines.

I mention these rumors to Julie. Smiling, she retorts, *"Nakakainis, the way it is sensationalized. Pero wala akong inis kay Ara Mina o sinuman* (It's irritating, the way it is sensationalized. But I'm not irritated at Ara Mina or anyone)." Julie explains that their opponents will grab any opportunity for slanderous propaganda.

In the public conversation, Joma is always the obvious target, while Julie is collateral damage. She may not be in the headlines like her husband, but she still has to deal with her marriage being regularly mocked and denigrated by their political opponents. She says these cheap efforts at vilification have not weakened their resolve as partners, nor slowed their pace in accomplishing tasks.

A lot of people might not have a clue of how valuable Julie is to the national democratic movement. I would even go so far as to say that the public persona of Jose Maria Sison is a two-person job. "We're a team," she tells me when I approach the subject of their relationship. Not a word of the commentaries and statements issued under Joma's byline escapes Julie's scrutiny.

On accounts about herself including our interviews, Julie prefers to keep each statement concise, thinking like an editor in advance. On the challenges in editing statements in tandem with Joma, she shares, *"Mag-a-assert siya na tama. Sabihin ko, napaka-Tagalog no'ng syntax* (He'll assert that he's right. I'll say the syntax is too Tagalog)." End of story. Sometimes, she'd deliver a punchline after a descriptive build-up by Joma. For instance, when I asked her to comment further on Paco Lava's version of a political report she had prepared with Joma in 1965, she looked at me and declared plainly, *"Bagsak* (Fail)."

* * *

A workhorse is how those close to Julie have unanimously labeled her. Julie nods in agreement when I mention the term. Reflecting on my own encounters with Julie, I realize I've only ever seen her either at the office or at home, which itself resembles a workplace more than a residence. Her reluctance to join social gatherings complements her workaholic nature.

Activists, migrants, and all kinds of guests often come to meet the famous couple. Even public officials who happen to be in town on a junket or some other delegation will pay Joma and Julie a visit, especially during elections. *"Wala naman kaming tinanggihang bisita* (We haven't turned away any guests)," she says. Julie isn't a recluse, but she does think Joma can be too generous with his time. The constant engagements can take time away from his long-term writing projects.

At present, Julie is editing twelve books by different authors, including her husband. She also proofreads his less political endeavors. "He even tests his jokes on me. *Bago kami matulog. Iisipin na niya 'yong jokes na gagawin niya sa susunod* (Before we go to sleep. He'll come up with jokes he wants to say next time)," says Julie fondly.

Julie also manages the International Network for Philippine Studies as well as several committees within the NDFP. She leads the committee drafting the Comprehensive Agreement for Socio-Economic Reforms (CASER), the document at the crux of peace negotiations between the CPP and the Philippine government.[1]

At 4:55 p.m., Julie notices the time and rises to check on Joma's temperature. When she returns, the sun has begun setting. The living room is lit by a couple of warm lamps, but the cold has also crept in. It's almost audible, like a soft hum inside the apartment.

Julie falls into her chair, looking careworn. She does her best to stay healthy and active by preferring to walk or jog when she goes out for quick errands, but at her age, she can tire easily. I inquire about how long she thinks she can carry on with this kind of workload in her advanced years.

She replies, *"Si Joma, parating mine-mention kung ilang taon na lang expected mabuhay. Ako, walang ganun* (Joma always mentions how many years he has left. I don't do anything like that)."

It's a typical Julie de Lima response: expounding on the other person's traits and preferring to keep her own identity self-

---

[1] Since August 2020, Julie has been assigned as the interim chairperson of the NDFP Peace Panel.

explanatory. More than once, Joma has mentioned that if Julie were to pass away before him, he wouldn't last very long. No doubt Julie is equally devoted to her husband, but that particular sentiment is one she doesn't share.

We've been talking for four hours. By half past six, her energy dwindles. She sinks further into her chair. Her arms begin to droop, only lifting when she needs something for her chin to lean on. She assures me she can continue with our talk. When we touch on the subject of retirement, she shifts in her seat and pulls herself upright.

Julie wants to retire someday. She wants to tend to her plants and spend more time with her grandchildren. She identifies being a grandmother as the peak of her personal life, awaiting a visit from grandchildren. They used to come by regularly, sometimes staying for a month or so, although things changed after the terror listing.

She says, *"Ayaw ko na iparito ang mga apo dahil baka kung ano pa ang mangyari. Natakot din ang aking anak. Huling dalaw ng mga apo ay 2013.... Napaka-relaxing ba na para kang utusan ng mga apo at nakakatuwa 'yong watching them grow, 'yong discovery nila ng mundo* (I didn't want to let our grandchildren come here lest something untoward happens. My children were also scared. The grandchildren's last visit was in 2013.... It was very relaxing to have our grandchildren ordering us around, and a delight to watch them grow and discover the world)."

Julie also looks forward to more recreational reading in her retirement. Once in a while, when Julie has some free time, she ventures out into the city to look for secondhand books, whetting an appetite developed in her teenage years. Every month, she puts away some money towards her book fund. She tells me about a Saturday morning book market in the small square near the Hoog Catharijne shopping mall. Years ago—she refuses to disclose exactly when—she even wrote drafts of three short stories and considered submitting them to free-press journals, the same way her father's commentaries got published when she was a child. One of them involved a *"barrio girl na napadpad sa Maynila. Disappointed at lalong oppressed sa Maynila, nag-*

ing kasambahay siya (village girl who traveled to Manila. She was disappointed to find more oppression in Manila, where she became a house maid)." Unfortunately, she has kept these creative works private. She mulls releasing them under a pseudonym, but eventually decides against it because of the time it might take to rework her drafts.

I ask about her current recreational reading. She says James Joyce's *Ulysses* is sitting on her bedside. Immediately, my millennial mind jumps to a question worthy of *BuzzFeed*.

"Top book recommendations for activists apart from national democratic literature?"

She laughs more loudly than I've ever heard her. Up to the challenge, Julie's first pick is *Revolution and Counter-Revolution*, a quick and informative text from the Beijing-born Maoist author Professor Pao-yu Ching.

The second is *Wind in the Tower* by novelist Han Suyin. *"Maganda iyon. Tungkol sa latter days ng tagumpay sa China* (That's a good book. It's about the latter days of the victory in China)," she says. With barely a glance, the trained librarian, still facing me, stretches out an arm towards the bookshelf behind her. She pulls out her copy of the novel and shows it to me.

Her next choice is *Crimes of Empire,* by political scientist Carl Boggs, a comprehensive account of American imperial history. *"Maganda iyong economic analysis niya* (Its economic analysis is good)."

She ponders for a moment, then names her final pick: *"Slaughterhouse-Five."*

It's a choice I wasn't expecting. The Kurt Vonnegut classic, Julie stresses, is an appropriate book for young people looking to question their own environment and actions.

Eventually, the conversation turns away from literature, and I ask what she considers her most prized years in the revolution.

"All of them except the ones when I was in jail," she says in a tone implying the obvious.

Julie has the same straightforward manner in all her responses. *"At least, nakaka-contribute ako nang very concrete sa pagyabong ng kilusan. From the beginning ng pagiging tibak hanggang sa pagtayo ng Partido, sa full-blown, hanggang mahuli kami at after niyan* (At least, I've contributed very concretely to the growth and progress of the movement. From my beginnings as an activist, to the founding of the party, to seeing it grow into a full-blown movement, until we were arrested)," she adds.

I repeat a question I've asked her and Joma previously. *"Hindi po ba talaga kayo nawawalan ng optimism kahit minsan* (Have you really never felt your optimism falter, even sometimes)?"

She looks down at a spot on the floor, something I notice she does when she's deep in thought. After a pause, she confesses, *"Minsan. Frustrated din ako minsan sa visibility ng prop, pati iyung suppression sa kaniya. Minsan napakatagal bago makakakita ng statement. Nakakabahala.* (Sometimes. I'm also frustrated with the visibility of propaganda and how it's being suppressed. Sometimes it takes so long before a statement is published. It worries me.)"

Frustrations can be disheartening, but it also means there's always more to be done. It's clear that for Julie, the opportunity to enjoy her eighties — retired from work, and in the company of her grandchildren and the rest of her family — is not an option. Yet there's no regret or resignation in her demeanor. Even now, she claims more of her "best years" are still ahead of her.

I say goodbye at half past eight. I'm sure Julie will slip back in front of her computer once I'm out the door, delaying dinner. She will check on Joma as the evening passes, maybe have some oatmeal past nine. And she will stay up late, occupied with her tasks. She doesn't mind. There's work to be done.

Throughout our interview I think I was subconsciously probing for an amazing, unearthed factoid to show how underappreciated she is, some unknown colossal feat of singlehandedly changing the course of the revolution. And maybe there is, but knowing Julie, she wouldn't bother sharing that, probably thinking it would be beside the point. She's right.

There is a great and oftentimes overlooked value in diligence and a great immensity in consistent hard work — something I'm sure the working class and other oppressed sectors can appreciate. For Julie, there has never been a need to seek out history's validation or acclaim. No need for clever allegories or epic tales, just a list of tasks, perennially stacked.

Baptism by War

Little Julie de Lima scurried through the shrubbery on a windy December night. Her father carried her baby sister atop a carabao that pulled the family's belongings in a four-wheeled cart. Julie's mother walked beside her. The family was leaving the barrio of Sta. Justina, Buhi, Camarines Sur where Julie's mother worked as a schoolteacher. They were traveling toward the remote barrio of Delos Angeles, hoping for some refuge from the invasion.

Julie was bemused as to why they had to take such an unfamiliar route to a familiar destination. Why did they have to circle northwest at such an odd time of night, instead of heading directly south? The cart looked like a nipa hut on wheels. Inside, their belongings were held together by string and barely covered by the improvised thatched roofing. She could hear the rattling of all their possessions in the cart as it rolled up and down the winding paths. Nevertheless, the curious child relished the trip, refusing to be carried and savoring the newness of their trail. The trip was an immense journey for the toddler. She was so small she had to run to keep up with the longer strides of her companions.

Her eyes widened as they prepared to cross a small river. A makeshift bridge of two slender bamboo poles bound by rattan vines stretched over the water, and two thick pieces of abaca rope tied to trees on each side of the river served as handrails. Julie had no qualms about crossing, eager to see what was on the other side. Her father had a more difficult time as he guided the carabao along the riverbank, searching for a shallow area where he could maneuver the cart across the water.

It was 1941. Julie de Lima was three years old, and war had come to the Philippines. On December 8 the Japanese bombed Manila Bay, Baguio, and Tuguegarao from their airbase in occupied Taiwan. Four days later, the invaders landed to no opposition in Legazpi, the capital of Albay province that skirted the edges of Buhi. The de Lima family sought to avoid Japanese troops through a circuitous route to Delos Angeles. The swift and unchallenged capture of Albay signaled the completion of the invasion in Luzon. North of Manila, the central provinces had quickly fallen, pounded by aerial bombardment.

"Istorya ng mga taga-baryo, mababangis ang Hapon, nang-aagaw ng mga gamit at pagkain. Pupunta sa mga bahay, kukuha ng mga manok. Hindi nila nirerespeto ang kultura natin. Kailangan sumaludo kundi sasaktan ka. Tapos may raid sa mga palengke. Ganoon ka undisciplined ang mga tropa nila (According to the stories of the locals, the Japanese were cruel and would steal the people's food and other supplies. They'd enter houses and take chickens. They didn't respect our culture. Everyone had to salute them or you would be hurt. They raided our marketplaces. That's how undisciplined their troops were)," Julie tells me.

As a child she thought of Japanese soldiers as monsters who made life hard for her family and people. Years later, during her time as an underground activist in Central Luzon where the famous anti-Japanese guerrillas of the HUKBALAHAP were born, Julie would hear the locals use *Hapon* to refer to postwar oppressors, especially the troops of the dictator Ferdinand E. Marcos. They uttered *Hapon* as a curse against the soldiers, blurring any distinction between past and present enemies. The trauma of World War II was so painfully branded into the public consciousness, it became an epithet against new enemies, a cultural reflex of condemnation.

The de Lima family settled into their new home at the now abandoned school of Delos Angeles, a small rectangular hut with straw roofing. To earn a living, Julie's father, a skilled outdoorsman, went to the nearby pond to gather swamp grass. Julie accompanied her father's expeditions and watched him cut the leaves into smaller, inch-long portions. He would leave them out to dry for a few days before opening each blade of grass to remove the piths. The absorbent insides of the plants were easily recovered once purged of moisture. He then wound piths together to make a wick for oil lamps and other kinds of handicrafts which could be sold at the market. On his bike he had to search for the marketplace each week, as locals changed its location and hours to avoid Japanese attention.

Classes were suspended during wartime, but Julie's parents—both schoolteachers—taught her how to read and write. She was given introductory readings from a text used in schools during the 1940s and '50s. The short story "I am Pepe, I am Pilar," written in English by a Filipino author instead of an American, was a breakthrough of the period. As opposed to the children's literature depicting American lives and values, that story described a family in the Philippines.

"*Tawa nang tawa nanay ko sa translation ko, kasi ang sabi 'we have a house, I live in it.' Sabi ko 'dito kami tumitira, at kumakain ng dahon.'* Lives *kasi parang* leaves (My mother laughed at one of my translations, because the text said 'We have a house, I live in it.' But instead I said [in Irigueño[1]], 'We live here, and we eat leaves.' Because *lives* was similar to *leaves,* as in the leaves of a tree)." Later in life, Julie continued to translate texts into Irigueño, almost as a habit. It would prove useful in keeping her mind active during her time in solitary confinement under the Marcos regime.

A year later, the de Lima family returned to their native barrio of San Agustin in Iriga, reuniting with most of their relatives. Among them were the family of future senator Leila de Lima, whom Julie recalls to have had one of the nicest houses in the

---

1   Irigueño is a dialect of Rinconada Bikol, a language in southern Luzon.

neighborhood. However, by the time Leila was born, Julie had already left the barrio for good.

Julie remembers her childhood home in San Agustin as huge, but concedes her memory is probably distorted by the exaggerated perceptions of childhood. As she grew, her father remodeled the house several times because parts of the roof had been blown off by annual typhoons until only the main house remained with its thick planks of narra wood flooring. Julie reminisces how the wood darkened temporarily whenever they mopped. In a bid for a better livelihood, Julie's parents shifted from oil wicks to manufacturing and selling hand-rolled cigarettes. They hired two extra workers to help slice and roll the tobacco leaves. They also started weaving abaca to make mosquito nets, setting aside the finer abaca threads to help make kamisolas, dress shirts for women. As usual, Julie apprenticed with her parents, becoming quite adept at connecting strands with her little hands.

"*Marami akong skills* (I have a lot of skills)," Julie says, laughing through her own boast. She explains to me that her upbringing allowed her to learn a variety of trades well before the start of her formal schooling.

By 1942, Bicolanos were beginning to push back against Japanese troops. Both Julie's uncle and father joined the United States Army Forces in the Far East (USAFFE) guerrillas in the region.[2] The former rose to guerrilla leadership in Camarines Sur and the latter used his commerce activities in San Agustin as a cover for gathering intelligence.

But a year of relative calm was broken by troubling news: in 1943, the Japanese continued to advance northwest, expanding their areas of operation. The colonizers were closing in on the de Lima family. Once more, they had to evacuate. At that point

---

[2] Totanes (1999) describes how unprepared Bicolanos were for the Japanese invasion and thus allowing for a swift entry of the Imperial Army. He also shows that guerrillas of the USAFFE, while present, were confused and fractured up until the latter parts of the war and resistance effort.

the family had grown larger, with the birth of another daughter in January 1942.

The de Lima family retreated to their small abaca plantation on the lower slopes of Mount Iriga near the great Buhi Lake, which shielded them from the eyes of roaming Japanese scouts. Her parents, with Julie as their learned assistant, created a clearing and erected their most isolated dwelling yet, made of wood and bamboo with nipa thatched roofing. They set aside and terraced a plot of about a hectare for growing fragrant upland rice, sweet corn, *gabi* (taro), *kamote* (sweet potato), cassava, squash, and all sorts of vegetables and root crops. They also raised pigs and chickens and hunted small animals.

They stayed there until the end of the war. Fighting intensified with the retaliation of re-conquering American troops, and their makeshift home and farm was thrice strafed by American planes. In one instance, bullets almost hit Julie's sister, who ducked just in time after hearing the deafening rattle of whizzing planes and the cracking of automatic gunfire.

Julie came face to face with the wartime colonizers just once, in 1944. She was collecting eggs from the hen house, located in a dense, wooded area a few meters from their home. A heavy tap on her shoulder startled the then six-year-old child. She turned around to see a gaunt Japanese soldier, dressed in a ragged uniform, and with a rifle slung over weary shoulders. "Taiwan, Taiwan," he muttered.

Julie stood motionless, eggs in hand, her initial feeling of shock replaced by pity for the man who looked as though he hadn't eaten in days. He pointed frantically at the eggs, and Julie surrendered them without a word. He sped off in the direction from where he had come. Julie ran in the opposite way, toward the house of her uncle, the guerrilla commander. Upon hearing her story, he called a few of his comrades to hunt down the enemy.

That afternoon, her uncle returned with the news of a successful kill. Only later did Julie surmise that the soldier's hysterical yet non-threatening approach was maybe because he had been conscripted, someone who was compulsorily drafted into service. Perhaps he hadn't been Japanese at all. There was a good chance he was indeed from Taiwan, and not molded like the Japanese troops to commit unspeakable acts in pursuit of Empire. *"May riple pa siya, iyon siguro mali niya kasi may dala siyang riple* (He had a rifle. That was probably the mistake which got him killed, carrying a rifle)," Julie contemplates. She made sure to tell her uncle the man was armed. Whichever the case, an enemy had strayed into their territory and no one considered any other option but death for the hated *Hapon*.

"I felt so guilty for having reported the incident to my uncle when he came back to tell my parents that his unit had killed the poor straggler. I still feel that way," she tells me. Later in life she learned that deserters from the Japanese army purposefully identified themselves as Taiwanese conscripts so USAFFE forces would take them in as prisoners of war.

The war finally ended in 1945. Julie now had four sisters, and the bigger de Lima family returned to San Agustin to resume their normal life. Her parents went back to teaching in the town's small gabaldon hut, an American architectural trend introduced for schools and intended to resemble a *bahay kubo*. Its concrete walls and corrugated iron roofing had been hit by shelling. Its surface was lined with craters the size of adult fists.

Julie was supposed to enter the first grade the year the war ended, and she was eager to come home. By that time, she had deft hands and was reading at a more advanced level than the rest of her age group. She was a child, no longer a toddler, by the end of her baptism by war. Imperialist powers had clashed and reclashed on her homeland and she had seen the ruins with her own eyes. She didn't know it yet, but the experience prepared her for a different kind of conflict, one that would govern the course of her adult life.

Off-Center

Julie de Lima wasn't a troublemaker, but she was headstrong. She wasn't exactly a naughty child, but she wasn't an obedient one either. From her earliest memories, she was driven by some irrepressible force to learn what was yet unknown.

Julie is the only one of her sisters to ever be spanked — partly because she was the eldest of eight girls and thus expected to be the most responsible, and partly because, like most children, she engaged in a bit of mischief every now and then. She was the only one of her father's children to ever bolt in the middle of a scolding.

Often, instead of joining her sisters during nap time, Julie got up and sat by the window. With an elbow on the windowsill, she gazed out at the vast expanse of coconut trees near her house. It wouldn't be long until she was exploring the surrounding wilderness. Her relatives told her legends of the *aswang* and *duwende* lurking in the area, scaring children and stealing them away from their parents. But Julie was unafraid. She carried around cloves of garlic, confident it was enough to keep the monsters at bay as she wandered and played as she desired. "*Segurista ako* (I don't take chances)," she assures me.

In the wilderness, she dug out termite mounds, hunting for the queen in its smooth cave-like nest. She picked guava and *bignay* from trees or scanned the ground for fallen *pili* nuts.

Before heading back, she scavenged for wood mushrooms growing beside termite mounds, bringing them home to share with her siblings.

Julie was a curious child. When World War 2 ended, the Philippines was granted independence by the United States, but only on paper. In practice, the Americans still held dominion over domestic affairs. On the global stage, another conflict was brewing. The Cold War was about to break out between the world's top superpowers, sending its tremors across the globe.

Young Julie didn't yet have a grasp of these historical events, or the role she'd play in them. In 1946, she was only seven years old, about to enter first grade, and glad to be back in her family's San Agustin home of *narra* and concrete.

"*Mabuting estudyante po kayo* (Were you a good student)?" I probed.

"*Oo naman* (Of course)."

"*Masunurin* (Obedient)?"

"*Ibang bagay naman iyan* (Well, that's a different matter altogether)."

When she wasn't perfecting her *trumpo* (spinning top) or *jolens* (marbles) skills, she sprinted for sport. She even won competitions at the barrio level. But she lost interest after meeting her new classmates. Many had just resumed school after the war, and they were older and taller than her, easily able to outpace her with their longer legs.

One such pupil was an eighteen-year-old who sat next to her in first grade class. Perhaps he was very bored. Perhaps he resented having to sit through lessons with children when he was already a young man. For whatever reason, he made a habit of teasing Julie. He must have thought she was a harmless little child who couldn't stand up for herself.

But she had become very good with knives at a young age; she could chop wood and carve like her father. In the classroom, she practiced these skills on her pencils. One day, when her seatmate started to tease her again, she thrust her sharpened pencil into his arm. After that, he never uttered anything to displease her again. In later years, when they were both adults, he showed

Julie the scar she had given him: a black dot in his inner arm, a reminder to keep his distance from the formidable little girl in his class.

Outside school, Julie's love for literature blossomed. She remembers sitting on her grandfather's lap as he read her epic ballads in the form of Spanish *corrido*—the tale of Don Juan Tiñoso was one of their favorites. When she was in her fourth grade, her uncle, the former USAFFE guerrilla, came home after a stint with the US military with sacks full of paperbacks. Within the year she finished the *Decameron,* along with many others of the books.

By the time she was enrolled in Albay Provincial High School, she had gotten into the habit of skipping school to spend the day at the United States Information Service (USIS), a small hub for US cultural exports. Among the selection of Americana items were shelves of classical fiction, which to Julie were far more interesting than her classroom lessons.

Those first few visits quickly increased in frequency. Soon she found herself dropping by several times a week. Each book Julie devoured left an indelible mark on her. She learned there was so much waiting to be discovered and experienced in the world beyond her barrio; there was a wealth of stories to be lived.

The works of Mark Twain, Harriet Beecher Stowe, Louisa May Alcott, John Steinbeck, William Faulkner, and Ernest Hemingway are what she remembers best. Most of their plots contain destitute protagonists standing up to the establishment. Ironically, these might not have been the ideas US colonizers wanted to plant in impressionable brown minds.

On the days when she did attend class, she headed for the school library, borrowing as many books as she could bring home. Julie urged her parents to subscribe to *Reader's Digest.* She perused the magazine and took note of monthly literary recommendations so she could hunt down copies of acclaimed ones at USIS.

Somehow, in her third year of high school, she came across the short but enticing *Communist Manifesto,* written by Karl Marx and Friedrich Engels. Around the same time, news of Mao

Zedong leading the Chinese people to revolutionary victory was broadcasted on US radio programs heard in the Philippines. She also read about Mao in the pages of the *Philippines Free Press,* to which her parents had a subscription. Julie followed these developments with great interest.

Julie smirks when describing her introduction to political life. *"Nauna pa ako kay Joma na maging seryosong aktibista* (I became a serious activist before Joma did)."

Teenage Julie already knew what she wanted to do. *"Noong last years of the fifties, naghahanap talaga ako ng grupo na masasalihan. Napapanood ko na at nababasa ko ang tungkol sa rebolusyon sa China* (In the last years of the fifties, I was actively searching for a group I could join. I was already watching and reading about the revolution in China)." During that youthful period of discovery, she crossed over from adolescent mischief into political awareness, and grew mindful of social inequity around her.

Because her family lived close to peasants, she was aware of the oppression afflicting the barrio. She saw the many landless families who suffered through exploitation, debt, and hunger. She had learned about the plight of the farmers working in the same land she had explored with garlic in her pockets. *"'Yong mga magsasaka na tenants, mangungutang sa amin tapos mag-istorya sila kung bakit sila nangungutang. That was my first encounter with oppression. Kung minsan, 'pag bumagyo, siyempre mahina ang harvest and yet maririnig mo na dine-demand pa rin ng panginoong may-lupa ang dapat ibayad sa kaniya* (The farmer-tenants in our village would borrow money from us, then share why they had to. That was my first encounter with oppression. Sometimes, when a typhoon strikes, of course the harvest would fall, yet the landowners would demand the same payment from the farmers)," Julie recalls.

Julie ranked fourth in class when she graduated from high school. She didn't attach too much significance to her academic standing. She may not have garnered any major academic honors, but she'd learned a lot about the world she had yet to explore for herself.

Julie wanted to continue her studies at the University of the Philippines (UP) in Manila and she wanted to join a group that was critical of the Philippine establishment. Fearing his eldest might run into trouble in the unpredictable city, her father persuaded Julie to remain in Bicol instead. She conceded, enrolling at Albay Normal School.

But when her father allowed Julie's younger sister to enroll in UP the following year, Julie was indignant at the unfairness. She says, *"Umayaw na ako…. Umalma na ako, umuwi na ako. Sabi ko ayaw ko na pumasok. Kinukumbinsi na akong tapusin ang second semester. Basta ayaw ko. Walang nakakapilit sa akin* (I decided I didn't want to stay there anymore…. I protested, I went home. I said I don't want go to school anymore. They tried to convince me to finish the second semester, but I refused. No one could force me)."

Her parents conceded to Julie this time. She applied to UP and dropped out of Albay Normal School in the middle of the second semester, seeing the rest of the school year as unnecessary. While waiting for her studies in UP to begin, she busied herself by reading and gardening. She tried to grow the biggest squash, the corn with the biggest cobs, the longest *sitaw,* the fattest *ampalaya.* She tended to her garden before breakfast, when the sun was barely out, or early in the evening when the nightshade plants bloomed. "I enjoyed that school break and learned much more than what I would have in formal classes," she says.

In the summer of 1956, she transferred to UP Diliman, where she planned to enroll as a third year Foreign Service student.

The enrollment process in UP was notorious for its long lines. Students stood in queues for hours and traipsed back and forth across the 493-hectare campus in search of signatures and stamps of approval. While waiting in line, Julie met a girl who told her about Library Science, a course to which only a few students applied. The girl also assured her that if she didn't like it there, she could easily shift to a different course in the future.

So Julie pushed through with Library Science. She explains, *"'Yon kasi ang may pinakamaikling pila* (That course had the shortest line). I later found Library Science interesting, so I went on to choose that as my specialization."

At first, Julie spent most of her time within the spacious Diliman campus. Within the classrooms and halls and the expansive tree-lined avenues of the university, she was shielded from the hubbub of Manila.

Eventually, she started leaving the campus to go to Recto Avenue, known at the time for its secondhand bookstores. For ten centavos, she'd board the JD Bus to Quiapo, one of the busiest commercial areas in Manila. Then she'd wander through streets filled with neon signs and back-alley vendors to reach her beloved shops, buying books priced from fifty centavos to one peso each. She recalls fond times when customers were allowed to return books to the secondhand bookstore after they'd read them, and she could get up to seventy cents for a book if she returned it in good condition.

Neither her studies nor her explorations of the metropolis detracted from Julie's original goal — she wanted to be part of an organization, one where she could learn and contribute as a young intellectual..

Then, in a Spanish elective, she met a lanky classmate with thick-rimmed glasses who introduced her to other students with the same inclinations. His name was Jose Maria Sison. They quickly fell in with the growing crowd of dissenting students and formed study circles. Why did the Philippines, despite gaining independence after World War II, remain beholden to the whims of the United States? Did the patriotic push for democracy end after the 1896 revolution? How would the application of Marxism take form in their country? They sought a revolutionary inquiry beyond the constraints of academics and careers that were expected of them.

The Cold War was in full swing during the mid to late 1950s, and the competing ideologies of capitalism and socialism had become a hotly contested global debate. At the same time, upheavals in Asia brought the conflict close to the Philippine archipelago. The Vietnam War broke out in 1954, and America deployed troops to eliminate Ho Chi Minh and the Viet Cong.

Meanwhile, revolutionaries founded the People's Republic of China, sparking hope among the proletariat worldwide. In the Philippines, officials mimicked the "red scare" propaganda of the United States. The government pledged its support for American aggression in Vietnam, and Congress set up a committee to investigate "anti-Filipino" activities, proceeding to demonize and hunt down young activists for any speech that hinted at sympathy for communist ideas. On June 19, 1957, President Carlos Garcia outlawed the Communist Party of the Philippines, and declared the "fight against communism [as] a matter of national policy."[1] The young radicals in UP were undaunted; the government threats seemed to harden their resolve.

According to Julie, she and Joma began preparing to establish the Student Cultural Association in UP (SCAUP) at around the same time they became a couple, soon after they had both graduated. From there *"siyempre mas nag-develop ang kamulatan* (our consciousness developed further)."

Often considered the precursor to the mass organization Kabataang Makabayan (KM), SCAUP was instrumental in developing the blueprint for the national democratic movement. Student-led demonstrations were increasingly common, and alternative ideas were being popularized in massive teach-ins. The allure of revolutionary groups was contagious.

Although I knew Julie had taken a key role in the movement, her name rarely came up in the materials written about this period. I try to imagine where Julie was in these scenes of bubbling tumult, when mass leaders were radicalizing the university, and a nation took notice of noisy students with new ideas.

She's kept her hair short since high school. A mishap at the parlor when she was a teenager caused her to trim her hair short to try and fix the problem, but then she grew to like the look. She also made many of her own dresses, each in a different shade of blue.

---

[1] President Garcia said this in his speech after signing House Bill 6584 "Outlawing the Communist Party of the Philippines and similar organizations."

I imagine the scene. A fresh graduate, wearing a blue dress, stands in the back of a small auditorium during a SCAUP Assembly. She observes the proceedings quietly, never seeking to draw attention to herself. But she's done a lot of the work to ensure this assembly runs smoothly. She's right at home among rowdy student intellectuals, just as she would be among the farmers in the countryside and the guerrillas in the jungle.

After graduation in 1959, 21-year-old Julie gave birth to their first child. She moved into a home along Retiro Street in Quezon City with Joma and landed a job as a librarian at UP. These responsibilities meant she seldom joined mobilizations, even the large, historic mass demonstrations against the passage of a McCarthyist anti-subversion law in the Philippines. Instead, she used her time at home to work on SCAUP documents, education and propaganda materials, and left-leaning periodicals, including the popular campus-based *Fugitive Review*.

At the UP College of Law library, Julie took charge of cataloguing their selection on international law. She says, *"Nag-enjoy din ako sa pag-catalogue. Hindi naman napakahirap, siyempre i-classify mo, mag-aayos ng mga abstract, basahin muna introduction, tingnan ending at subjects covered tapos i-classify kung jurisprudence o kung anong klaseng law* (I enjoyed cataloguing. It wasn't very difficult. You had to fix abstracts, read introductions, look at the endings and the subjects covered, then classify them as either jurisprudence or another type of law)."

In the following years, she had other stints at the Institute of Hygiene in Padre Faura and the National Science Development Board. She even rejected a position at the library of the law firm headed by Alfonso Ponce Enrile, father to current Philippine senator Juan Ponce Enrile. Eventually she was employed as the first librarian of the Pamantasan ng Lungsod ng Maynila. *"Masarap noon, kasi hindi ikaw ang mag-a-apply. Ikaw ang hahabulin* (It was fun, because you didn't even need to apply. They would be the ones chasing you)," she recalls.

"Maraming advantages sa library, makakakuha ka ng mga papel, mga supplies (You get many advantages in a library, like a steady supply of paper and other items)," laughs Julie. They

needed stacks and stacks of paper to sustain the publications and releases SCAUP was producing.

By 1962, their home in Retiro had been unofficially annexed as a headquarters by young activists. The radicals stayed for dinner, followed by intense and protracted political discussions. Julie was a little bugged at how their sacks of rice meant to last for months sometimes never made it past a few weeks. "*Umaangal nga mother-in-law ko, kasi siya taga suplay ng bigas namin mula sa Cabugao, nauubos kasi agad. Marami rin kami noon na natitipid na nagmumula sa kanilang lupa, suplay ng monggo, sibuyas at iba pa* (My mother-in-law complained because she sent us rice from Cabugao and was dismayed at how quickly we finished up our supply. We used to save a lot of money nonetheless because we could source things like monggo, onions, and other produce from their land)."

By the time KM was founded in November 1964, Joma and Julie were neck-deep in the tasks needed to coordinate the birth of mass struggles and campaigns across schools, factories, and rural communities. Amid political tasks, they juggled parental duties for their now two children. When pressed for time, both kids joined in the work, placing stamps on letters sent to activists nationwide. Once the couple had prepped all the required documents, Joma pawned off his typewriter to pay the rent for the YMCA auditorium where KM held its first official assembly.

Once established, KM propaganda and literature were sent to student councils and publications at the secondary and tertiary levels.

"*Ang reasoning ay para ma-familiarize ang kabataan sa materials, at kapag interesado sila, kokontak sila o makakausap ng iba pang organisador* (We reasoned that it would help young people become familiar with the materials, and if they were interested, they'd contact us or speak to another organizer)," Julie says.

The political situation was tense and the atmosphere was electric with urgency, culminating in what became known as the First Quarter Storm (FQS) of 1970. The FQS was a series of massive youth-led demonstrations against the Marcos regime. Joma was in the thick of it — he stood front and center at many mass assemblies and press events. For most of those occasions, Julie was the silent engine, taking care of many preparatory and logistical duties. She led the production of documents, publications, flyers, and organizational materials. She reviewed and reworked the speeches of various mass leaders. She had materials reprinted and distributed at a frantic pace, to keep up with the growing interest in the movement.

Julie had a hand in almost all defining steps of the national democratic movement since its early years. She helped to found the youth movement and the party, produced its early publications and study material, and charted the growth of the struggle for many years. Yet in so many instances, her role has been left undocumented.

She was there for almost all of it. She was always in the frame, but somehow off-center.

In 1968, when Joma and eleven others went to Alaminos and took the biggest chance of their lives, Julie stayed at home. As Joma's group reestablished the Communist Party of the Philippines with an updated ideological line of Marxism–Leninism–Mao Zedong Thought, Julie kept busy with other work in Retiro. Of course, much of the documents and other materials they were using in Alaminos had gone through Julie's sharp eyes beforehand.

She explains, *"Wala ako sa First Congress, bihira din sa mga demo. Nandoon ako sa bahay, madaming trabaho. Kailangan din bantayan talaga ang bahay kasi may mga nag-a-attempt na pasukin, na magpapanggap tapos manghihingi ng kung anong material para sa intel nila or maybe something worse* (I did not attend the First Congress. I also seldom attended demonstrations. I often stayed home, busy with work. Someone needed to watch over the house because there would be attempts to break in, by people pretending to be sympathizers. They would ask for materials, probably for their counterintelligence operations or something worse)."

Back then, despite their firm belief in the validity of the revolution in the Philippines, none of them could have imagined the scope the movement would take, the incalculable number of lives and beliefs it would alter forever. Julie saw the breadth of unfolding events but focused on the details, establishing routines that underpinned the maturing CPP–NPA.

In recounting these events to me, Julie does not express surprise at the bold trajectory of her life. She sounds calm and unruffled—as though she expected all of this to happen, as though she willed it to be so.

No Binaries

I hear Joma jog to the door of their apartment to answer my knock.

"*Meron ba tayo today* (Do we have a session today)?" he asks, a bit confused, glancing at his watch but eager to participate in another interview.

"*Kami lang po ni Ka Julie* (No, just me and Julie)."

"*Ah, OK. Julie! Dito na si Michael* (Ah, okay. Julie! Michael is here)."

He rushes back to his chair to resume a post-meal and pre-work routine of singing along to *kundiman* playing. Meanwhile, Julie and I sit across from each other and pick up where we left off — the founding of the CPP in Alaminos, Pangasinan, in 1968. Julie was home in Quezon City.

Joma, trying to be unbiased at the Party's first congress, considered withholding Julie's nomination to the Central Committee of the CPP during its first year. But no one could deny her contributions. Months later, either Monico Atienza or Rodolfo Salas (the couple couldn't agree which one) nominated her to the party's Central Committee.

In 1969, she became the first woman elected to the Central Committee of the CPP. Today she is the longest serving woman in the revolution, a feat that might put her on par with the likes of Tandang Sora.

Julie was indifferent to me broaching the subject of this accomplishment. She thought joining the Central Committee was somewhat inconsequential. Her duties before and after the "promotion" remained practically the same. One of her tasks was to head the translations made under the CPP's education department, and another was to work in tandem with Joma in the international relations department. She says, *"Marami, maraming trabaho… ako pa din ang nag-aasikaso ng imprenta ng libro, paglalabas ng progressive review* (There was a lot of work to be done… on top of that, I was still the one in charge of printing books and releasing progressive reviews)."

For the next few years, well into the mid-1970s, she led efforts to release some of the most important manuals of revolutionary work in Filipino. Her department translated seven volumes of selected works by Mao, including *Combat Liberalism, On Contradiction,* and *Where Do Correct Ideas Come From?*

As a sidenote, she recommends, *"'Yan ang advice ko sa gustong mag-aral ng Mao, 'yang* Where Do Correct Ideas Come From?. *Ito ang pinaka-truthful niyang work, and introductory to understanding all his other works* (That is my advice to those who want to study Mao, to read Where Do Correct Ideas Come From?. It's his most truthful work, and introductory to understanding all his other works)."

With good humor, she thinks back to when her committee was stumped searching for the right word for "specter," which they encountered at the first sentence of *The Communist Manifesto.* After an all-night debate, they settled on *multo* instead of *halimaw.*

Many generations of activists in the subsequent decades have huddled around these translated texts in school halls, public parks, shanties, picket lines, and bahay kubo. Newcomers have Julie de Lima and her comrades to thank for their introduction to national democratic literature. Julie emphasizes, of course, these texts are the work of a committee and not an individual. She says, *"Kino-correct din ako ng iba, kasi minsan pang-Bicol ang syntax ko. Inaayos ng mga Tagalog* (The others would also correct me occasionally because my syntax drew from Bikol. The Tagalogs would fix it

Julie fulfilled these obligations on top of taking care of her family. Being in the movement didn't exempt her from the traditional pressures society exerted upon women. As a mother, she was expected to put her children's needs ahead of the demands of the struggle. Caught between revolutionary prospects and the traditional restrictions on women, Julie refused to see these as her only absolute choices. She had the will and capacity to do both, just not at once. With a plaintive yet assuring voice she tells me, "There are no binaries, only dialectics."

By 1969, remaining an aboveground activist was no longer a viable option. For security reasons, they moved their operations underground. Joma was the first to head for the mountains, where he joined the other cadres laying the foundations for the New People's Army. Julie soon followed. This led to what she described as the single toughest separation of her life — when she left their three children in her parents' care in Camarines Sur.

After leaving Bicol, her life had turned quite eventful: she'd gotten a degree and an education in political work, started a family, and helped found a revolutionary movement. Her return was brief and bittersweet, fraught with the tensions of upheavals brewing elsewhere. Peasant folk nationwide were hearing of a guerrilla army expanding from Central Luzon. Julie was needed in so many places, but for a momentary interlude, she needed to be with family.

Julie's parents welcomed her home. They accepted that their daughter was off to war — they'd all been through it once already, baptized together as a unit. They understood the merits of the war, and shared Julie's resolve to keep her own children far from its perils.

This reunion was a prelude to a long separation. "You do not have the luxury of getting depressed about it," she reflects. There are far too many goodbyes in a revolution. She would not be fully reunited with her whole family until 1986.

The risks and sacrifices they took were for future generations, including her own children. Later, there would be a time and a place to be a family once more.

* * *

The Philippine revolution spotlights the question of women's liberation and overcoming gender-based oppression. Addressing these issues wasn't an easy feat during the 1950s and '60s, especially in the most Catholic country in Asia.

Today, Julie defers to Coni Ledesma as the NDFP's more ardent advocate of women's liberation. Those who know her say Coni is always the first one to highlight any concerns or questions regarding women's organizing in meetings. She has also taken the lead in establishing solidarity with other feminist groups around Europe. Julie and Coni cannot disclose exact figures, but they agree the party's efforts to be gender-inclusive have made positive strides.

In a separate interview, Coni shares, "Many of the leaders in the guerrilla army are women. They occupy positions of leadership not only at the national or regional levels, but in smaller areas, in areas where there are organs of political power. Women have assumed major tasks and responsibilities in their field of concentration." In contrast, she observes, the Philippine military seldom deploys female soldiers for their combat operations. By most accounts, state troops considered it a worse humiliation to be defeated by NPA platoons when those units were composed mostly by women.

The national democratic movement believes the oppression of women is rooted in class struggle or the division of people into the exploited and exploiters. "Women and Revolution," a transcript of a 1986 lecture by Julie unearthed by Coni among her personal files, presents a picture of CPP's appreciation of the emancipation question.

The transcript records one of the few instances through the years where Julie delivers a public lecture. Julie was speaking to an audience of Australian comrades, drawing upon her experiences fighting in a war against a dictator. She says:

> The struggle for women's rights is interconnected with the struggle for national freedom and democracy. Women liberate themselves from oppression and rise to a level of equality with men, by participating actively in the struggle to overthrow foreign and feudal domination [...]. The issue of women's rights and equality has the potential of uniting women from all classes in a struggle to strike at the roots of the socio-economic system that has nurtured male dominance. This potential, however, should not obscure the necessity of grasping the class line in the women's liberation movement. We must recognize that it is among women of the exploiting classes that the schizophrenic culture of Philippine semi-colonial and semi-feudal society is most entrenched.

Julie admits even in the revolutionary movement, in over five decades, there have been obstacles when it comes upholding women's rights. Every cadre makes mistakes, the kind that spring the patriarchal conditions afflicting every human being in history. At one time or another, many male comrades have underestimated their female counterparts. *"Maski na qualified ang babae, na o-overlook, madalas. Kun'di man, ang binibigay na trabaho ay sa finance* (Even when women are qualified, they are overlooked. More often than not, they are given work related to finance)."

Before the CPP's reestablishment in 1968, Julie and a few others took it upon themselves to establish a core group of women organizers. *"Kaso hindi nag-take off, kasi ako naman noon, marami akong iba't ibang tungkulin at hindi ko talaga napagtuunan 'yon* (But it didn't take off, because at the time, I was busy with other duties and was unable to devote myself to that task)," Julie says. Still, their efforts were the forerunner to the formation of MAKIBAKA, the first militant organization of women in the national democratic movement.

I ask what she thinks of a common—and often criticized—adage among some activists that male comrades see the bigger picture, while female comrades are more focused on the details.

Julie straightens in her seat, and quips, "I object. I always have a bird's-eye view." She raises her eyebrows and adds, *"Pero sa pagiging babae, advantage ang alam mo ang detalye dahil kailangan mong maintindihan kung anong parte ng detalye ang dapat aralin. Kailangan mo din ang bird's-eye view. Sa mga obserbasyon, talo ko pa sa broad view ang maraming comrades na lalaki* (A woman can use her awareness of details to her advantage and study what parts need to be examined further. But you also need a bird's-eye view. In my own observations, I have a broader view than many of our male comrades)."

She backtracks, smiling. *"Mayabang, ano* (It sounds boastful, doesn't it)?"

I tell her that at 81, with over fifty years spent for the movement, there's no doubt about her revolutionary acuity. *"Okay lang magmayabang nang kaunti siguro* (I think it's okay to boast a little at this point)."

The ideas Julie debunks are outdated views on gender that nonetheless linger in proletarian warfare. She argues, however, that these can be overcome by an ideological insistence on the importance of women to the revolution.

Coni explains that the CPP has veered away from rigid structures or fixed roles for women in the movement, which bore the Spanish colonizers' legacy of patriarchy. Female cadres are deployed to all areas. Coni stresses that for the CPP, resisting centuries of oppression against women requires an appreciation and recognition of equality in duties. There is a conscious effort not to assign such tasks as housekeeping or financial work to cadres simply because they are women. All cadres, men or women, are links in a chain—equally crucial, and equally responsible.

Coni compares the CPP's practices with other organizations. "For example, fifty percent of women must comprise the leadership. Or preferably, a woman should head the organization.

While we respect that practice and it can lead to good results, in our case, it can also lead to not-so-qualified women being put in positions of enormous responsibility. The revolutionary movement in the Philippines is different. Women are appointed or elected into positions of responsibility solely because they are qualified for the position. That there are so many women in such positions shows there are many qualified women in the revolutionary movement."

The sun is fading fast. Julie relaxes in her chair, unbothered by the huge pile of papers waiting for her once I conclude the interview.

As for the prospects of women's liberation, Julie's 1986 lecture is a reminder of where to direct indignation. She said:

> The end of foreign and feudal domination will not automatically result in women's full equality with men. Deep-seated prejudices against women will still tend to be nurtured by backward elements of society. However, the biggest obstacles to women's liberation and equality with men are removed, and the women can vigorously fight for their rights in the continuing struggle for the total transformation of our society into one that is truly independent, democratic, just, progressive, prosperous, and peaceful.

Out of the Attic

The NDFP's beginnings in Europe is also the tale of Coni and Louie breaking through the Martial Law travel ban before settling in Utrecht. Long before the Dutch city became home to a thriving Filipino community and an important base of operations for international organizers, Coni and Louie set out with the intentions of establishing a broad solidarity network. This task was made all the more challenging by the volatility of the situation — Marcos had outlawed all travel by Filipinos abroad, except for those on "official missions."[1]

The account of their escape from the Philippines to Europe begins in 1974, where they first met Joma and Julie under a bridge in the countryside.

Coni and Louie take turns speaking, connecting each other's sentences to piece together the entire story. They might as well be the same person switching between two distinct tones of voice. Fast-talking Coni contrasts Louie, who releases his

---

[1] In a letter addressed to the Secretary of the Department of Foreign Affairs, Marcos instructs the agency to "not to issue travel papers of any kind such as passports and other like documents to any citizens of the Philippines who may wish to depart from the Philippines for any foreign country after the date of this order." However, he did leave room for government business and "exceptional cases" (Office of the President of the Philippines, 1972a).

words gently, as though you're conversing beneath the shade of a strong *narra* tree. Together, they tell me how the Philippine revolution slipped through enemy detection.

After eleven months of detention for organizing farmers in Negros, Coni and Louie travelled to Nueva Ecija, eager to return to political work. Joma and Julie, both in hiding at the time, had asked for a clandestine meeting, the norm for activists in the underground movement.

Among wooden huts of farmers under the bridge, Joma, Julie, and few others welcomed the newly freed pair. With amusement, Coni describes how she tried to reconcile her presumptions with the reality of her host. *"Kasi ito ang famous Joma Sison, pinaka-wanted, tapos ganun parang 'nye, nye, nye,' talking-talking. Sobrang daldal* (Because this is the famous Joma Sison, one of the most wanted people in the country, and he was just like 'nye, nye, nye,' really talkative)!" Joma wanted to learn every minute detail of the peasant struggles blossoming on Negros island.

It was the first in a series of meetups that year. The whole group threw around ideas such as sparking a faith-based protest movement against Marcos, and a human rights referendum to indict the dictator for his crimes, among others. Eventually, they reached a consensus on one of the proposals: Coni and Louie were given the assignment of leaving the country to be ambassadors of the revolutionary struggle.

Missionaries from abroad were one of the few people able to enter and exit the Philippines during that period. They knew Louie and Coni, who were no longer clerks of the cloth, but still of the same faith. With their assistance, Coni was first to leave the Philippines. In 1976, she slipped out of the country with their firstborn child, escorted by Irish clergy who had secured a real passport for her under a fake name. Her getaway was smooth. Later, she speculated the authorities probably thought — erroneously — a woman, much less a nun, did not warrant any sustained investigation.

Louie's situation was more complicated because he was under a lot of heat from the government. He first tried to obtain a passport through a syndicate in Manila. But the gang's leader recognized the priest-turned-activist and rejected his request. Under Marcos, even organized crime groups sometimes avoided the attention associated with rebels. The gang feared the falsified document could be traced back to them. Louie remembers hearing, *"Ay, hindi p'wede ito, too hot a potato ito* (No, we can't do this, it's too hot a potato)."

As a last resort, Louie managed to link up with a foreign missionary who squeezed in some work as a photographer. He took 120 passport photos of Louie, each with a small modification of the latter's facial features. Louie enjoys recounting that experience, narrating it as something like a heist movie. *"Lagay cotton dito, tanggal buhok dito, pag-iiba ng anggulo at ilaw. Ang sabi niya sa akin, 'these minor changes will give you a new appearance'* (A bit of cotton here, a snip of the hair there, adjustments in the angles and lighting. He told me 'these minor changes will give you a new appearance')." They narrowed it down to five photographs before choosing the winner. *"It was a masterpiece, parang ako, pero hindi talaga ako* (It was a masterpiece, it was like it was me, but it isn't really me)!"

The long-haired ex-preacher, clad in a Hawaiian shirt, sandals, and sunglasses arrived at the airport flanked by three foreign missionary companions. *"Tantiya ni Joma, 'baka 75 percent lusot ka.' Sabi ko, sa tingin ko, dahil very detailed ang preparasyon at pagsisiyasat sa airport ang ginawa, sabi ko 95 percent lusot* (Joma estimated there was maybe a '75 percent chance you could slip out.' I said, in my view, because of our detailed preparation and investigation of the airport, my own estimate was that I had a 95 percent chance of success)," boasted Louie.

Louie was right, following Coni a few months after she'd left. Both had agreed to a massive mission, something no other Filipino movement in history had ever done. If they succeeded in drawing support for the Philippine revolution in Europe, a continent where most people knew nothing of the country before, it would be an unprecedented triumph.

Irish missionaries hosted the pair when they first stepped foot in Europe — the same friends who later hatched an aborted plan for the discreet return of Joma and Julie to the Philippines. Politicized Irish clergy members were no strangers to covert operations. However, the UK was just a landing spot, not a permanent base. Soon, Coni and Louie moved to Utrecht, where they stayed with Dutch missionaries who'd been to the Philippines and seen the despair under the Marcos administration first-hand. From a committee of about two dozen volunteers ready to campaign against the dictatorship, they'd founded the Filippijnengroep Nederland (FGN, Philippines Group Netherlands). Back then, there was a warmer climate of support for Third World liberation movements, and the Philippines was about to enter the European activist spotlight. Part of the committee's work was to translate and distribute *Ang Bayan,* the CPP's main publication, and hold discussions with European sympathizers, using standard study materials for Filipino activists such as the book *Philippine Society and Revolution.*

Once they settled their asylum papers, the two sought a dedicated and secure workspace. They found a flat in the tourist-filled Oudegracht area downtown. In the attic of the Surinamese solidarity group near the old canal (the literal translation of Oudegracht), the NDFP made their first home in Europe. It was a discreet workspace. To enter, one had to tug on a string from the ceiling which released a narrow wooden ladder.

Back in the Philippines, the public was unaware of the quietly developing NDFP abroad. Coni and Louie held all their meetings and produced propaganda materials in the attic, away from watchful eyes.

In the early 1980s, when the Surinamese organization moved to a new location, the NDFP switched as well. They moved to another attic, still near the old canal.

The heightened political activity in Europe did not go unnoticed in the Philippines for long. In 1986, the People Power uprising in the Philippines led to the overthrow of Marcos, and the instatement of Corazon Aquino as president of the republic. The following year, one of her generals, Fidel V. Ramos — who would later succeed her as president — publicly accused the

NDFP of extorting the European public.[2] He claimed the NDFP was sending weapons and resources to the NPA in the Philippines. He condemned the NDFP for bankrolling the murder of patriots in the armed forces.

In stepped attorney Bernard Tomlow, a Dutch cowboy if there ever was one. Tomlow was also a motorcycle enthusiast and occasional film producer. He tells me how he conteded in many "big mouth" cases where trials could be won within hours. He professed to be a part of Joma, Julie, Coni, and Louie's family as the NDFP's "house lawyer," and thus prepared to deal with backlash from the Philippine or European governments against his clients. By the late 1980s, the hulking attorney had already been to the Philippines on an exposure trip, and was astounded by the inequalities. During my interview with Bernard in Utrecht, he mentions many of his observations including disbelief at the sight of Smokey Mountain and cramped makeshift slum dwellings along the train tracks of Blumentritt Road in Manila.

Perhaps the only thing that left a stronger impression was the armed resistance in the countryside. He shares, "In Negros, I went with a squad of the NPA. We went through the jungle at night and stopped at a clearing. I was almost about to collapse from exhaustion. Then they asked me, 'What do you want?' I said, 'a cold cola.' Ten minutes later, a young guy handed me a cola in the jungle. It was the best cola I ever had! And another time, we were at a valley with a stream. We went inside a farmer's home on stilts. Down through the bamboo floors you could see the pigs and chickens. And we ate a small meal with the farmers. There was a very big plate of rice and one piece of chicken for all of us." He lets out a big sigh. "There, you get humbled."

---

[2] The Dutch newspaper *NRC Handelsblad* (1987) reported on allegations made by Ramos against the NDFP. The matter made waves in Dutch parliaments as then member of the House of Representatives Frans Wesiglas "asked the Minister of Foreign Affairs Van den Broek whether he was aware of the accusation of the Philippine general Fidel Ramos that the resistance movement NDF in Utrecht is involved in illegal arms supplies to the communist insurgents. NDF Representative L. Jaladoni categorically denied this accusation yesterday."

When Ramos flung his accusations against the NDFP, Bernard knew he had another "big mouth" case on his hands. It would be a high-profile contest — his loud mouth against that of the Philippine military. In the small attic office of the NDFP, Bernard called a press conference. He charged Ramos with slander and argued the NDFP did nothing wrong because their funds were for general operations and support to barrio-level programs for farmers in "red areas." Besides, most of the NPA's weapons came from raiding military caches and camps as part of the ongoing civil war. He warned Ramos that his allegations of criminal activity were not founded on evidence, and thus warranted a swift rebuttal in the form of a countersuit.

The next day, Bernard found himself on the front pages of Dutch newspapers. Ramos backed down, but his crusade would be taken up by many succeeding military chiefs and Presidents. "It's like the sea. Every few years you get a new wave of threats, arrests, and intimidation," says Bernard.

Then in 1988, Joma met up with Louie and Coni fourteen years after they'd engineered a route to Europe. He was in Utrecht and the administration of Cory Aquino cancelled his passport. Again came Bernard serving up another "big mouth" press conference in the small attic where Joma officially announced his intentions to apply for political asylum. It was those two media events which announced the NDFP's European presence to the world.

By the late 1980s, Coni and Louie felt they'd laid enough groundwork to enter the public sphere of activity from their Utrecht base. They had carved out a second home for themselves and a portal for the Philippine revolution outside the nation's borders.

Today, Coni and Louie's popularity has grown to the point where even their neighbors have grown somewhat protective of the couple. When a friend from the Philippines came to visit in those days, asking for directions to the Jalandoni residence, one would give the same feisty answer: "I know, but I will not tell you."

Murmurs on a Train

It's nearly December and the holiday season has been making its decorative presence known around the city. On a foggy afternoon, I stop by a bookstore in downtown Utrecht. Julie recommended it. Inside are messy piles of old books while others sit on antique bookshelves. Flipping through some vintage Dutch comics, I pause on one with a curious cover.

I stare at the battered children's comic book. I'm not entirely sure, but I feel like I've made some kind of discovery about Holland's colonizing past.

On the cover is an illustration of a slender Caucasian man on horseback, old enough to have a long and well-maintained beard. He's dressed like a religious figure in a white gown and pointed headdress with black and orange accents, a cross between a wizard and the Pope. On the inner pages, written in Gothic-style lettering, is the word *Sinterklaas*. Dutch Santa, perhaps? But unlike his more popular counterpart, Sinterklaas is quite regal, holding a glowing scepter. Maybe this image is what brings comfort to children and families here, as opposed to the overt glee of the more common pot-bellied, bootstrapped cookie extortionist.

Accompanying the Dutch Santa is a smaller, more cartoonish character, a young lad with his hand on the horse as if guiding it through the snow. What strikes me is the boy's face: Sinterklaas's companion has inked black skin, a stout nose, and lips like a curved hotdog slit through the middle. He resembles many of the blackface caricatures now considered offensive in many parts of the world. But what is something like this doing in a bookshop in 2019? Am I the only one who sees that Sinterklaas seems to have a slave? I want to rush into the streets and confront a Dutch pedestrian about this disquieting image.

I ask Luningning's eldest daughter and her husband — both filmmakers — about Sinterklaas, and they answer my queries by showing me a short documentary. I learn that Sinterklaas indeed has a slave, and his name was Zwarte Piet or Black Pete. Always in chains and sometimes lugging around a heavy steel ball, Black Pete is a lasting reminder of the deeply rooted racism in the country. The December holidays, sadly, were another occasion for colonizing powers to spread racist propaganda.

In a bid to temper backlash against the racist imagery, some loyalists of Sinterklaas folklore claimed Pete's black face was merely the result of his many trips up and down the chimneys. They tried to make "Sooty Pete" a thing, but it never caught on (Henley 2019).

Slightly less tolerant locals opted for a white Pete with a smudge of soot on his face. Others debuted a multi-colored "Rainbow Piet." Still, the annual appearance of Black Pete in some cities has sparked protests over the last eight years against systemic racism. This November 2019, a coalition called Kick Out Zwarte Piet plans to hold another demonstration.

When the coalition held a public assembly earlier this month in The Hague, they were assaulted by aggressors from the Dutch extreme right. The assailants pelted the gathering with bricks, stones, Molotov cocktails, and other explosives, injuring dozens. The police arrested five attackers (but released them shortly after). The youngest aggressor was a thirteen-year-old boy (*NL Times* 2019). He must have loved Sinterklaas, and perhaps felt aggrieved that the Black Petes or Zwarte Pieten of his country didn't feel the same way.

Despite the attack, the coalition is pushing through with more protests across six cities, including another demonstration in The Hague. I have to be there — this is a chance to take a closer look at domestic tensions with movements. Luckily, a bunch of young activists called Revolutionaire Eenheid (Revolutionary Unity or RE) are willing to have me tag along. Among the broad range of organizations set to join the protests, RE is among the more Marxist-minded, and I've been intending to interview them.

RE was founded on January 1, 2016 in the NDFP office, coinciding with a Filipino-hosted New Year's Eve get-together. Thomas van Beersum, one of its first members, tells me all of them that night had come to feel dissatisfied about their experience with other activist groups, and wanted to take part in something with a "more mass line approach."

At the onset, RE members were interested in aiding revolutionary movements abroad, such as those in India, Nepal, Kurdistan, Palestine, and the Philippines. They consider themselves an anti-imperialist mass organization. Thomas tells me, "We looked for groups that are active in the Netherlands and had worked with comrades from different nationalities. But the Filipino comrades have been the most open in regards to allowing [use of] their offices and venues, open in helping us politically and ideologically without ever imposing when we'd ask for an interview, lecture, just about anything." I wonder, how was this group of young European activists working alongside the Philippine revolution on the other side of the planet?

I'm set to meet more of the RE crowd at the demonstration today. Willem, one of RE's Utrecht-based members, arrives 11:30 a.m. sharp at the NDFP office to escort me. He is skinny, and the portion of his face visible under his thick bonnet is very pale. He looks worried for me and a bit annoyed to be put in charge of keeping me from being arrested and deported. I try my best to match his solemnity and not act like a tourist as we make our way to Utrecht Central Station.

Before boarding, he asks me to write down a lawyer's number on my hand. It's easier that way, since an arrest would involve confiscating my phone and other belongings. Inside the train, Willem grows relaxed, leaning back into his seat and removing his bonnet to reveal cropped purple hair. With us are Willem's friends — Ying, an artist, and Jilles, a journalist, also off to the rally. Judging from their conversation, there is a potential three-way clash between the protesters, the right-wing fanatics, and the police.

Ying mentions she's never joined a protest on racial issues without being confronted by the rightists. The campaign against Dutch colonial and racist history tends to unite the various progressive forces in the country. Anarchists, socialists, liberals, opposition parties, and like-minded passersby join forces and march together in anti-racism demonstrations.

The train is packed, by local standards. A handful of people are already standing. I can't understand everything they're saying. I can only note an alertness among the passengers. There are murmurs among comrades in the train, like a thin fog of indignation, barely audible but unmistakable. Willem, Ying, Jilles, and I aren't the only ones headed in the same direction. The train comes to a complete stop, bringing all the car passengers to a stiff rise, coats on and banners on standby.

The whole station is a state of unrest. Police and their barking dogs are manning checkpoints or roaming through the interiors. Everyone walks in a clipped rhythm, their heads either bowed or swinging left and right to scan the perimeter.

Ying and Jilles head straight for the protest site. Willem and I walk into a square of cafes and restaurants. As soon as we enter, about a dozen customers from all sides stand up. RE members have been waiting for us. They look young, unencumbered, of various ethnicities, and ready to go at a moment's notice. After a quick head count, we're fourteen, we head to the park.

The Koekamp (Cow Camp) is a long and plain grassy knoll with several benches. The stage is lined with banners saying KICK OUT ZWARTE PIET and NO MORE BLACKFACE while reggae music blares from the speakers. Someone from the Kick Out Zwarte Piet coalition delivers an opening speech; the police arrive. I thought Jilles was joking when he told me earlier that some cops patrolled protests atop horseback, but before me now are some of the biggest behemoths I've ever seen. Steeds on steroids. The saddles must be over six feet high, hovering over my head. The thought of one these cavaliers lunging at me is enough of a warning to stay alert.

Three perimeters surround the mass action. The first, set up by the protesters themselves, runs a few meters from the crowd, with marshals donning black leather jackets, tinted sunglasses, and berets. They looked like a brigade of the Black Panther Party straight out of the 1960s. The second perimeter is made up of the armed cops on their war horses strutting around the park. Behind them lies a moat flanking each side of the grounds. Across the waters are about two dozen pale, skinhead "observers," standing in pairs, motionless and staring at the crowd. Willem whispers to me, "Those are the fascists."

I stay with the RE bunch near the moat. They unfurl a colorful hand-sewn banner bearing the crowd's chant: "Zwarte Piet is racisme!" Many of them subscribe to Maoist thought, which I'm told is somewhat uncommon in the landscape of Dutch political movements.

I get a chance to speak with Yasmin Ahmed, an RE organizer of Pakistani and Irish descent who looks excited to be here. Jumpy and talkative, she delights in not having to spend the day as a clerk at her shoe store job.

Yasmin shares that RE doesn't yet have its principles codified in any charter or document. Although all members acknowledge the group's orientation is to support revolutionary efforts. According to her, the group is working through its "infancy," while committed to political discovery through struggle. Most of their members have ties with activists from around the world, students looking to soak up what they can from more experienced rebels, including Joma, Julie and the rest of the NDFP.

"I learned so much from my Pinoy comrades, not just theoretical stuff, and not just from the ones here in the Netherlands," says Yasmin.

"We're everywhere."

"And everywhere organized," she emphasizes. "It's how the organizing feels. It feels like a community, as opposed to activism in this part of the world where it can tend to be more competitive. Here, there is not much strategizing, and actions are isolated. There's also a lot of emphasis on not burning out. There is a big conversation on self-care and it's quite individualistic. Filipinos emphasize collective care. It's interesting how extremely individualized societies interact with activism."

Mike, another RE member, has been translating the speeches of speakers at the rally for me. He's visited the Philippines before, and agrees with Yasmin's assessment. "It's a different vibe. The collective culture is really different to what we are used to here. It's hard to pin it down to just one thing."

Thomas has a familiar word for it. "It's like being among family," he tells me. I've heard *family* before in relation to the Philippine revolutionary movement, but only from other Filipinos. He adds, "The Filipino movement has been so welcoming to everyone. There's a social aspect which has an equal influence on us along with the political aspect. Every event you go to, you feel like you're with people you can trust. There's food, and everyone wants to help each other out, as opposed to just being told what to do. That's very special. All of the most effective groups, like Black empowerment groups, Palestinian groups, and of course Filipinos, they have their social aspect among them."

Thomas attests this "social aspect" to organizing has been more helpful to them than anything else. Throughout RE's existence, they've held meetings, discussions, and film screenings, among other activities at the NDFP office, bringing along new members. Plus "Hanging out, eating dinner, or birthdays — that's really a big part of it."

That "vibe" is a rare find in many mainstream left movements in the Netherlands, according to my companions. Mike describes local Trotskyist movements, for example, as "bureaucratic." Some of their members are even discouraged from any recreational time together.

Making a connection with people is certainly an effective way to organize, but Thomas shares that it isn't easy for a lot of Dutch folk. He recalls how one of their members, who was looking to join another popular activist organization, met with one of its officers to get acquainted over drinks. It was just one beer, and the officer took care of the bill. A few days later, however, the officer sent the fledgling RE member a receipt for the beer — about five euro. The underlying demand was for him to compensate the officer for it. Thomas noted, "It's a really Dutch thing. Everyone must pay for their own thing and no one does anything for each other, and that's the standard here, but it doesn't help movement-building."

In the Netherlands, you wouldn't be able to go door to door, workplace to workplace, spreading information about certain issues. To do so would be downright bizarre, the RE members explain. There aren't many big concentrations of people here, and there definitely isn't a conversation on collective life and struggle like there is in the Philippines.

The notion of *bayanihan,* especially present in the backstreets and barrios of the archipelago, has been a conduit for political expansion. Capital pushed out mini-cities to the peripheries of metropolitan areas, where the hungry and destitute live. In areas like these, ideas about resistance can resonate the strongest. The Filipino tendency to band together makes for an environment conducive to the struggle. But what feels commonplace to Filipinos is a rarity in the West, according to organizers like Yasmin.

Solidarity doesn't always have visible tethers but carries a tangible impact. Like Mike, Thomas has visited the Philippines before, eager to learn from the movement. "It was very energizing to see the movement in practice, to see so many layers in society that are organized and are able to do a lot more with a lot less," he says.

At the same time, Yasmin believes there is still much to be done about getting the Philippine revolution some sustained global attention. "Sometimes I wonder why there isn't more [attention] for the longest revolution in the world, and a contagious one at that."

As soon as the program ends most of the protesters scatter, but those heading toward the train station begin to mass up, determined to reach more people with their message.

The smaller contingent — fewer than a hundred demonstrators — advances with strong and steady stomping, turning the five-minute stroll back to the station into a half-hour march. I walk right in the middle of the crowd, my ears sandwiched between people's shoulders. The continuous chanting led by RE reverberates like an ear-splitting blast heard from inside a tunnel. The cops escorting the crowd plead for us to stop, making gestures of disapproval, but their shouts are drowned out.

* * *

Fast forward to 2020, and the subject of racial injustice has gripped movements globally. I reach out to Yasmin during the height of the protests sparked by the murder of George Floyd by a police officer in the United States. In Amsterdam, a mobilization on June 10 drew an impressive number of fifteen thousand people. "It was incredible to see such a strong emotive response in a country where racism is often talked about as a problem that exists only elsewhere," Yasmin says. She was proud of participating, but wore a daunted expression once our conversation turned to the task of getting a comparable number to even think of standing up to capitalism.

The rally on June 10 was held in the Bijlmer, the largest Afro-Dutch neighborhood in the Netherlands. Initially the protest site was supposed to be at the Anton de Kom Plein, a square named after the Black Surinamese communist resistance fighter during World War II. However, it was moved to the Nelson Mandela Park to accommodate a larger crowd. At the demonstration, the speakers marked the occasion by announcing that every year henceforth, the date would be commemorated as Anton de Kom Day. "While this is a wonderful gesture," Yasmin says, "I fear his communist background will not be at the forefront of his remembrance. It is something that is weirdly avoided a lot in justice spaces in the Netherlands, and other places too no doubt. The lack of ideology to lay the groundwork and direction for racial justice is missing and this is something that is essential for racial justice work to transform into revolutionary aspirations."

For Yasmin, despite the stirring show of solidarity for Black lives and against racial oppression, huge gaps remain in the efforts to form a collective revolutionary consciousness to overhaul the social order.

Unlike the Philippine resistance, which has endured for nearly half a century, RE is in its early stages. Yasmin wonders aloud how much further they need to go before confronting the capitalist state becomes a national concern. When will race and revolution become intertwined?

She tells me, "Here in the Netherlands, the issues at the forefront don't necessarily challenge the Dutch capitalist imperialist system. That is to say, the bridge between racial justice and revolution is a long one."

Turning Back the Tide

"The world revolution over the past fifty years has not advanced in a straight line, but through twists and turns," Joma tells me one afternoon at his home. I've steered toward this line of questioning because tomorrow I will be traveling to Belgium to interview other proponents of revolutionary change outside the Philippines.

The subject of our conversation is the current state of the global socialist revolution around the world, which has suffered major setbacks amid the rise of modern revisionism and neoliberalism. In the 1950s, a full third of the world's population lived under socialist governments, and in the 1960s, national liberation movements advanced in various colonized countries. However that hopeful period was eclipsed by capitalist restoration in Russia, Eastern Europe, and China, with the United States grabbing the chance to fill the power vacuum created by this shift.

According to Joma, these developments were driven by the emergence of revisionists — "traitors to the masses," as he calls those who cloak their obedience to the status quo with agitating rhetoric.

However, he is adamant about the perseverance of the revolution. He expounds, "The capitalist crisis of overproduction has worsened since the financial crash of 2008, neoliberalism has become bankrupt, and US imperialism has further declined strategically. The US has lost its sole superpower status. Regardless of setbacks, the workers and other exploited people will always struggle for liberation. The escalation of state terrorism and fascist reaction in all countries is the prelude to the resurgence of the world proletarian–socialist revolution."

After the interview, as I head back to my quarters at the NDFP office, I wonder if I pressed Joma too hard to say something too candid about the state of the global revolution. Was I trying too hard to find any sign of doomsday or defeat? He remained upbeat, smiling through each answer, but I am cautious about his optimism. Over the next few days, I've scheduled appointments with members of the liberation movement of Kurdistan and the local worker's party, and I'm eager to ask them about Joma's perspective.

At 4:10 a.m., my phone buzzes, waking me. Joma has sent me an email:

> Do not miss having your photo taken in Brussels (Le Cygne at Grand Place) where Marx stayed and held meetings with the Communist League before writing *The Communist Manifesto*. You do not have to eat at Le Cygne which is now a gourmet restaurant.

I appreciate the gesture, and I fully intend to have my picture taken there. However, I can't help but take note of the unsettling irony. That the place where Marx and Engels had made their breakthrough has now been converted into some kind of opulent landmark for tourists doesn't seem to be the most encouraging sign of victory.

Brussels is engorged, overwhelming; a multicultural city of steel, glass, ghettos, granite, and graffiti. Buildings rise from the bloated cobblestoned pavements to almost block out the sky. Brussels is a proper metropolis — unkempt, littered with trash, with grime lodged in the crevices of roads and gutters, the marks of inequality visible through the precipitating vapors greeting you at street corners.

Capitalist globalization has unequivocally triumphed at this moment in history. With authoritarianism on the rise, people's movements are up against the wall. And yet, Joma admires the "thriving" revolutionary movements in Asia, Africa, and South America. Hope is far from extinguished. Here in Belgium, I want to ask comrades for an internationalist perspective on this dilemma: how do you keep fighting while you're suffering great losses?

* * *

For centuries, the people of Kurdistan have been besieged by simultaneous conflicts. Bordered by Iran, Syria, Iraq, and Turkey, the Kurds have faced conquerors and despots, from Alexander the Great to the Ottoman Empire to early-twentieth-century rulers of the West. Now, imperialist powers are conspiring to keep them from ever achieving any semblance of independence and self-determination.

The division of Kurdish land in 1923 by the Lausanne Treaty of Allied Forces resulted in their geographic assimilation into neighboring countries. In a bid to annihilate their people, the nearby countries have systemically assaulted Kurds for decades. Turkey's extermination policy has perhaps been the most vicious. On top of these issues are the repeated interventions by the United States, Russia, and European powers. Persistent conflict has scattered the roughly fifty million Kurds across the world even as most are in Turkish-occupied areas, spawning generations of families in diaspora, according to the Partiya Karkerên Kurdistanê (Kurdistan Worker's Party or PKK).

Abdullah Öcalan, detained founder of the PKK, wrote from prison that "to learn about the Sumerians and their state [...] amounts to learning about ourselves and the times we live in" (2007, 5).

Since its establishment in 1978, the PKK has organized for the self-defense and liberation of the Kurdish people. It has set up communes, political coalitions with other ethnic and religious groups, and a guerrilla army renowned for its ferocity and gender equality. Most notably, from 2014 to 2017, PKK-led guerrillas took the lead in defeating ISIS presence in the region. Women headed key offensives against the terrorists, emphasizing the role of the emancipation of women in Kurdish liberation.

All organizations, coalitions, and village associations under the PKK adopt the cochair system, where leaders must always consist of a man and a woman on equal footing. Along with the People's Councils (comprised of both men and women), local Women's Councils are among the decision-making bodies in their communes, tackling everything from economic production to social education and reports of domestic abuse. Such measures are intended to counter over 1,400 years of Islamic patriarchal ideas and culture that shackle women.

Among the Kurds, revolutionary women are particularly familiar with having to fight their way through society's obstacles. Fascism begets misogyny, and many of today's authoritarian regimes possess a distinctly macho bravado, from the Philippines' Duterte who ordered the army to shoot female insurgents in the vagina to Turkey's Recep Tayyip Erdoğan who believes women who assert their rights are some form of subhuman species.

In June 2019, I had the pleasure of a chance meeting and interview with Nilüfer Koç, co-chair of the Kongreya Neteweyî ya Kurdistanê (Kurdistan National Congress or KNK), a coalition spanning Asia and Europe to unite advocates of Kurdish independence. I spotted her smoking outside the premises of an event we had both attended and approached her to request an interview.

"Hello, my name is Michael Beltran, I work with urban poor movements in the Philippines, and I am also a freelance journalist. I heard you talk earlier about the Kurdish struggles and it got me thinking..." I droned on for a couple of minutes or so.

"You've said a lot without really saying what you came here to say," she responded bluntly.

I got to the point. "I want to interview you for a possible story on Kurdish liberation," I said, explaining that I wanted to write about the radical reshaping of women's liberation by the Kurdish rebels, and she was a noted authority on the subject. She agreed to meet me later.

Nilüfer is a tall, broad-shouldered and unflinching woman. She states, "Kurdish society has changed. We are a much more open-minded society now. We have had forty years of de-colonization coupled with women's liberation. I think this is the main point of Kurdish revolution. We cannot accept that the man is the ruler and woman the ruled one; the man the owner and the woman the slave."

Even in the early days of the movement, Kurdish women flocked to the PKK to be activists and freedom fighters, almost as an escape from patriarchal bondage. Nilüfer recalls some of the problems the PKK encountered when traditional gender roles seeped into their organizational structures. She said, "Women became fighters, and men the commanders. This shouldn't happen. Most of the women joined the PKK because of backward reactionary traditional structures in family. The role model of society was just repeated in the mountains, so it was a time of harsh critiques. The Kurdish women together with Abdullah Öcalan on their side decided to build up the base of autonomous women's structures within the party."

The women's army operates autonomously from the men's. They have separate squads and platoons. Both sets of rebels collaborate in their operations, sharing tactical information and launching joint offensives. The distinction has boosted women's morale and productivity. She looks straight at me before summing up her thoughts, "individual freedom is not possible for men or women. We work to liberate each other."

On a more concrete note, I asked Nilüfer to elaborate on their 2014 battle with the ISIS in Syria.

"The highlight for Kurdish women was the defeat of ISIS in Syria," says Nilüfer. "I think besides the military bravery, it was the ideological importance of the women's movement that led to our victory. Because ISIS also represented the highest level of patriarchy and its brutality. Being challenged by women was their weakness because they haven't accounted for the possibility of being defeated by women. So there were two reasons for

Kurdish women to have courage to defeat the ISIS, because the ISIS is an enemy to Kurds and to women."

The popularity of ISIS was, in the first place, a reflection of the increasing marginalization of working-class movements in certain places — even if there was an ongoing pushback from the PKK, women especially. Nilüfer presented an inspiring but incomplete picture. We didn't have the time and there was still more to uncover. For further discussion, she said I was welcome to visit the KNK Headquarters if I ever found myself in Brussels.

* * *

Today, I am taking her up on that invitation. I make my way to the KNK offices around one of Brussels's shopping districts. I buzz in at two huge double doors, which seem sturdy enough to withstand a bomb blast. Erdelan Baran, of the KNK's foreign relations committee, lets me inside. He offers to take me on a short tour of the premises.

We walk through an old and expansive house, previously owned in the early twentieth century by a wealthy attorney. There's a wide, ornate staircase leading to a landing with a nobleman's portrait. Narrow shafts of sunlight enter through the windows, illuminating intricate wooden carvings and displays of nineteenth-century Christian art. Overall the somber house only survives by the care given to it by the Kurds.

The three-story house with high ceilings and multiple rooms is large enough for several meetings to be held simultaneously. There's even a small reception area close to the front door, as well as a commemorative altar devoted to fallen Kurdish fighters. Erdelan points to the pictures on it. "My friends."

I'm here to interview Zubeyir Aydar, an Executive Council member of the Kurdistan Communities Union (KCK), the umbrella group for all progressive Kurdish forces. He joins us inside a study, which the former owner used to store his collection of Renaissance art pieces — most of them are still on display.

Zubeyir with his grey moustache looks stubby in his black suit, but stands poised with an air of authority. He responds to my questions in Kurdish, and Erdelan translates.

I ask about their take on right-wing authoritarians popping up everywhere throughout the world, and the supposed defeat of people's movements. Over the past decades, communist parties have degenerated in Russia, China, and other parts of the world. Among those affected were the Communist Party of Turkey, which lost broad public support in the aftermath of Mikhail Gorbachev's peace-making with Ronald Reagan, the reentry of capitalist enterprises, and the rise of bureaucratic governance.

"After the Soviet Union collapsed, Western powers said to the world, 'Look, we were right, we were the progressives.' And there was nothing to prevent them from designing the world as they wished. Normally it's the Left who presents the answers and provide solutions. But the Left had also a psychological collapse," Zubeyir says.

He points to the Middle East, which has long been a site for military interventions of the United States and NATO countries. "To find solutions, Muslim countries went back in time and radical Islamist groups like the ISIS and the Taliban started to appear," he says. "The West has been saying that socialist hopes and desires do not exist there anymore, and portrayed socialist values in a bad light. That influenced society psychologically, parallel to the political defeat. Both of which, morally, meant that in the eye of the people, the Left was not seen as an alternative."

For him, the Left has been scarred by ideological degeneration, damaging to the struggle and traumatic for the soul. The setbacks of socialism throughout the globe provided a bigger space for fascists to step in.

However demoralizing, hearing revolutionaries talk of the realities of facing historical ebbs can be refreshing. There are no overused slogans or stagnant rhetoric, just the truth. To say the revolution is on the verge of victory would be delusional and even counterproductive.

The PKK's ideologue and founder Abdullah Öcalan is now a political prisoner of the Turkish government. He pushes for revolutionary innovation following the ideological and economic shifts of Russia and China. Taking Öcalan's cue, since 2005 the PKK has leaned toward democratic confederalism, an idea that in broad strokes marries Marxist organizational principles with an emphasis on democratic freedoms. Zubeyir describes how Öcalan "necessarily distinguished between administration or governing, and power. When there is a society, there is a need for a governing system, but the structure of power is a tumor which leads to domination. We must weaken the power structure that is the state so society can make its own decisions," Zubeyir admits, though, that these ideas are still far from being realized in practice.

Since its inception, the Kurdish liberation movement has reached out to revolutionary forces worldwide. It made contact with Filipinos through Kurdish women's groups during the early 2000s and formed ties with the NDFP in 2010 through joint statements of support on a variety of issues.

Erdelan has been to Manila, where he visited Filipino activists from Indigenous people's communities. The resemblances between Filipino and Kurdish children left an emotional impression. "What I felt that we had in common was the spirit of struggle, which was very pure. The interest for women to be free was also something we had in common. Another instance, when I visited the Indigenous people, I thought that these Filipino children are like Kurdistan children. You could see in their eyes that they were searching for a beautiful world, because their present world had been turned to hell."

After Zubeyir left, I probe Erdelan about their attitudes on gender and emancipation.

The most surprising thing he shares is that activists in their movement see romantic relationships as inessential. Erdelan explains they bear no condemnation for romance but in principle, "reproduction of traditional relationships or the traditional family in a revolution contradicts the revolution as a progressive process. We need optimal time for the revolution."

Strengthening marriage and childrearing can be time-consuming activities, but relegating them as mere distractions to revolutionary activity is something I'm not completely on board with. One of my eyebrows rises and my lips crumple with doubt. Erdelan sees this and decides to share from his own life that he ended a long-term relationship with a fiancé to focus on his political duties. He adds, "Emotions are political. Capitalism and the mentality of the patriarchal system have coded our relations in the worst way. We need to depoliticize from fundamentalism and capitalism."

According to him, a revolutionary must prioritize liberation from traditional roles where reactionary power is reproduced.

Their cadres need to "recode" to adapt to what the revolution needs, and such "recoding" is like waking up a "walking dead person." He means someone who has been made to live with a blind eye to the misery of oppression.

Movements worldwide have unavoidable likenesses and ideas, but they also sprout from unique conditions, providing each with certain characteristics. What may be unthinkable for Filipinos may be a rational step toward advancement for the Kurds.

In any case, I have all the information I came for, plus something extra. The ability, even policy to "recode" and adapt was apparent in their pursuance of democratic confederalism and even the conduct of those in their ranks. They squared off against the worst the enemy can deliver, survived it, and are looking to make a leap forward with new ideas. This was happening where conditions were harshest, and it makes me wonder how coping with reactionary bombardment would take shape in Europe where life was easier by comparison.

* * *

My next stop is the office of the Parti du Travail de Belgique (Belgian Workers' Party or PTB), one of the few influential workers parties currently left in Europe. Whereas many workers parties, communist or otherwise, have dissolved into the margins, the Belgians have managed to stay afloat in one of the richest countries of the continent.

Their own pamphlets describe the PTB as a "Marxist party" of the working class fighting for a "socialist society." From Palestine to the Philippines, the PTB supports their friends in places where revolution is waged. Founded in 1979 amid the Cold War fever and student protests in Belgium, the PTB has only recently emerged into mainstream public consciousness through participation in general elections. It catapulted to record success in the May 2019 general elections by raking in 8.6 percent of the total vote, quadrupling its presence in parliament. According to the PTB these figures only averaged around 0.5 percent to 1 percent in previous electoral outings.

I walk toward Maurice Lemonnier Boulevard. In between an Asian fusion restaurant and an indoor fish market are the wood and glass doors of the PTB's plain white four-story building. Inside, the receptionist tells me that PTB cadre Bert is expecting me.

Bert arrives wearing a dark turtleneck sweater. He also has light hair, spectacles, and a stern expression. It startles me to be staring at some kind of Steve Jobs lookalike in these communist headquarters. But he offers me a warm hand then gives me a short tour of the office, and the vivid splashes of red, yellow, orange, violet, green, and blue throughout the interiors, including décor and furniture, make me wonder if I'm in the right place. I think, "Is this really the headquarters of communists, or is this some kind of a socialist ad agency?"

One hall is reserved for people brainstorming social media content, showing graphic designs on flat Apple computer screens and exchanging multicolored papers and pens. Most of them are young and dressed in checkered sweater vests, with well-groomed hair, tight-fitting long-sleeved shirts, and pressed khakis. These are some of the trendiest communists I'd ever seen.

Each room is dominated by bold, colorful images of popular historical figures with their famous quotes spelled out in comic-book fonts. The design makes me stop and stare. Karl Marx is depicted in pointillist red above the office sink, flashing a peace sign.

Until now my mental picture of communism in Europe has been one of dreary houses crowded with furious cadres in thick, drab coats, slamming on typewriter keys, preparing posters and pamphlets to paper walls and streets with. No doubt this is an outdated trope, drawn from stereotypes in mass media. Once I get over my surprise, I begin to enjoy the office design, appreciating the visual impact of their effort. These decorations display a dedication to communicate effectively with twenty-first-century audiences and reimagine tired propaganda tools.

I sit down in a small conference room with Bert. Boudewijn "Bouddy," a retired party cadre in plain clothes and a pointed beard joins us. Still reeling from that dip into my media-polluted subconscious, I see two gentle and kind-looking veterans sitting across from me. They look happy to share their thoughts, remaining steadfast even in what some might call bleak times.

I ask Bert and Bouddy the same thing I had asked the Kurds, albeit in a more European context: how can a revolution survive this authoritarian onslaught?

"After the collapse of the Soviet Union, the Left movement of Europe almost disintegrated. Then, social democracy became more and more a notion in support of the bourgeoisie," Bouddy groans. The PTB is considered one of the last of the old guard, as many of its European counterparts were caught in the disarray caused by the Soviet disintegration. Bouddy estimates workers parties lost about 90 percent of their mass base.

Unintentionally echoing the Kurds, Bert expands on how Belgium has fallen prey to right-wing vultures who've been expanding since the early 1990s. "Because the system is in crisis, it looked to drastic solutions as a reserve option, including fascism or more overt forms of bourgeois class rule."

In Belgium's northern region of Flanders, ultra-nationalist parties dominate the political landscape. One of these is Vlaams Belang (Flemish Interest), the rebranded Vlaams Blok (Flemish Bloc), which disbanded in the early 2000s after being convicted of racist actions. Essentially, Vlaams Belang holds the same platform as the Vlaams Blok, although it is now more careful about engaging in altercations with the immigrant population. Its biggest victory came in the 2019 elections when it garnered the second-highest number of votes that year in Belgium, bagging eighteen seats in parliament from a previous three (BBC 2019).

Another political party surging to dominance is the Nieuw-Vlaamse Alliantie (New Flemish Alliance or NVA), founded in the early 2000s. NVA preaches more moderate conservative thought and is now the most widely supported party in the country. Its leaders champion the peaceful secession of the Flemish region, the exclusive use of the Dutch language in their multilingual country, and the imposition of limitations on the influx of immigrants, especially those from Islamic backgrounds, into Belgium.

In contextualizing this trend, Bert insists, "As austerity policies have been imposed, more people are seduced by fascist parties and leaders with so-called easy solutions. Most of those parties are using social demagoguery to win over the working class, because the latter is rightly fed up with the establishment and the political elites. But these parties don't analyze it as a capitalist crisis."

I ask how the PTB navigates through this mess. In 2008 they held a "Renewal Congress," which proved to be a course-altering decision for the party, leading to, among other things, their animated and rebranded headquarters.

Bouddy asserts, "The party had been built on a solid theoretical base. The backbone was strong. But post-Soviet Union, it took us a few years to realize that the situation has totally changed, so we also had to change."

The PTB adopted a more flexible approach. They recruited more openly and tried modern design styles in their propaganda. As a party participating in bourgeois elections, they opened up to various levels of membership. For instance, they no longer require someone to be a devout Marxist before joining. Unlike in previous eras, now they also make use of small-scale actions to get people involved, such as petitions to generate broad participation. In the past, they'd devote all their efforts to pressing for mammoth demonstrations like general strikes. Right now, they have a campaign to raise the pension of Belgian workers.

Bouddy contends they have not relaxed their grasp on core ideological beliefs. "We are definitely in a defensive position now. In the 1960s and '70s, and the time we went to the Philippines, it was easy to speak of revolution. Now we have to go to the level that people can understand. We have one foot in the legacy of Marx, Engels, and Lenin, but in another, we really have to reach out to the people." They know where they want to take the masses, but they also know where the masses are coming from. They are working on a premise of a general distrust for socialism.

Bert clarifies that the PTB doesn't consider itself primarily as an electoral force. But participation in the polls has also opened the door for deeper connections with factory workers and even European movements outside of "tiny Belgium."

The PTB has also maintained relations with liberation movements across the globe. In the Philippines, right after the ouster of Marcos in 1986, Bouddy acted as emissary between the PTB and the national democratic movement. That was when he met Joma and Julie, beginning the longstanding camaraderie between the two groups.

During the first peace negotiations with the Cory Aquino administration, Bouddy came to the Philippines to touch base with the national democratic movement and observe life of the peasants in the rural areas for himself. After his initial trip, delegations of young Belgian activists traveled to the archipelago for exposure and solidarity visits.

"I really admire the courage of comrades in the Philippines," says Bouddy. "Until now, there is a lot of militarization. In our country it's not easy to be a communist because of the stigma, but in the Philippines, you really risk your life. So to see so many young people really dedicated to their revolutionary work was very inspiring for us."

Bert, meanwhile, lived in the Philippines with his wife from 1988 to 1996. During those eight years they had three children, and their family returned to Belgium with many new friends and lessons. He published a book about his experiences, entitled Kasama (Comrade), translated and edited by the NDFP's late penman Antonio Zumel.

He shares, "The experience I found to be most inspiring was living among the masses — the urban poor, workers, and peasants — to really feel and experience that you are waging a revolution. All the discussions and debates during the great rectification were also very important for my own learning."

The PTB leader's relationship with Joma and Julie was professional at first, as he helped organize talks and seminars across Belgium for the pair after they were stranded in Europe. The Belgians filled the couple's schedules with one speaking engagement after another, prompting even Julie the workhorse to call Bouddy a "slave-driver" in jest. Bert enjoyed having Joma at his house, saying, "He likes to tell many stories. It's never-ending, but always entertaining."

"I think the adage of simple living and hard struggle applies to Joma and Julie," Bert says. "There is all this propaganda that they live in luxury in Europe but that is the farthest thing from the truth."

A good number of Filipino revolutionaries have also been welcomed as overnight guests by Belgians. The visitors are always easy to host, even if they arrive in large groups, as most of them are willing to sleep on the sofa, the floor, or basically any surface, according to their hosts.

Interactions with contemporaries worldwide have helped the PTB affirm their sense of internationalism. They still send their members to places like the Philippines, educating them that many revolutionary people's movements thrive in the planet's peripheries. With this understanding in mind, and their recent positive experiences, they expect favorable years ahead.

Bouddy says, "We are not pessimistic about the masses in our country, because you always find points that people want to struggle for. We face harsher times, but we won't always be on the 'losing' end. Mao says that in the South, illegal rebellion is the main form of struggle but in the West, the main forms of struggle are legal. So we don't have a protracted people's war. We have protracted legal struggles until we reach the point where we can say the masses are ripe for a fundamental change of society."

* * *

The post-Soviet and post-Mao era is characterized not only by a breakdown of socialist and communist movements worldwide, but by the absence of any international political centers to guide them. Instead, according to its documents, the NDFP and CPP adhere to a principle of "mutual support and non-interference" in international relations among parties and movements.

Joma says "the integrity, self-determination, and independence of organizations must be respected before they can engage in mutual support and cooperation. Interference by any organization in the affairs of another organization should be eschewed." Nobody has, at the moment, the ascendancy to claim the universality of their analysis and practices. Criticisms are accepted, but formulas for success cannot be proffered.

I remember one adage attributed to Vladimir Lenin, a favorite among Filipino activists: "Marxism is not a dogma, but a guide to action."

One might say the strength of the Kurdish revolutionaries lies in their determination to uphold women's liberation. Likewise, the PTB has adapted their tactics to their unique political arena. Both are changing with the times at one level and remaining unyielding despite the times at another.

From both the Kurds and the Belgians I gathered that even when revolutions can be losing, they are far from defeated.

Joma, for his part, isn't thinking of turning back the tide of defeat at some indefinite and opaque time in the future. He is studying the present situation. He says, "The addition of two imperialist powers in the world capitalist system has aggravated inter-imperialist contradictions, the contradictions between the imperialist powers and their own proletariat, as well as the contradictions between the imperialist powers and oppressed peoples and nations who now suffer worse conditions of oppression and exploitation and are being driven to rise up. Great victories are in store for the proletariat and people of the world within the current decade."

Even for many of its defenders, the cracks in the bourgeois ruling system may still be too painful to accept, but they have also become too visible to ignore.

The concreteness of people's triumphs can oftentimes be blurred by distance and the frenetic pace of changes. It can be hard to find hopeful examples, but they are there. As Joma insists, "The objective conditions for people's resistance worldwide are exceedingly favorable." The rest is up to the people.

The Polite Man

Whenever I read anything—a book, a newspaper article, a statement—I tend to imagine the author's appearance. I'm not sure if this is common. Whenever I am unfamiliar with the face behind any text, my mind pieces together an image of the writer from just their choice of words.

In the case of Alex de Jong, I have had a distinct preconception of him for some time now, threaded from his articles disparaging the record and foretelling the CPP's failure. I visualize a grizzled man with stiff lips. Because of constant stress, he has gained more wrinkles than was common for middle-aged men. He is balding, with shrubby eyebrows and gray hair. I can see him sitting with one shoulder tensed up, typing away at his laptop and pressing his jaw up his teeth.

In a 2015 piece published by the online magazine *Jacobin*, De Jong wrote, "The decline is slow, but despite CPP-NDFP-NPA attempts to forestall irrelevance, 'the world's longest running communist insurgency' is being worn down by the passage of history." He characterizes the theoretical principles of the CPP as "intellectually stagnant." In a more recent article for New Politics, he suggested that many Filipino cadres are driven not by the real possibility of a better future, but by the "myth of the people's war, certain of final victory." He wrote that this inevitability is emphasized by the commemoration of the struggle's martyrs, aimed at enforcing strict agreement with the party line.

De Jong has already made public his vehement opposition to the subjects of my study, but I want to dig deeper. From what I've gathered, he's pretty popular among a section of the global Left in the developed world for his stirring indictments of the Filipino revolution. He has his fans and, undoubtedly, his critics. He's also a train ride away from Utrecht. I have to meet him.

De Jong is an academic by profession and spends much of his time at the International Institute for Research and Education (IIRE) in Amsterdam. When I send him an email requesting an interview, I want to avoid any misunderstanding, so I disclose upfront that I am documenting the lives of political exiles and the bulk of the work will be devoted to Joma and Julie.

A few days pass with no answer. I get anxious. In less than a week, I'm flying home to Manila. I wonder why I even thought De Jong would entertain my request in the first place. Why would he? He has nothing to gain from agreeing to an interview with a journalist of a national-democratic inclination. Again, I picture the grizzled man frowning at his laptop screen, reading my email then scoffing at it.

Several days later he replies, agreeing to meet with me on November 27, a few days before my flight to the Philippines. Of course, I find a way to squeeze our meeting into my schedule. We have two hours to speak at his office in Lombokstraat, Amsterdam. I arrive ten minutes early, in time for a pre-interview cigarette, still curious as to what made him agree to our meeting.

The IIRE office is located inside a rectangular building with red brick exteriors and tinted windows. I press the buzzer and an accommodating voice lets me inside. It's Alex. His appearance throws me off. He looks nothing like the image of the man I concocted in my head.

He's actually quite handsome, young, and clean-shaven, with a head full of brown hair carefully combed to the right. He's wearing a sky-blue shirt and half-framed eyeglasses. Inside, we climb to a mezzanine, where his office occupies one corner of the floor.

To dispel any lingering confusion — as I'm still only half-convinced that the man who has hurled such insults against the national-democratic movement will want to speak with anyone associated with it — I explain my purpose to him again. I don't want to be accused of doing anything insidious. Partly also because I'm still unsure as to why he agreed to meet me. I'm not here for a debate or some ideological duel. My primary intention is to gather his views and tally their divergences with those of the CPP. He assures me it's no problem.

Alex has had an eye on the Philippines and the Filipino revolution since his student days around twenty years ago. "My primary interest is the ideological debate within the Left," he says. "The movement that I'm part of and part of my political identification is in the Trotskyist tradition, which doesn't really exist in the Philippines. But of course, the tradition that the NDFP comes from, Maoism, has always had very intense disagreements with Trotskyism about what socialism is, the role of the party, and which social classes should lead the revolution. These debates help me think about these questions."

Alex concedes that the CPP's revolution has made unquestionable strides in terms of growth and influence over the decades. "You can't just dismiss them as you would a small sect in Europe that you disagree with." However, he is firm on his judgment of the party. "I fundamentally disagree with their analysis and strategy."

Alex seems to be well-versed in the subject. He has been to the Philippines on a few occasions, never staying very long. I ask whether he has taken part in extensive discussions with Filipino revolutionaries. He admits his engagements have been confined to Filipino academics who share his abhorrence of the Communist Party.

I ask if he's ever had even a brief immersion with the Filipino masses or with members and cadres of the movement. He responds that he's read many published materials as far back as the 1970s since the CPP "uniquely produces a lot of paper and of course Joma is very productive." So the answer is no.

Can a distant observer undertake an efficient deconstruction of the movement? Is being in or near the revolution a requirement for understanding it? Frankly, I am underwhelmed by the efforts he put into learning about this subject matter, but I am impressed by the confidence and diligence with which he dissects the CPP.

Alex feels the CPP is repetitive and formulaic in their messaging, always extolling the advancing revolution, always condemning the exploitation foisted by the ruling system. The same content rehashed and recycled for newer generations.

"Yet the CPP appears to be genuinely advancing, so might they be doing something right?" I probe. The current Duterte administration has singled out the CPP many times, declaring Filipino guerrillas to be the single most dangerous threat to the status quo. In June of 2020, President Rodrigo Duterte even claimed they are "a bigger threat than the coronavirus" (Gotinga 2020). For the NPA, that must have felt very validating. Apart from the reception of the masses, the degree of attacks coming from the ruling state is, I suspect, also an indicator of the revolution's progress. I wonder aloud how a *Trotskyite* defines revolutionary success.

Alex says, "If you define socialism as the self-emancipation of the working masses, then the success of a movement cannot be determined by how many rifles it has, how many party members it has, or how many people it can mobilize. You measure victory based on the rights which are won, and how confident the working masses are to mobilize on their own terms, without being led by a vanguard party."

He stops for a moment, interrupting himself. "By the way, that's an issue of language. The term *Trotskyite* is used by people who are hostile to Trotskyism."

"Really?" I gasp, worrying that my attempts at politeness may have been perceived as rude due to my ignorance.

"Yeah, no Trotskyist would ever call himself or herself a Trotskyite."

"You'll have to excuse me."

"You know something about a text when you see the term *Trotskyite*."

"Learned something new today," I say, making a mental note to shift to the proper Trotskyist from here on out.

Alex returns to the subject of how the CPP appraises their accomplishments, explaining that it diverges fundamentally from Trotskyist ideology. His understanding of CPP publications and other texts is that the party weighs its achievements using quantitative and ultimately shallow measures, such as the number of new recruits, new guerrilla fronts, or new rifles acquired over a given period of time. I listen, thinking back on my conversations with Joma and Julie, but I've never seen them fixate on counting such things.

In a separate correspondence, Joma counters Alex's assertion. "The CPP has never said that the number of rifles that the NPA has is the sole determinant of the advance or success of the revolutionary movement of the people. That is not the way the CPP thinks and acts." He clarifies that the revolutionary forces are more focused on assessing their level of organized strength, as well as the effectiveness of their programs and campaigns, adding the CPP "would not have survived and overcome all the US-directed campaigns of military suppression since the time of Marcos if not for the political work of the CPP." Far from having a myopic obsession with militaristic indicators such as army size and weapons count, the CPP has engaged for decades in organizing and education work, resulting in "a wide and deep mass support for the revolution."

Joma also points to "the fact that the revolutionary organs of political power are already governing thousands of barangays, hundreds of municipalities, and scores of districts within the range of more than 110 guerrilla fronts. They are busy with administration, land reform, and other social programs, production campaigns, health work, self-defense, judicial work, disaster relief, environmental protection, and so on — all with the support and participation of the masses."

This is evidenced by a rebel countryside significant enough to assert a status of belligerency, or existing as a popular and sovereign force in conflict with the Philippine government. Since entering formal, on-and-off negotiations with the Republic, the rebels have invoked Article 96, Protocol I of the Geneva Conventions on International Humanitarian Law, which posits their armed struggle as an "exercise of the right of self-determination." The declaration may be unilateral, however the existence of peace negotiations underpins the mutual recognition of their respective jurisdictions.

But Alex stresses that the CPP, using its current methods, cannot hope to push forward or even lead a socialist revolution, as it is "happening behind people's backs." The CPP organizes people, such as the peasant sector, "on the basis of 'land to the tiller' and the ND [National Democratic] revolution. But when does the revolution transform into the socialist one? The vanguard party carries an idea of a socialist future and consciousness, but this is not the consciousness of the masses that they organize in the present."

I suggest the CPP is pushing the socialist alternative forward, by way of actually waging a revolution. Indeed, they do so despite the life-threatening risk faced by anyone who associates with (or is accused of associating with) a communist party. Many CPP cadres and members — hunted by reactionaries, their lives and liberties at stake — do not make their identities publicly known.

According to Joma, claiming that Maoists promise land for peasants during the struggle then take it away once victory is won is a classic and tired Trotskyist argument. He brands it a cheap parody of the CPP's principle on land reform. Revolutionaries must struggle for land, achieve victory, and educate and encourage the peasant population to undergo various levels of land collectivization.

Redistributing land to the peasantry is indeed not a socialist measure per se. However, the CPP contends through its annual reports to the public that without this undertaking through proletarian guidance, there can be no prospect of collectivization.

Without this nonsocialist measure, socialism is impossible. In order for socialism to have a chance at survival, a revolution must first strip the oppressors of the source of their powers. Socialism is the direction as well as the perspective of a long process where peasants break free from feudal bondage.

Alex's position reminds Joma of a fib told by his landlord relatives who liked to frighten their tenants sympathetic to the Huks and who might have a hint of something better than feudalism. They'd say giving land to the poor would send the whole land into disarray and make them un-Christian. Joma questions whether the Dutch intellectual wasn't able to grasp these fundamental facts due to his outsider perspective, as a European, in relation to the Philippine revolution.

"The CPP never conceals the socialist direction and future of the people's democratic revolution. They explain fully the two stages of the Philippine revolution: the new democratic stage and the socialist stage, even to Filipino farmers. And they always answer questions about socialist revolution in study meetings as well as in public meetings. There is no 'socialism happening behind people's backs,'" says Joma.

There is a near unanimous verdict among the Left that since the 1980s movements have weakened worldwide. Hence De Jong believes there is value in pursuing debates on what shape the revolution should take now. He doubts anyone claiming to have all the answers. He pushes for "recognizing the value of pluralism within the revolutionary Left. I think vanguard parties are created in the course of the struggle, but it's rare that only one exists in history. Parties go through a process of merging, splitting, changing. And that's a necessary process everywhere, too. That means we have to relearn and figure out a lot of things."

* * *

Perhaps what De Jong is saying is that the CPP, at present, is opposed to the plurality of views and opinions, and is "claiming to have all the answers." For De Jong then, the natural conclusion is that the CPP should undergo a new process of "splitting" and "changing."

As a Maoist Party, the CPP adheres to the principle of unity through struggle, which relies on its members coming together and resolving differences to strengthen the party. With so much bombardment from the enemy already, it finds wisdom in being as firmly bonded as possible. It's hard to imagine the CPP entertaining a Trotskyist formula for political fission.

The CPP has never imposed a single approach in terms of global strategies and tactics. However, Filipino leftists are pushing for a single answer, one they feel is right for the specific conditions in the country. That incenses Alex, who feels that the CPP is claiming their methods to be the most advanced.

To be fair, one need only examine the history of the CPP to see a process of reshaping. Joma says, "It is absurd for anyone to claim that the strength of the CPP comes in spite of denying the need to cooperate with others and from presuming that it knows all answers to all questions." He charges De Jong with "[caricaturing] the CPP as denying the need for these diverse forces of the Left to be put into revolutionary play and be aroused, organized, and mobilized for the purpose."

Both Alex and Joma agree that communist parties must usher in a stronger left-wing movement, although they have divergent ideas on how to go about it.

"How do you get to these strong parties?" reproaches Alex. "If parties are the expression of a certain relationship of forces, of social mobilization and awareness, then the first step is to gauge the ability of the popular and working classes to fight."

He drives his point home by contrasting the evolution of the CPP with Mao's communist party in China. "I don't think you can start this process by declaring a party and start recruiting people bit by bit," says Alex. "Real mass parties are the expression of social contradictions. Take a look at Mao's original party and army. He didn't start with a small group. They had three hundred thousand soldiers who came out of nationwide insurrections. You see that also with the Bolshevik party, which had sixty thousand members before the First World War, and then it ballooned." Maybe he was just trying to illustrate a point, but I couldn't help but note how Alex was tallying party members despite his earlier statements against making assessments on the basis of quantity.

The protest movements in France, Chile, and the US seem to support Alex's ideas. He trusts these unaligned demonstrations fighting back against neoliberalism are the best chances of a left-wing revival because they are "formless." This underlines his analysis of the "self-emancipation" of the working class operating autonomously from existing, parallel left-wing channels. According to Alex, communist parties can emerge during these processes as more of a helping hand, rather than a leading figure.

On the other end, Joma's experience with the reestablishment of the CPP in an immensely more exploited Third-World nation differs from Alex's hypothesis on the necessary conditions for the emergence of strong communist parties. How did the CPP go from a small militia then to the formidable force it is today? How did it spread out from its beginnings in Central Luzon to a nationwide assault?

"In 1968, the CPP was so small and weak, with only a few scores of members. But it based itself on, and was benefited by, the mass movement of workers, peasants, and the middle social strata in the entire 1960s," Joma describes. He attributes the rapid growth to the revolutionary will and expertise of cadres who led mass struggles in various settings, causing bursts of political awakenings throughout the Philippines. The conditions create the ferment.

In contrast, no Trotskyist can point to any victory of a Trotskyist movement or party that can be considered universally, regionally, or nationally significant. Perhaps Trotskyists' insistence that communist parties are but a small and derivative component of any mass movement has rationalized their absence from the front lines.

As someone who proclaims to have distanced himself from orthodox interpretations of Trotsky, even Alex admits, "Trotskyism has failed to make an adequate analysis of the Global

South and the role of national liberation and peasant struggles and the broader struggles." While he would like to do away with the notion of models — Lenin's Soviet Union, Mao's China, and so on — his ideas feel confined to this indefinite period of theory and reflection. His recommendations hold up like a faulty prosthetic, seemingly assuring but ultimately unreliable.

Alex endorses political unity among forces on the Left. Joma agrees this is possible within a broad united front against fascism. Yet Alex remains equally intent on debasing the CPP, regarding it as a threat to society at large even after affirming a "heterogenous" view of the Left, in which the CPP is supposedly included. His criticism has trespassed into opposition, treating the CPP as a danger on par with Duterte. He is mistaking pluralism for factionalism.

In between questions I turn off my recorder. In those interludes, Alex and I try to make small talk but inevitably drift back toward more serious topics. Among the subjects to come up are the supposed alliance between the CPP and Duterte in the early stages of the latter's presidency. For Alex and many of the party's detractors, the alliance was solid, a hypocritical cooperation enabling the regime to consolidate itself.

Joma maintains "the people's war never stopped" and the CPP never held any formal alliance with the Duterte government. The closest that the two parties were ever brought together was during peace negotiations and pressures from the NDFP to grant amnesty to political prisoners. Any hopes of either were dashed by the regime quite callously in November 2017, when Duterte called off peace negotiations with the rebels.

Members of the Left were appointed on their personal merits to Duterte's cabinet early on. At the same time, any moves by the regime detrimental to the people's interests were met with protests by the Left and other political forces. When the president promised land reform, an end to "contractualization" (the practice of short-term contracts for workers to prevent them from being regularized), and nationwide wage increases, among others, it made sense for much of the Left to support those specific initiatives. Why not? At that point, it was better to pressure the regime to implement these policies than to reject any notion of reform.

As we know now, Duterte didn't fulfill his promises and the Left didn't just play along. Various leaders and organizations condemned the president for his anti-people actions. The CPP also told Duterte not to appoint anyone to his cabinet as CPP or NDFP representative in order not to prejudice the ongoing peace negotiations and trap the armed revolution in an unprincipled compromise or capitulation in effect.

To me, this debate feels tiresome, bloated, and irrelevant. This discussion drags on even after most progressive forces in the country have already unified against the president, relatively early in his term. Who stands to gain from the constant slander against revolutionaries who sought to find a common ground with Duterte? Militarists and anti-communists will surely be rubbing their hands with glee if they heard what Alex was saying.

Alex's other controversial accusation is that the CPP has a standing order to physically hurt and even assassinate activists outside of their ranks. I've never heard of any such policy. In a 2018 commentary published in *Jacobin,* Alex wrote, "The international Left should support Philippine Leftists when they are threatened by the state or by the NPA."

Joma feels such an accusation inflates the importance of the CPP's critics. "They are so few, and they have been ineffective in their counterrevolutionary activities. Thus they've been generally ignored by the CPP and by the revolutionary mass organizations. Even if they are rabid anti-communists in the clothing of super-communists or overanxious socialists, they do not deserve any kind of physical punishment so long as they use only their mouths and computers against the CPP."

I enjoy Alex's company. He shakes my hand and I thank him for his time before leaving. His words may read like that of an infuriated man with all the answers, but the person I met was nothing but pleasant and searching for the right path like everyone else. I think it'd do him good to be a little more concerned about the ramifications of his indignation towards the Left in general. I hope he can try to see how far the Philippine revolution has come — where it's going, its sincerity and conviction. I really do hope. It's with some sadness that I acknowledge a few borderline antagonistic disagreements between us, which (as expected) were not resolved during this interview. I respect his willingness to be interviewed. Ultimately, however, his ideas fall short of persuading me. In fact, they've succeeded in doing the opposite. He does not say so, but it's clear Alex expects the CPP's supposed inherent faults to lead to the eventual end of the organization, vindicating Trotskyist scholars in the West.

After my interview with Alex, I make a final visit to Kanaleneiland to bid my goodbyes. I mention some of his accusations to the couple, including attacks and threats by the NPA against those aligned with De Jong. Julie's disinterested sigh is telling. She replies, *"Masyado kaming busy. Wala kaming time para diyan* (We are too busy. We don't have time for that)."

The CPP is often faulted for having a "monopoly of truth," but Alex has not been denied the opportunity to speak his truth. His claims, however, are bound to be challenged. Were I him, I would ask myself: Are my ideas encouraging debate or enabling reactionary forces? Am I chastising the outdated, or am I the one who has been left behind?

Parting Suggestions

There is a pack of cigarettes beside my pillow. I pick it up, wondering where it came from — I already finished the last of my stash the night before. I stagger out of bed in the cold. The next thing I hear is an irritated voice. *"Para tumigil ka na sa kakahingi sa akin* (So you will stop asking me for some)!"

It's Fidel Agcaoili, calling through the open door. He sleeps in the room across mine in the NDFP office. Only he can manage to turn a generous gesture into a vaguely threatening and humorous one.

He walks back into the room, where my bags are already packed. "Michael," he says, gripping my hand, *"pagbutihin mo iyang blog mo. Basta 'wag mo ako isama* (Do a good job on your blog. Just don't include me in it)." He likes to describe my journalism as blogging, though I know he knows I don't even have a blog. I've spent considerable time with him at the office since I got here, and by including him only in this final chapter, to some extent I am honoring his request.

By now I've come to enjoy his harmless surly jabs. I'm going to miss them. I certainly won't forget how we met. On the day I arrived, he waved his fist at me and demanded, *"Gusto mo bang bugbugin kita? Itanong mo sa lahat ng ospital dito sa Utrecht kung bakit may injury ang mga pasyente nila. Lahat iyan binugbog ko* (Do you want me to beat you up? Ask all the hospitals here in

Utrecht why their patients got injured. I beat them all up)." We shared many post-meal cigarettes together soon after.

It's my last full day here, and I have one more visit to make before I leave.

I grip my jackets (plural) as I walk from the Kanaleneiland bus stop to Joma and Julie's apartment. It feels like a shroud of sharp icicles is attacking my every step on the dusky street. It's 4:00 p.m., the interval between the setting of the sun and the lighting of the streetlamps. I won't miss the glum weather, but I will miss these sessions with Joma and Julie.

Only a few lights have been switched on. They might not have noticed that the sun was setting. Heaps of papers, clothing, and dishes sat on various apartment surfaces like an overgrowth of clutter. "*Pasensya ka na sa gulo, ha* (Sorry for the mess). My mornings are reserved for Duterte," says Joma. The morning ended hours ago, but maybe his opponent has him working overtime. He collapses onto his favorite couch, as though he's taking his first break from work today.

Julie looks up to greet me. She is sitting on a stool, holding a screwdriver, crouched over the skeleton of a processing unit.

I worry about what I should say, and what gesture I can make to express how much this visit has meant to me. A few days ago, Kim told me I was worrying too much about my final meeting with the couple. She was right.

Luckily, in the absence of a prepared topic, Joma always has something ready to discuss.

Joma begins tapping his foot with excitement. The conversation turns from routine questions about my flight home to a flurry of recommendations. Acting like an old man grumbling to the younger crowd, he jests, "*Alam mo, may mga reklamo ako na ibabahagi sa iyo* (You know, I have some complaints I would like to share with you)."

He proceeds to shower me with suggestions to relay to activists back home. I can tell he's been thinking about this for some time and eager to hear feedback. Now that I'm returning to the Philippines, I have transformed from chronicler into courier.

Reflexively I switch my recorder on. Julie sees me and comes over to join us, switching on her own recording device.

"If the people fail to oust Duterte this fourth year, other political forces might say, especially conservative opposition, 'Let's just wait. Only two years, and he'll be finished by the elections,'" Joma says.

He continues, "Fidel got it correctly. *Minsan may mentalidad tayo na sumunod sa rules of legalism, like getting a rally permit, na dapat lang naman para iwas pambala sa atin, pero 'wag din iyong sumunod lagi sa sinasabi ng pulis. 'Pag sinabi ng pulis na 'dito kayo, tigil, tabi,' susunod ka. Kailangan imaginative ang pamamaraan, e* (Sometimes we tend to have a mentality that follow the rules of legalism, like getting a rally permit, that we should be doing to avoid more interference, but not to a point where we'd be always following the wishes of the police. When the cops say 'go here, stop, step aside' you might even follow. We need to be more imaginative in our methods)."

Joma laments how the Duterte regime managed to sidestep the public's outrage during the political flashpoints that could have indicted him. *"Marami nang inciting moments na dumaan, 'di natin nasagpang. Nariyan iyong kay Kian, bakit 'di tayo lumagablab* (Many inciting moments have passed that we weren't able to seize. There was the killing of Kian. Why weren't we outraged enough)? How do we multiply the protests against extrajudicial killings? *Bakit seven hours nawala ang election count, 'di pa nasagpang* (Why weren't we able to seize the moment after the seven-hour glitch of the election count)?"

Joma is referring to seventeen-year-old Kian delos Santos, one of the victims of Duterte's bloody drug war. He was murdered at point blank range by cops in 2017. He also mentions the notorious "glitch" during the 2019 mid-term elections, when the government mysteriously lost count of the ballot due to unprecedented seven-hour technical difficulties. People were outraged, but not enough to pour into the streets calling for Duterte's ouster. In doing so, the president is free to commit more atrocities. Perhaps activists can and should do better.

Joma hopes the Philippines can study some of the explosive demonstrations over oil prices hikes in Chile during the latter part of 2019. *"Biro mo, thirty pesos pinag-umpisahan sa Chile, sumiklab na! Naging matalas na paglalantad sa neoliberalism* (Can you imagine, it began because of a thirty-peso price hike, and then the movement ignited! It was a sharp exposure of the failures of neoliberalism)."

"May reklamo din ako (I have complaints too)," Julie inserts dryly. She adds, "The current crackdown is an indication that worse things can and will come. It supports the contention that there is already de-facto martial law, a precursor to all-out martial law. *Dapat pag-igihan ng mga solidarity groups at kilusang migrante na talagang palakasin ang paglaban sa administrasyong Duterte. Sa maraming talakayan, palaganapin ang panawagan para sa ouster.* (Solidarity and migrant groups need to strengthen the fight against the Duterte administration. In many discussions, let's drumbeat the call for an ouster)."

When I get a chance to scan my notes after their "complaints," I come across a question in my notes I think I needed to ask at some point. "How've you kept your marriage going?"

Joma scratches his chin for a moment, then answers, "To develop high levels of mutually assured tolerance!" He laughs and claps his palms together like he's cracked some code. His wife of over fifty years nods in agreement. Lest I get the wrong idea, Julie amends, "Of course, there must be more fine moments than quarrelling." Whatever the obstacles, if there is even the smallest chance things can get better, then it's still worth a try. I think that's how waging a revolution works, too.

There is much to contest back in the Philippines. On a personal note, during my time in the Netherlands, I've missed the chaos of my homeland, the fast-paced and high-blood pressure-inducing political upheaval. I'm sure Joma and Julie miss it too. They've been missing it for over three decades.

After all our sessions, I've gained some insight into their acute sense of mortality. In the past I've heard the pair accused of "rushing the revolution" to obtain some historical absolution and even fast-track their homecoming. But there is a difference between rushing and pushing. They've been doing everything possible to launch the struggle into its next stages, without trying to force it. There is courage in fighting and in knowing the ultimate victory will always be beyond their years. There is a calmness underlying their daily work, an acceptance that there is no foreseeable end in sight.

Joma and Julie have been contributing to the revolutionary cause in the Philippines longer than almost anyone else in history. To put in perspective, only Francisco Dagohoy's rebellion lasted longer — he led an uprising that carried on for eighty-five years.

Listening to their final words of advice, they aren't adamant about returning to the Philippines, nor are they planning to gather any accolades and sit on some kind of pedestal. They sounded more concerned about me, about everyone else back home, about the possibilities, about letting the revolution unfold, letting it discover new people and letting them find a place within its restless temper.

Half a century's worth of waging a revolution is a constant reminder that both life and the struggle can take a long time. Yet there are so many fine moments in between.

I shake both their hands, thanking them for their time. Julie hands me some tea packets for the road. The couple walk me to the door as I leave. It has gotten quite dark outside. Their apartment window glows bright yellow against the dimming street. I suppose the lights will be on for some time.

References

Ang Bayan. 1978. "CPP, MNLF Deal Heavy Blows on Common Enemy in Mindanao." October 31.

Bantayog ng mga Bayani. n.d. "Pedro, Purificacion A." http://www.bantayog.org/node/172.

BBC. 2019. "Belgium King Meets Far-Right Vlaams Belang Party Leader." May 29. https://www.bbc.com/news/world-europe-48454034.

Beltran, Michael. 2021. "Activist Recalls 1971 Manila Blast as Marcos Jr Candidacy Looms." *Al Jazeera,* November 12. https://www.aljazeera.com/news/2021/11/12/philippine-socialism-and-the-threat-of-marcos-return-to-power.

Bulletin Today [*Manila Bulletin*]. 1977. "Sison, Top Red Leader Is Captured." November 20.

Cantos, Joy, and Malou Rongalerios. 2001. "Joma Planong Iligpit." *Philstar,* February 2. https://www.philstar.com/bansa/2001/02/02/125852/joma-planong-iligpit/amp/.

Corrales, Nestor. 2019. "Palace Hits 'aging armchair passé rebel' Sison over Remarks vs Duterte." *Philippine Daily Inquirer,* September 2. https://newsinfo.inquirer.net/1159896/palace-hits-aging-armchair-passe-rebel-sison-over-remarks-vs-duterte.

Dalisay, Jr., Jose Y. 1998. "The Lava Brothers, Blood and Politics." *Public Policy* 2, no. 3: 87–112. https://cids.up.edu.

ph/wp-content/uploads/2022/03/The-Lava-Brothersl-vol.2-no.3-July-Sep-1998-5.pdf.

———. 1999. *The Lavas: A Filipino Family.* Anvil Publishing.

Gotinga, JC. 2020. "Military Vows More Offensives as Duterte Insists NPA Top Terror Threat in PH." *Rappler,* June 23. https://www.rappler.com/nation/264603-military-vows-more-offensives-duterte-insists-npa-top-terror-threat-philippines/.

Guda, Kenneth. 2007. "Jailing Joma." *Bonfires Leaping,* August 31. https://krguda.wordpress.com/2007/08/31/jailing-joma/.

Henley, Jon. 2019. "Dutch Saint Nicholas Parade to Replace Blackface with 'Sooty Faces.'" *The Guardian,* September 18. https://www.theguardian.com/world/2019/sep/18/netherlands-ban-blackface-makeup-zwarte-piet-black-pete-christmas-parade.

Lacara, Cesar. 1988. *Sa Tungki ng Ilong ng Kaaway: Talambuhay ni Tatang.* LINANG (Kilusan sa Paglilinang ng Rebolusyonaryong Panitikan at Sining sa Kanayunan).

Laude, Jaime. 2007. "Ara Mina, Joma Dancing Partners." *Philstar,* March 3. https://www.philstar.com/headlines/2007/03/03/387596/ara-mina-joma-dancing-partners.

Lava, Jesus B. 2002. *Memoirs of a Communist.* Anvil Publishing.

Legaspi, Amita. 2017. "NDFP Insists It Has Factual Basis on Kill Plot vs. Joma." *GMA News Online,* August 10. https://www.gmanetwork.com/news_duplicate/topstories/nation/621335/ndf-insists-it-has-factual-basis-on-kill-plot-vs-joma/story/.

Matthews, Jay and Bernard Wideman. 1978. "Marcos Meets Opponents." *The Washington Post,* June 2. https://www.washingtonpost.com/archive/politics/1978/06/02/marcos-meets-opponents/cbc23e0d-88e4-4541-9dab-11d4a2916204/.

Mijares, Primitivo. 2016 [1976]. *The Conjugal Dictatorship of Ferdinand and Imelda Marcos.* Tatay Jobo Elizes Pub. https://archive.org/details/TheConjugalDictatorshipOfFerdinandAndImeldaMarcosByPrimitivoMijares.

NL Times. 2019. "Arson Attack on Anti-Racism Group in Den Haag Leads to Five Arrests." November 9. https://nltimes.

nl/2019/11/09/arson-attack-anti-racism-group-den-haag-leads-five-arrests.

NRC Handelsblad. 1987. "Weisglas vraagt naar activiteiten Filppijns verzet." August 26. https://www.nrc.nl/nieuws/1987/08/26/weisglas-vraagt-naar-activiteiten-filppijns-verzet-kb_000028874-a3553240.

Öcalan, Abdullah. 2007. *Prison Writings: The Roots of Civilization*. Pluto Press.

Office of the President of the Philippines. 1972a. Letter of Instruction No. 4. September 22. https://www.officialgazette.gov.ph/1972/09/22/letter-of-instruction-no-4-s-1972/.

———. 1972b. Proclamation No. 39, "Promulgation of Rules Governing the Creation of Military Tribunals, Etc." November 7. https://issuances-library.senate.gov.ph/legislative%2Bissuances/Presidential%20Decree%20No.%2039%2C%20s.%201972.

———. 1992. Proclamation No. 10, "Granting Amnesty in Favor of Persons Who Have Filed or Will File Applications for Amnesty Under Executive Order No. 350, Series of 1989." July 27. https://www.officialgazette.gov.ph/1992/07/27/proclamation-no-10-s-1992/.

PDI (Philippine Daily Inquirer). 1987. "Palace, AFP confused on Amnesty." August 19.

———. 1988. "Subversion Raps Filed vs Sison." September 16.

PILC (Public Interest Law Center). 2004. "Laws, Labels and Liberation: The Case of Jose Maria Sison." *JMS Legal Case Files*, May 29. https://web.archive.org/web/20221007001616/https://www.josemariasison.org/legalcases/related/LLL_jmscase_290504.html.

Time. 1964. "The Philippines: The Last of the Huks." June 5. https://content.time.com/time/subscriber/article/0,33009,938597,00.html.

Pugh, David. 2005. "William Hinton on the Cultural Revolution." *Monthly Review* 56, no. 10. https://monthlyreview.org/2005/03/01/william-hinton-on-the-cultural-revolution/.

Quimpo, Nathan, and Susan Quimpo. 2012. *Subversive Lives: A Family Memoir of the Marcos Years.* Anvil Publishing.

Rodriguez, Cristina, ed. 2015. *Ang Mamatay Nang Dahil Sa 'Yo: Heroes and Martyrs of the Filipino People in the Struggle Against Dictatorship, 1972–1986.* Vol. 1. National Historical Commission of the Philippines.

Romero, Alexis. 2018. "'50 Years of CPP–NPA a Failed Rebellion.'" *Philstar,* December 27. https://www.philstar.com/headlines/2018/12/27/1880201/50-years-cpp-npa-failed-rebellion.

Rosca, Ninotchka, and Jose Maria Sison. 2004. *At Home in the World: Portrait of a Revolutionary.* Ibon Books.

San Juan, Jr., Epifanio. 2007. "Dutch Fascism & Bush–Arroyo State Terrorism Attack Filipino Refugees." *Indymedia,* September 6. https://www.indymedia.org.uk/en/2007/09/380411.html.

Sangil, Max. 2012. "The Invisible Government of Kumander Sumulong." *Singsing Magazine* 6, no.1: 172–75.

Singsing Magazine. 2012. "Kumander Alibasbas and the Huks' Descent into the Maelstrom." *Singsing Magazine* 6, no. 1: 171.

Sison v. Council of the European Union. 2009. T-341/07, European Union: Court of First Instance. September 30. https://www.refworld.org/jurisprudence/caselaw/eucfi/2009/en/70213.

Sison, Jose Maria. 1993. "I Wish to Be Taken for Granted." November 5. https://www.josemariasison.eu/i-wish-to-be-taken-for-granted/.

———. 1994. "Sometimes, the Heart Yearns for Mangoes." March 30. https://www.josemariasison.eu/sometimes-the-heart-yearns-for-mangoes/.

———. 2017. "Kinship and Encounters with FVR." In *FVR XYZ Files: An Anthology of Controversies & Issues, Anecdotes & Trivia about Fidel Valdez Ramos,* edited by Melandrew Velasco. Media Touchstone Ventures Inc.

Tadem, Eduardo. 2006. "Peasants and Outsiders: Change and Continuity in Three Rural Villages in the Philippines." PhD diss., National University of Singapore.

———. 2019. *Living in Times of Unrest: Bart Pasion and the Philippine Revolution.* University of the Philippines Press.

Tantingco, Robby. 2012. "The Fall and Rise of the Communist Party of the Philippines." *Singsing Magazine* 6, no. 1: 179–80.

Totanes, Stephen Henry. 1999. "Ang Pagbabagong Anyo ng Principalia sa Kapanhunang Amerikano: Kabikolan, 1900–1946." PhD diss., University of the Philippines.

Villa, Benjie. 2003. "NPA Admits Kintanar Slay." *Philstar,* January 27. https://www.philstar.com/headlines/2003/01/27/193010/npa-admits-kintanar-slay.

Warner, Denis. 2012. "Sex, Lies and Insurgency." *Singsing Magazine* 6, no. 1: 176–78. Previously published as "A Lewd Embrace," *The Ottawa Citizen* (1971).

Wurfel, David. 1988. *Filipino Politics: Development and Decay.* Ateneo de Manila University Press.

www.ingramcontent.com/pod-product-compliance
Lightning Source LLC
Chambersburg PA
CBHW050105170426
43198CB00014B/2466